Finding the Weight of Things

Finding the Weight of Things

Larry Eigner's Ecrippoetics

GEORGE HART

The University of Alabama Press Tuscaloosa

The University of Alabama Press
Tuscaloosa, Alabama 35487-0380
uapress.ua.edu

Typeface: Minion Pro

Cover image: Larry Eigner, May 1959, photographer
unknown; courtesy of the Poetry Foundation
Cover design: David Nees

Cataloging-in-Publication data is available from the Library of Congress.
ISBN: 978-0-8173-2113-0
E-ISBN: 978-0-8173-9386-1

for

‡‡my
SUSAN favorite
person‡‡

as Larry Eigner the one day yet, so many years ago I
read in Gloucester—to half a dozen people still—
                                                                asked me
why, meaning my poetry doesn't
help anybody.

Charles Olson, "(Literary Result)"

What does literature do to help ecology?

Larry Eigner, Letter to *Wild Dog*

Contents

Preface

A Note on Citing Eigner's Poems

Since the layout of Eigner's poems on the page depends on the monospaced Courier font, block quotations are presented in that typeface. Run-in quotations of Eigner's poems, as well as quotations from his published prose and his unpublished correspondence, do not attempt to reproduce the spacing, so they are presented in the standard font chosen for this volume. All citations of Eigner's published poetry are from the four-volume *The Collected Poems of Larry Eigner*, edited by Curtis Faville and Robert Grenier (Stanford, CA: Stanford University Press, 2010), referred to by *CP* and volume and page number in parenthetical citations.

A Note on Transcriptions

Eigner's capitalization, punctuation, and spelling have all been retained in my transcriptions of his unpublished correspondence. Obvious misstrikes on the typewriter keyboard have been silently corrected. Where a key failed to make an impression, but the intended letter is determinable, that gap has been silently filled in with the appropriate letter. Eigner's variable paragraph indents and margins have been standardized. Illegible strikeouts using typewriter keys have been omitted; strikeouts in pencil have been retained and indicated with an overstrike line. Illegible notes in pencil have been omitted, and some typed notes have been as well. Brief marginal notes have been inserted in-line in brackets; longer marginal notes appear at the end of the body of the letter. Eigner's use of spaces between letters to indicate poem titles has been retained, but other irregular spacing has been standardized. Eigner created his own punctuation mark for asides and afterthoughts by overstriking an open and closed parenthesis; these marks are represented by double daggers (‡) in the transcription. Eigner's use of a two-point ellipsis to abbreviate words and names has been retained. Double hyphens have been converted to em dashes, but at times Eigner used a single hyphen with space on both sides to indicate dashes, and these have been retained. If Eigner indicated a title or emphasized a word with partial or full underscoring, the title or word appears in italics here. Quotations of published letters are as they appear in those publications.

Acknowledgments

My first publication on Larry Eigner predates this book by two decades. Reading Eigner's poetry through these years has convinced me that he is our great poet of interconnectedness. That article on Eigner's postmodern "nature/ poetry," as I then called it, connected me with more people than anything else I have written. The article derived from research in which I was applying my mentor Albert Gelpi's distinction between postmodernist and neoromantic strains of postwar American poetics to nature poetry. I came across the lovely Black Sparrow Press edition of Eigner's *Waters / Places / A Time*, edited by Robert Grenier, in a used bookstore in Palo Alto, and I realized I had found the poet I was looking for to extend Charles Olson's projective verse into a postmodern ecopoetics. Bob was a former student of Al's, at Harvard, and he had recently just ended a nearly ten-year stint as Eigner's roommate and helper (along with Kathleen Frumkin) across the Bay in Berkeley. I never met Eigner through this connection, but Bob generously and fully replied to my inquiries about Eigner when Al put me in touch with him after I left the Bay Area. I presented a paper based on this early research at the Association for the Study of Literature and Environment conference in Missoula, Montana, in 1997. Also on the panel was Matthew Cooperman, presenting on Charles Olson and ecology, and both of our papers were selected for publication in *Reading under the Sign of Nature: New Essays in Ecocriticism*, edited by John Tallmadge and Henry Harrington, the conference hosts. Once that collection was released, Jonathan Skinner hailed me from Buffalo, New York, sending copies of his *ecopoetics* journal. I was just catching the wave of interest in Eigner and ecology, and it was encouraging to find other surfers there, too.

Poets and scholars who knew, worked with, wrote about, and cared for Larry Eigner have offered me nothing but encouragement for my work on Eigner's poetry. Michael Davidson, whose essay "Missing Larry" began as a keynote at the National Poetry Foundation's North American Poetry in the 1960s conference in 1999, has supported many of my publications on Eigner, and I cannot thank him enough (the only other paper on Eigner at that conference was mine). A few chapters in *Finding the Weight of Things: Larry*

Eigner's Ecrippoetics began as presentations at the Louisville Conference on Literature and Culture since 1900, one of the livelier venues for work on experimental poetics thanks to Alan Golding, and other panelists that I have presented with there include Jennifer Bartlett, Barrett Watten, Ondrea Ackerman, and Andrew Rippeon. Barrett is also one of the original "Eignerians" who helped me greatly in thinking about his poetics. Part of the introduction was presented at the University of Pennsylvania's New Disability Poetics Symposium in October 2018, organized by Jennifer Bartlett, Ariel Resnikoff, and Orchid Tierney.

I do not use social media, so I am grateful to my good friend Glenn Bach, who saw Jennifer's posts about her Eigner biography and put us in touch. Jennifer is now a dear friend, without whose interest in and encouragement of my work this book would not have come to be in that way that it has. Since Jennifer lives in Brooklyn and I am in Southern California, we have traded archival materials that the other would not have easy access to, and sharing our ongoing mutual discoveries from Eigner's vast correspondence has been one of the true delights of writing this book.

I would like also to thank the librarians and staff members of the various archives that I consulted during my research. These include the Library Special Collections, Charles E. Young Research Library, University of California, Los Angeles; the Department of Special Collections, Stanford University Libraries; the Archives and Special Collections at the Thomas J. Dodd Research Center, University of Connecticut Library; the Harry Ransom Center at the University of Texas at Austin; the Fales Library and Special Collections, New York University; and the Henry W. and Albert A. Berg Collection of English and American Literature at the New York Public Library. I want particularly to thank James Maynard at the Poetry Collection of the University Libraries, University at Buffalo, State University of New York; Lynda Claassen at the Special Collections and Archives, University of California, San Diego; and Elspeth Healey at the Kenneth Spencer Research Library, University of Kansas.

Richard and Beverly Eigner are owed a huge debt of gratitude for always granting permission to quote from Eigner's published and unpublished work, and I am sad that Richard passed away before this book was finished. I want also to thank Jack Foley, Charles Bernstein, and Hank Lazer for their support and encouragement; Dan Waterman, Pete Beatty, and the staff at the University of Alabama Press for their assistance; and Jessica Hinds-Bond for her excellent copyediting. The two anonymous reviewers who read the manuscript made many useful suggestions that helped me improve the writing and argumentation, for which I am grateful.

This book is dedicated to my favorite person, Susan Wiggins, who, lucky for me, is also my wife.

Finding the Weight of Things

INTRODUCTION

Finding the Weight of Things

Eigner's Ecrippoetics

> You play and feel your way by ear and eye. But always you have hindsights, if not insights.
>
> Larry Eigner, "Qs & As (?) Large and Small"

There are many definitions of ecopoetry and ecopoetics, but none quite fits Larry Eigner's work.[1] John Kinsella goes so far as to say that he has "grave doubts that an 'ecopoetics' can be anything but personal."[2] If this is so, then Eigner's personal ecopoetics could be called his *ecrippoetics*, as I propose. The ungainliness of the term marks the intersection of the poet's physical abilities, writing technology, and ecological crisis. As Eigner was a person with disabilities whose political interests focused on environmental issues, his use of a manual typewriter "crips" ecopoetics and "ecologizes" disability poetics. Eigner rarely mentioned his disability in his poems, but it is from such a disability perspective that his interest in experimental poetics and concern for ecology emerged, and the defamiliar body is the locus at which these approaches to poetry—eco and crip—merge into Eigner's idiosyncratic ecrippoetics. Eigner's disability informs his practice of shaping a material page, but it does not determine how he writes or what he chooses to write about. Because he *plays* and *feels* his way "by ear and eye," Eigner's ecrippoetics makes poems that are rich in both aural and visual texture. It is what Timothy Morton's deconstructive ecocriticism calls an "ambient poetics," the main elements of which "reflect[] the significance of multi-media in general, and synethesia in particular."[3] The relationship between eye and ear, writing and speaking, necessarily involves space and time, and dividing eye from ear distinguishes what language in different mediums does in terms of space and time: graphic marks on a surface spatialize language and make it visible; articulated utterances happen in time and are invisible. "Ambience," Morton observes, "denotes a sense of circumambient, or surrounding, *world.* It suggests something material and physical, though somewhat intangible, as if space itself had a material aspect."[4] Eigner's ecrippoetics gives space a material aspect by creating a visual form, and that visual form, in turn, corresponds to an aural performance of voice in time. Because it presents an ecological content and produces an ecological form, Eigner's mixed-media poetry is the prime example of a poetry that thinks Morton's "ecological thought," in which inside and outside, content and form, foreground and background, ear and eye, voice and image come into an uncanny juxtaposition on the page and in the world.[5] This introduction will examine two overall elements of the *form* made by Eigner's ecrippoetics: the materiality of writing and embodied temporality. The chapters that follow are a literary-historical account of the development of Eigner's way of writing, focusing on both the ecological form and the ecological content of the poems, using various archival materials for information and context.

I can only play one note at a time

Eigner's ecrippoetics thinks the ecological thought, which can be defined as open and unending interconnectedness, by producing defamiliar textual bodies.[6] Michael Davidson guardedly introduces the idea of the "defamiliar body" in the afterword to *Concerto for the Left Hand: Disability and the Defamiliar Body.* He is wary of reproducing the ableist tendency to see "proper" embodiment as conforming to a "normate" body, "but," he writes, "as much as the aesthetic is underwritten by an able body, so it is revised when the photographer is blind, the poet is deaf, the pianist has one arm. The defamiliarization of the normate body is also the generative force in new cultural production."[7] Davidson argues for a disability poetics that complements a disability politics, a poetics that would allow for this new cultural production to register. Davidson describes Eigner's compositional practice:

> Eigner used his limited mobility to create a highly idiosyncratic pattern of lineation. . . . His lines tend to slant gradually across the page, each line indented a few spaces further toward the right to indicate both the onrushing force of his perceptual awareness as well as his physical difficulty in returning the carriage to the left margin. Because his typing was limited to his right index finger, he painstakingly measured each word and phrase, often isolating individual words on a single line or using the space bar to mark changes of attention. And in order to avoid having to put a new piece of paper into the typewriter, he often continued the poem in the space vacated by his rightward tending lines. In short, Eigner's material page became a cognitive map of his relationship to space, phenomena, and physiology.[8]

In this account, Eigner's typing oscillates between intention and chance, control and contingency, deliberation and serendipity.[9] The spacing and indentations depend on the limits of his abilities, but they are also "painstakingly measured." His ability to type with only one finger slows the speed at which he can capture "onrushing" perceptions, but that pace also allows for sensitively marking shifts and changes inside and outside the poet's mind. When Eigner shapes his "material page" into a "cognitive map," he "defamiliarizes not only language but the body normalized within language."[10] Eigner's friend, fellow poet, and editor Robert Grenier emphasizes that Eigner is "*not 'handicapped'*" but, rather, "empowered by his / ability" to type and "shape the page."[11]

Because Eigner developed his poetics on a manual typewriter—he could write, but his handwriting is barely legible—the shape of his poems on the page is determined by the interaction of his intentions as an artist and his body's ability to control the typewriter, as in Davidson's account. Just as his experience in the external world is mediated by the prosthesis of his wheelchair, his experience in language and textuality is mediated by the prosthesis of the typewriter. Discovering this parallel, Eigner once remarked, "The typewriter is the only machine controls I am familiar with, except for the control stick on the electric wheelchair. Ah!"[12] The typewriter ambiguously records both Eigner's disability (partial returns of the carriage, misstrikes on the keyboard, irregular spacing) and his intentional choices (the place where the poem begins on the page, groupings of lines, nonlinear arrangement of text). Such elements create the distinctive shape on the page as Davidson describes; therefore, Eigner's ecrippoetics produces what Jacques Derrida calls an "irreducibly graphic text," one that achieves "its 'modernity'" by exposing the "purely graphic stratum within the structure of the literary text."[13] For Derrida, modernism's textual materiality is the first successful challenge to the metaphysics of presence because it scrambles the logocentric distinction between speech and writing, invisible and visible, inside and outside: "This is the meaning of the work of [Ernest] Fenollosa whose influence upon Ezra Pound and his poetics is well-known: this irreducibly graphic poetics was, with that of [Stéphane] Mallarmé, the first break in the most entrenched Western tradition."[14]

Editors and publishers of Eigner's poetry are well aware of this tradition. In "The Text as an Image of Itself," Curtis Faville, one of the editors of *The Collected Poems of Larry Eigner*, points out that Eigner's typographic play follows in the line of "early modern departures from the traditional presentation of distributed text formalities [such as] Mallarmé's *Un Coup de Des*" (*CP* 4:xxviii). Faville also sees Eigner's typewriter as "the key 'prosthetic' link between Larry's disabled body and the universe of print media," but, in claiming that Eigner's texts are images of themselves, Faville runs into some trouble with terminology (*CP* 4:xxxii). Clarifying what it is we are seeing or hearing when we read or listen to an Eigner poem will help us understand this visual component of his ecrippoetics and its relation to his defamiliar body. Faville begins, "Historically, the content of a text has generally been considered as having a separate existence from its physical manifestation as print. . . . The spoken word . . . was long thought to precede, or lie outside the parameters of the physical text" (*CP* 4:xxvii). The first problem is that a spoken word is also a "physical text"; it's just not a mark on a surface that we can see. Textual editing provides many more terms for the interaction of intangible language with its material manifestations, and Jerome McGann makes a useful distinction between a written text's "linguistic code" and its "bibliographic code"; the former being what the words mean linguistically and the latter being the material history and context of the text's physical form.[15] In Eigner's work, along with that of other exceptions such as Mallarmé, Emily Dickinson, or E. E. Cummings, the significance of the bibliographic code is greater than in other poet's. Faville's collapsing of "a text" into "the physical text" is confusing because all texts are found in physical documents. Using the terms according to the methods of textual editing, however, makes a clearer distinction. A text is a particular arrangement of marks on a surface that represents a work of art. Poems are not *texts* in this sense, but *works* that are, or can be, represented by a variety of texts (as well as in a variety of media, such as printed matter or recorded sound). We find those texts in *documents*, physical containers that hold the text. None of these are the work. Faville's gambit is to reduce everything to text in order to confirm the "irreducibleness" of Eigner's graphic form, but unless we destroy every other version of an Eigner poem aside from the "established texts" that are the basis for *The Collected Poems of Larry Eigner*, a text cannot be an image of itself.[16] It is a copy of a copy of a copy, ad infinitum.

Peter L. Schillingsburg, using terms parallel to McGann's, emphasizes the importance of documents as intermediaries between the linguistic and bibliographic codes:

> It will be useful . . . to have a term for the union of Linguistic Text and Document. I call it the Material Text. It seems clear that a reader reacts not just to the Linguistic Text when reading but to the Material Text, though it be subconsciously, taking in impressions about paper and ink quality, typographic design, size, weight, and length of document, and style and quality of binding, and perhaps from all these together some sense of authority or integrity (or lack thereof) for the text. These aspects of the Material Text carry indications of date and origin, and social and economic provenance and status,

> which can influence the reader's understanding of and reaction to the Linguistic Text.[17]

The "indications" conveyed by the material text (I will drop Schillingsburg's capitals) made by Eigner's typing are the indexes to his disability, among other things. Therefore, Eigner's material texts defamiliarize language by being "irreducibly graphic texts," and his defamiliar body makes the linguistic text's relationship with the documents it is found in also irreducible.

In other words, the material text is the work's defamiliar body. Normate bodies and normate texts attempt to make their material instantiations invisible, transparent; as Lennard Davis observes, disability can be defined as a "disruption in the visual, auditory, or perceptual field."[18] A linguistic text can be invisible in a significant sense: even when memorized and recited, a poem's linguistic text is still physical in that it is made of synapses and sound waves; it is just not visible. It is easier for a visually impaired person, for example, to interact with a written work's linguistic text read aloud rather than to interact with its visual material text. But a material text, such as one rendered in Braille, is physically available (i.e., readable) to a visually impaired reader; it's just not visible. Reading an Eigner poem aloud liberates its linguistic text from its visual material text, despatializing it, making it purely linear. An Eigner poem printed in Braille would preserve its spatial aspect, but can we say that this material text is an image of itself?

Some readers and critics propose that the material text constituted by sound is the better way to experience the materiality of an Eigner poem. Stephen Ratcliffe considers Eigner's poems to be equivalent to musical scores that "represent in notational form the sounds of a voice that otherwise would not be heard."[19] In *Bodies on the Line*, Raphael Allison proposes that a recording of Eigner reading a poem indicates how he "crips" the lyric. Turning the tables on critics who fetishize what Eigner once wryly called his "momentous layouts," Allison argues that "the repeated and uniform emphasis on Eigner's graphic aesthetic erases his physical self."[20] As in Faville's formulation, however, the term "physical" here is problematic. Certainly one's "self" has a material basis in embodied perceptions and experiences, but the self and the body are not identical. Allison and Ratcliffe both claim that hearing a recording of Eigner reading aloud is the means by which we hear his authentic voice because this voice is marked by physical disability.

Ratcliffe writes, "To *hear* Eigner's poems read aloud *in his own voice* (inaccessible to most listeners, those at least not used to his speaking habit) is to come face to face with the power of words to convey sense by sound (alone)."[21] Allison privileges a recording of Eigner reading a poem over the printed poem because he finds that it "show[s] the awkward, lumbering, sometimes indecipherable, and error-prone voice sounding a language that it finds a challenge simply to express."[22] I believe that both critics intend to offer a way of acknowledging disability in Eigner's work, but these statements strike me as just as ableist as saying that his typing is determined by his disability. They mean to accommodate Eigner's manner of speaking, but what they are actually doing is reducing the meaning of his poems to disability.[23] This is the tricky ground that I hope ecrippoetics can help us navigate to the extent that it is a deconstructive practice. A recording is a representation of Eigner's voice; it is a text, not the actual voice of the poet. The illusion that sound is the "natural," physical link between language and its signs is at play here, and the logocentric privileging of speech over writing reinstates an ableist norm against which Eigner's spoken words are measured.

In Allison's account, Eigner's vocal performance of a poem clarifies and corrects his ambiguous syntax and ellipses on the page through intonation and pacing as he reads the lines. The meaning is derived from normalizing and stabilizing the visual text.[24] Relying on his notion of Eigner's poems as scores, Ratcliffe locates meaning ("sense") in sound itself: "if one cannot 'understand' Eigner speaking his poems—cannot make out what the words are—one nonetheless hears what is essential: pace, tone, pitch, pause, silence read (pronounced) according to the poem's (page's) direction."[25] Eigner himself is skeptical of claims such as Ratcliffe's: "It's fairly incredible to me that the only thing to be had from a piece of writing is sound."[26] Both Allison and Ratcliffe treat Eigner's actual voice as a generator of meaning, whether or not meaning is intended. But sound and voice are not the same thing, as Eigner himself recognized in an early poem that ends: "After trying my animal noise / i break out with a man's cry" (*CP* 1:140). Sound without meaning is an "animal noise"; the subject must "break" from that noise not just to make his complaint about the world sensible, but to make it make "sense."

The poem as musical score is a standard trope for projectivist poets; it is based on Charles Olson's claim that the typewriter, for a poet, is "the stave and the bar a musician has had," and that modernist poets were using "the machine as a scoring to [their] composing, as a script to its vocalization."[27] Ratcliffe, however, goes further by equating the score with the poem (indeed, his essay is titled "Eigner's 'Scores' "), compounding the confusion between texts and works. Can poems be scores? Again, textual editing can help here. In "The Textual Criticism of Visual and Aural Works," G. Thomas Tanselle writes,

> The points that can be made about the nature of verbal works are directly applicable to thinking about music, even though the medium of music, sound, is less enigmatic than the ontology of language. What is immediately

> comparable about the two is that in each case the notation present on paper provides instruction for some kind of performance and is not in itself . . . part of the work of art. . . . Another similarity between musical scores and verbal texts on paper is that each can be the basis for a silent performance as well as a rendition out loud. Many people are adept at "hearing" music by reading scores, though when they do so, they are not experiencing the work in the medium in which its creator intended it to be experienced (unlike the silent readers of verbal texts). No two performances, silent or aloud, can ever be precisely identical, for the most that a score (like a tangible verbal text) can do is to provide a framework that encompasses, and delimits, a variety of performances.[28]

So, in Ratcliffe's model, each reading of the poem, silent or aloud, is the poem (work), and the text is the notation for its performance. Yet, Eigner's material page is intentionally "part of the work of art"; it is not merely notation for performance, so it is not exactly a musical score.

Tanselle acknowledges that both verbal texts and musical scores can have visual elements, that such texts or scores should be considered works of mixed media, and that the degree to which these visual features add to meaning would depend on the author's or composer's intention. Therefore, it is best to think of Eigner as a mixed-media poet, who has chosen (and not chosen) to add a visual component to his verbal texts. As Tanselle points out, most authors expect their readers to "hear" the verbal text silently. Eigner likely had this expectation as well, as indicated in this poem from the 1970s:

```
interior
  speech,
 thought
sweet and
 silent
```

(*CP* 3:1326)

Although Allison's intention is to show us how Eigner crips the lyric, an insistence that the slurred and hesitant enunciation *heard* on the tape is the *real* voice of disability seems to me to deny the voice Eigner hears in his head, which is "sweet and / silent," and just as real. "Interior / speech" is, in fact, one of Eigner's definitions of poetry: "Thought voiced and/or in the mind."[29]

Eigner looked to the visual texts of other poets for models for his own practice. In a 1985 essay, he compares the standardized and edited versions of Emily Dickinson's poems as they were first published with the Thomas Johnson edition of *The Complete Poems of Emily Dickinson*, which attempts to reproduce the poems more closely to the poet's manuscripts. In a note, Eigner wonders, "As to her use of dashes, varying in length (not apparent from the books)—and there are her ways with capitals too—could Dickinson have possibly been careless more or less? How regular was her handwriting? Was Gerard Manley Hopkins a contemporary of hers, before the advent of the typewriter, or anyway the realization and use of its potential, who's known to have come up with a calligraphic system graphing more specifically, accurately, how to speak a piece (in the mind)?"[30] These are similar to the questions evoked by Eigner's ecrippoetics: What is deliberate or intentional? What is the consequence of carelessness, disability, or serendipity? Eigner wonders, was Dickinson using her idiosyncratic punctuation and orthography as scoring devices for performance? Is Hopkins's diacritic system of accents marking his sprung rhythm comparable to Cummings's and Olson's use of the typewriter as a substitute for metrical patterning? Eigner brings up Hopkins's diacritic marks in an interview, wondering whether a musical score might be a model: "You wonder how versatile musical scoring has gotten or could be."[31] But, rather than using a visual musical score, Eigner more often used "a calligraphic system" as a model of his practice of producing irreducibly graphic texts.

Eigner imagines a relationship between his use of the typewriter and calligraphy, confirming his sense that his poems must be seen on the page if one is to understand how they are to be voiced and heard. He coined a phrase for it in a poem, "calligraphy / typewriters" (*CP* 4:1359). If the calligrapher's brush is a prosthetic extension that allows her to mark the body's voice in black lines on white space, then Eigner's use of the typewriter is what allows him to do the same. Eigner's ecrippoetic practice realizes the world through typewriter calligraphy. The paradox is that we can hear the "voice of the body" only in our minds, but we can *see* it on the page.[32] If, in suppressing Eigner's visual text in favor of his oral performance, Allison untypes his typing, then he also denies us access to the gestures of form in the poem in favor of unitary meaning. So, Eigner's defamiliar body led him to develop a visual, graphic shape to his poems that he considered calligraphic, but in what way does calligraphy—the form or shape of letters and words—contribute to a text's meaning?

In the 1985 essay that inaugurated the academic study of Eigner's poetry, Barrett Watten uses structuralist linguistics, speech act theory, and Russian formalism to find the "formal meaning" in Eigner's syntax. Watten worked closely with Eigner as an editor in the 1970s, publishing his poems in the little magazine *This*, which he initially edited with Robert Grenier, as well as helping Eigner assemble a collection of his prose writings, so he is familiar with Eigner's material texts.[33] In his essay "Missing X," however, he provides a deep analysis of the linguistic code, rather than bibliographic code, of an Eigner poem. Watten does not neglect the visual layout of the poem or ignore its "nonformal" meaning (i.e., what it is about), but his main concern is to account for how Eigner creates meaning through manipulation of syntax and grammar, suppressing predicates and emphasizing subjects. One of Eigner's key techniques is ellipsis, leaving things out of the poem both grammatically and referentially, and this supports Watten's idea of the "missing X" in Eigner's poetry. He writes, "this X could be located in each case *outside* the poem," yet, "at the same time, X could be" one part of the poem in relation to another part of the poem. The X could also be "the non-infrequent location of an apposed subject element on an axis horizontal to the body of the poem."[34] The missing X is a central feature of Eigner's ecrippoetics because it frustrates any distinction between the inside and the outside of a text. Thinking the ecological thought, which entails "a radical openness to everything," means that "inside-outside distinctions break down."[35] Davidson, again with some hesitation, adapts Watten's figure for his interest in Eigner's disability poetics: "I want to extend Watten's useful speculations about predication to describe the ways that the 'missing X' could also refer to an unstated physical condition that organizes all responses to a present world."[36] For Davidson, in other words, Eigner's missing X is disability or the defamiliar body.

Therefore, Eigner's material page is the poem's "formal meaning" as he perceives and thinks about the world in and through his defamiliar body, and any of these things can be the missing X. For Watten, "the unity is in grammar, not objects, though there are 'things' in the poem."[37] For Davidson, the point is not to reduce the meaning of Eigner's poems to disability, "not simply to find disability references[,] but to see the ways Eigner's work unseats normalizing discourses of embodiment."[38] For both critics, Eigner's work is a defamiliarization of norms, either in language or embodiment. Watten writes, "the illocutionary act of the poem *is* the poem, accounting for its own existence, set against all else, as Eigner says, 'to find the weight of things.'"[39] In foregoing propositional acts (referring, predicating), Eigner makes illocutionary acts (stating, questioning) stand on their own as objects, which is the goal of projective verse, according to Olson: "For a man's problem, the moment he takes speech up in all its fullness, is to give his work his seriousness, a seriousness sufficient to cause the thing he makes to try to take its place alongside the things of nature. This is not easy."[40] This aspect of projective verse is also what makes it *formally* ecological, according to Morton: "Ecological art, and the ecological-ness of all art, isn't just *about* something (trees, mountains, animals, pollution, and so forth). Ecological art *is* something, or maybe it *does* something." The "ecological-ness" of an Eigner poem is its material page, but it can also be the voicing of that page in speech: "The shape of the stanzas and the length of the lines determine the way you appreciate the blank paper around them. Reading the poem aloud makes you aware of the shape and size of the space around you. . . . The poem organizes space. Seen like this, all texts—all artworks indeed—have an irreducibly ecological form."[41] Eigner's ecrippoetics is the defamiliarization of the normative form that insists on a distinction between inside and outside. Rather than making meaning by relating the objects (things) in the poem to a subject, ecrippoetics locates meaning in the weight of things (words) on the page.

So, as Morton insists, "if we restrict our examination to the citation of ecological 'content' . . . we hand over aesthetic form, the aesthetic dimension and even theory itself, to the reactionary wing of ecocriticism."[42] Although neither Watten nor Davidson read Eigner's poems for their ecological content, the "formal meaning" of an Eigner poem is also its ecological-ness. In an essay from the mid-1970s, Robert Grenier identifies the characteristic of Eigner's language that is Watten's main focus: "a 'syntax,' open/radically conceived as one & the same with the very ('real') shape/organization of objects on a page."[43] Explaining his approach to Eigner in a letter to Bruce Andrews, Grenier cites Heidegger's concept of "enownment" as described by translator Albert Hofstadter. He finds a pun on Eigner's name in Heidegger's German: "what's his *name*?—apparently German roots in *own* as *eye*—e.g., *Look at the Park, On My Eyes*."[44] Hofstadter writes, "*Das Eignen*—how, now, shall we read this? Of course, it is *owning*. But *das Eignen* is *das Äugen*, and so it must be *showing* as coming out to be seen or as letting be seen or as seeing or being seen or both. Appearing is owning and owning is appearing. The sameness of appearing and owning immediately strikes the eye here."[45] What Eigner sees with his *own* eyes thereby comes into its *own* presence in the space of the material page, making a place for thinking (dwelling).[46] As Morton observes, "Poetry *is* place, for Heidegger. In some deep sense, it actually saves the earth—sets it 'free into its own presencing.' "[47] Eigner captures this idea in lines from a poem dated December 19, 1976:

```
saying
  the words making
 things places
```

(*CP* 3:1301)

"Saying" the words can make things *and* places, or it can make things into places; owning and showing can only be the same thing in the saying: "What presences—what is essential—in language is this saying as showing."[48] And, "showing" is not describing (in the "show-don't-tell" sense) if Watten's claim about Eigner's illocutionary acts is true. If things are in the poem but are not its unifying factor, the meaning comes from the form into which the things are arranged, the way they "strike the eye." As Grenier notes in the letter to Andrews, "Eigner himself, etc., doesn't seem to want to talk about his own [poems] . . . *Eigner* will say, if you show him an old poem and ask, 'what did you mean there,' etc., he'll look at it & say, 'gee, what was I thinking about . . .' "[49] The implication, Grenier believes, is that Eigner is saying *you look at what is there and tell me what I meant.* If an illocutionary act such as a question stands on its *own*, then the saying is a showing. This question and questioning is central to the idea of place in Morton's dark ecology: "Place . . . is radically indeterminate—it is intrinsically in question, *is* a question"; "*environment is theory*—theory not as answer to a question, or as instruction manual . . . but as question, and question mark, as *in question*, questioning-ness."[50] Eigner's statements on poetry are filled with questions and "questioning-ness."

As they come, what can things mean?

Eigner often, like many poets, troped poetry as walking.[51] In a 1978 essay published in the inaugural *L=A=N=G=U=A=G=E* newsletter, he recalls that as he tried to write longer poems, it was "like walking down the street noticing things a poem would extend itself." The walking poet finds things as he goes. But sometimes, as Eigner thinks in the same essay, things come to him: "As they come, what can things mean? Why expect a permanent meaning? What weights, imports?"[52] The first stanza of Heidegger's "The Thinker as Poet," in Hofstadter's translation, combines all these ways of finding meaning: "Way and weighing / Stile and saying / On a single walk are found."[53] For Eigner, thinking and poetry are the same: "a poem can be assay(s) of things come upon, can be a stretch of thinking."[54] Eigner's method of "assaying" the meaning, as we have seen, is to weigh words on the material page. The phrase "to find the weight of things" quoted above by Watten, comes from this 1973 poem:

```
to find

     the weight

      of things

       the fish

         the air
```

```
          support

        the flower
              in the earth
                pot

                  the woods

                        the floors
```

(*CP* 3:1152)

It is not hard to read this as a poem about poetics, an *ars poetica* that proposes to discover what "things" mean (without imposing that meaning on them) by *weighing* them, finding what it is that they support and what they are in turn supported by.[55] Indeed, flowers need air and water to grow, whether they are outside ("in the earth" or in "the woods") or inside (in the "pot" or on "the floors"), and each of these things reciprocally supports the other. The poem's linguistic code is clear enough a reader can find the "meaning" there. *The Collected Poems of Larry Eigner* provides a glimpse into the poem's bibliographic code because it contains two versions of this text: the poem as quoted above (in volume 3), and a facsimile of its typescript (in volume 4). The facsimile shows one of Eigner's paratextual notes to the right of the poem, its missing X: "In an interview Anselm Hollo citing the Provencal for to make a poem, trobar, to find, sd maybe at that it's finding thngs and putting them together" (*CP* 4:1726). The parascript, in this case, confirms the reading of the linguistic code, and the only significant difference between the facsimile and the "established text" in volume 3 is that in the typescript the last word appears as "flo ors" with a penciled correction closing the gap in the middle.[56] So, in this case, these material pages do not produce much more in the way of meaning.

Eigner often reproduced poems in letters he was typing, so there are also other versions of this text in various archives. Writing to George Butterick in 1974, Eigner types the poem into the margin of the letter and tells him,

> I got it on reading Anselm Hollo's speculation in an interview, after he cited the Provencal *trobar*, that poetry is finding things and putting em together (and ma's inviting me to regard a pot of geraniums the man upstrs had just brought her, she held in her locked hands), and for seven months forgot abt Dr. Williams' imagination and invention. As I think I noted in comment for St. James Press' *Contemporary Poets* a few months ago, anyway I observed poetry for me has become thinking, a poem a course of thinking (and, e.g.,

> there's Rbt Frost's "The Figure A Poem Makes"), and sooner and sooner afterward a record or artifact of thought, while I'm pretty well incapable of long substantial poems. But, at that, how things go together or are put together is maybe pretty much of a piece with what import, aim, drift, vector, force, meaning, is discovered in them or given to them. Epistemology, oh well, and brdcast news![57]

The broader context supplied by this version of the material text—the Williams-esque moment of his mother showing him the pot of flowers—indicates what Eigner means by privileging immediacy and force over clarity and communication, which he often associated with his mother: "You know my mother said to me to communicate you must speak clear . . . first of all . . . though I soon realized immediacy and force take priority."[58] The force of the poem is the moment of realization that joins the pot of flowers to the idea of putting things together to find out what they mean, which Eigner has just learned is one definition of poetry. A different poet would perhaps provide some rhetorical framing to locate the scene and clarify meaning, but Eigner's ecripoetics works by compression and ellipsis. In his letter to Buttcrick, he admits that meaning may be "given" to things, but the way we know what we know ("epistemology") is a question, and sometimes we just learn things from the news.

Eigner restated his *ars poetica* over a decade later, invoking the notion of "finding" meaning by using a metonym for discovery as a title:

```
        E U R E K A

weight

  meaning

    import/ance

      assay, assessment
```

This poem is part of "an unpublished poetics statement by Larry Eigner typed on the back of an envelope postmarked 22 July 1987," according to Benjamin Friedlander, who holds the document in his personal collection (figure 1).[59] I have extracted what I identify as the "poem" above. The entire statement reads:

```
          E U R E K A    (Derrida?)
                      Retrospect frm
   weight              weiting poetry
```

if
meaning ~~yet~~ 1 thng np more
thn anothr, rliza-
import/ance tion
(aim of wrds, in-
assay, assessment tent/ion)

realizing or fully reconizing
thngs as come to (or not
too mch chased after?) -
ings
pple giving thns meaning
(wthin bounds ~~set by~~ they
set, set by unreacjanle
or unretainable or glimsd
and elusive reality?)

via emphasos, intonation
,

voice .[60]

Even when it is transcribed, the text emphasizes its own materiality by following the diagonal flap of the envelope from the top left slanting to the bottom right. "Retrospect frm / weiting poetry" classifies this statement as one of Eigner's hindsights that leads to insight. His typo functions as a Derridean metaplasm; the misstrike of *e* for *r* puts writing under erasure, and invokes the idea of weighing things to determine their value or meaning, or wei(gh) ting things to make them meaningful, and it also contains a pun on "waiting" that evokes a Derridean deferral. It is a trace figure; there is an unnegotiable relationship between writing, waiting, and weighting in this term. It is a mistake—certainly Eigner intended to strike *r* on his keyboard rather than *e*—that, being retained, becomes intentional and thereby signifies. The parenthetical statement that butts up against the poem, "(aim of wrds, in- / tent/ ion)," can be paraphrased as words aimed at meaning, a great definition of "intention" (Eigner called an essay on poetics from the early 1970s "Arrowhead of Meaning"). His questioning citation indicates he has learned a little something about deconstruction by hanging out with the Language writers.

"E U R E K A" is what Morton would call "medial writing." Although I can extract what appears to me to be the "poem" at the center of this arrangement, Eigner has made that move highly problematic by forcing the background

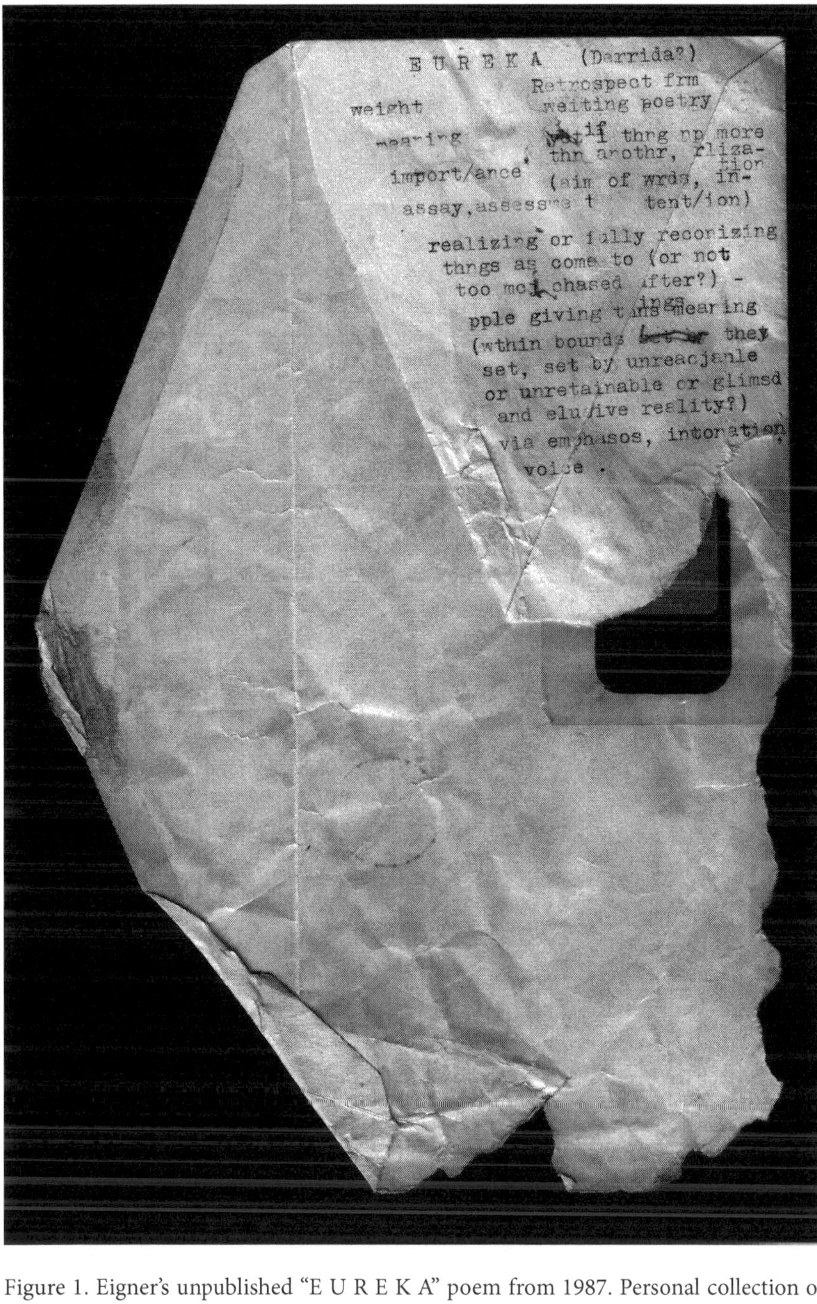

Figure 1. Eigner's unpublished "E U R E K A" poem from 1987. Personal collection of Benjamin Friedlander.

(context, explanations, mistakes, matter, noise) into the foreground (text, statement, intention, meaning, voice). Medial writing, according to Morton, "highlights the page on which the words were written, or the graphics out of which they were composed" because "ambient poetics seeks to undermine the normal distinction between background and foreground."[61] When everything is interconnected, we cannot draw clean lines between foreground and background, center and edge, inside and outside, intrinsic and extrinsic, text and context. Eigner himself wondered how much of the missing X to bring into the poem: "Distances between words are not negligible elements of a piece: pauses or silences. Punctuation can be intrinsic, as a title or heading can be, lacunae too can be, times when you (can) come up with such, ditto a parascript, and even a footnote has seemed nondistracting at least once."[62]

When we see and read the material text we can hear the poet's voice as he *intended* it to be heard rather than listening to a material text of his voice with its *unintentional* marks of disability. Meaning is found (or given) by the weighing of words through "emphasos, intontation / , / voice." Morton refers to this as the "timbral voice," which "far from the transcendental 'Voice' of Derridean theory . . . does not edit out its material embodiment." He continues, "One of the strongest ambient effects is the rendering of this timbral voice. Our own body is one of the uncanniest phenomena we could ever encounter. What is closest to home is also the strangest—the look and sound of our own throat."[63] Eigner's material texts are the defamiliar body that is the return of the repressed, the unfamiliar that is familiar, the writing that we can hear and the speaking that we can see.

Morton, in part, derives his idea of the timbral from Derrida's meditation on the tympanum, or inner ear. In "Tympan," Derrida notes, "it has been observed, particularly in birds, that precision of hearing is in direct proportion to the obliqueness of the tympanum. The tympanum squints."[64] If the tympanum squints, the ear becomes an eye that hears. As well as being a "sideways glance," a squint is "an oblique reference or inclination," and to have an oblique inclination means "having a slanting or sloping direction," which Eigner's graphically irreducible poems, as we have seen, often do. In the textual extract from *Biffures* that occupies the outer margin of Derrida's "Tympan" (as collected in his *Margins of Philosophy*), Michel Leiris writes, "in the final analysis caverns [such as the ear] become the geometric place in which all are joined together . . . the matrix in which the voice is formed, the drum that each noise comes to strike with its wand of vibrating air."[65] Eigner titled his first book *From the Sustaining Air*, and air, atmosphere, wind, weather, sound, noise, broadcasts, and birdsong are some of the "constant ephemerals" that his material texts realize.[66] Playing his poems by ear and eye on his typewriter all those years led Eigner to many hindsights and insights, which are to be found on his many material pages. Before I turn to the early work in the next chapter, I would like to look at one more irreducibly graphic text to examine how embodied temporality is a key component of his ecrippoetics.

another / time // in fragments

According to Michael Davidson, there are three modes of disability poetics: *metaphoric* (tropes of blindness, lameness, illness), *structural* (formal variations produced by physical or sensory conditions), and *sociological* (poetry as resistance and community formation). As the previous sections of this introduction have indicated, Eigner's disability poetics is structural rather than metaphoric or sociological, and this fact aligns Eigner's ecrippoetics with the language-oriented interests of readers such as Watten and Grenier.[67] "Perhaps the closest link between poetry and disability lies in the conundrum within the genre itself," Davidson writes: "poetry makes language visible by making language strange." By foregrounding language as the dwelling place on the material page, Eigner's ecrippoetics demonstrates that defamiliarization "applies in various ways to embodiment."[68] Along with making language visible, Eigner's ecrippoetics makes time visible on the material page. In her personal account of a defamiliar body's experience of temporality, Ellen Samuels writes, "*crip time is broken time*." Hillary Gravendyk proposes the idea of a "chronic poetics" to understand Eigner's experience of temporality. According to Gravendyk, a "chronic poetics [is] one that acknowledges simultaneity, chronicity, duration, and other forms of embodied perception." This "chronic poetics" comports with Davidson's "structural" aspect of disability poetics. Gravendyk explains that it is not "a theory of poetics that relies on knowing the physical conditions of poets but . . . a theory of the body that acknowledges disability, and particularity, as generalizable features of embodied experience."[69] Experiencing time as space on the page is one of the ways Eigner's ecrippoetics defamiliarizes normative and ableist notions of time and temporality, and Eigner's prosthetic relationship to his spatial environment brings him into a "time ecology," as Jesse Matz calls it, in which the "goal is to move beyond 'ecology *and* time' to the ecology *of* time."[70]

In *The Production of Space*, Henri Lefebvre observes how modernity corrupts the relationship between time and space. According to Lefebvre, before industrial time nature was the space in which time was visible. However,

> with the advent of modernity time has vanished from social space. It is recorded solely on measuring-instruments, on clocks, that are as isolated and functionally specialized as this time itself. Lived time loses its form and its social interest—with the exception, that is, of time spent working. . . . Our time, then, this most essential part of lived experience, this greatest good of

> all goods, is no longer visible to us, no longer intelligible. It cannot be constructed. It is consumed, exhausted, and that is all. It leaves no traces. It is concealed in space, hidden under a pile of debris to be disposed of as soon as possible, after all, rubbish is a pollutant.[71]

The commodification and regularization of time in modernity is parallel to ableist discourse and policies that enforced norms of transparency on defamiliar bodies. As Susan Schweik documents in *The Ugly Laws*, it was during the industrialization at the turn of the twentieth century that many American cities passed "ugly laws" based in "both a judgment about bodily aesthetics and the use of law to repress the visibility of human diversity in social contexts associated with disability and poverty—what we might call the sighting/citing of the ugly."[72] Cleanliness, healthiness, and able-bodiedness constitute a norm that justifies policing space *and* time. As Morton points out, "to allow things to get dirty is to allow that things are not at war with time."[73] Things themselves are this "time ecology," or "lived time," as we can see in one of Eigner's most admired poems:

```
Again dawn

        the sky  dropped
                its invisible whiteness

                     we saw   pass out
                                  nowhere

                          empty the blue

                                 stars

                      our summer
                                 on the ground

                like last night another
                                          time

                          in fragments
```

(*CP* 2:357)[74]

To speak in terms of "broken time," or "time // in fragments," is to acknowledge the essence of temporality as continuous flow, which, as Gravendyk notes, is an aspect of embodied perception ("crip time") rather than symbolically conceived temporality (that is, "clock time"). In order for a person to feel the continuity of time, there must be a break in that time, a discontinuity, that fosters an awareness of being in time, of experiencing temporality. In this way, Eigner's disability perspective does show us, in fact, that the experience of time is a time ecology, a temporality of interconnectedness, and this poem's meditation on time captures what William James called the "specious present." What we experience when we feel ourselves in time is not a moment like a "knife-edge," which slices through a continual flow to create a past and a future, but more something like "a saddle-back, with a certain breadth of its own on which we sit perched, and from which we look in two directions into time." On this saddle-back, "we do not first feel one end and then feel the other after it, and from the perception of the succession infer an interval of time between, but we seem to feel the interval of time as a whole, with its two ends embedded in it."[75] In other words, the present moment is specious because it is not a point in time but an interval, a duration "with a certain breadth of its *own*" that the subject determines not by clock time but rather by the experience of objects that emit time. Eigner's ecrippoetics allows objects to *own* their temporality by not imposing a uniform measurement of time on them.

In "Again dawn," which is dated "November 59," diurnal repetition (the sun is coming up again) evokes seasonality (the summer is the fall's "past"). Just as the summer is present in fall as pieces of it (in this case, as leaves on the ground), so the night is present in the dawning (the stars are still there but no longer visible). Temporal ecology in this poem is not feeling a moment in time (the "knife-edge"), but feeling a whole that seems less than the sum of its parts. As James observes, "the specious present has . . . a vaguely vanishing backward and forward fringe"; that is, it is an interval with an ambiguous beginning and ending.[76] The beginning of the interval is part of the future of the previous interval as it becomes part of the past of the present interval, and the future of the present interval is part of the past of the next one. In this way, we can think of James's "saddle-back" as a version of Derrida's "hinge," which is the "origin of the experience of space and time, this writing of difference." As Derrida explains, "this fabric of the trace, permits the difference between space and time to be articulated, to appear as such, in the unity of an experience (of a 'same' lived out of a 'same' proper body [*corps propre*])."[77] Eigner's "improper" body defamiliarizes the unity of the experience of the "proper body," thereby exposing the hinge that is both difference and articulation, that allows the invisible (speech) to be represented by the visible (writing) in space-time.

Although Matz acknowledges that spatializing time falsifies it, he concedes that "we cannot help but think of time in terms of space," and James's fringe, like Derrida's hinge, is a useful figure for thinking time ecology as the space in which we experience temporality. Matz writes, "The fringe is James's main concern because it creates the sense of time generally. . . . The fading is what gives us our sense of the past and our feeling of anticipation. Pastness and futurity have their originals in the fringes of the specious present, so that the whole of time begins here. . . . The specious present is 'specious' because it is not in fact the present but a longer moment, fringed by the senses of past and future and therefore verging well into time all told."[78] Morton describes this process as "a kind of relative motion between the two sliding trains of past and future" and says, "I call it *nowness* to differentiate it from a reified atomic 'present' that actually I don't think truly exists."[79] Eigner's *nowness* is also his *own-ness* in the Heideggerian sense Grenier gave to it. In making the words into things (places), spacing them out on the page to weigh(t) them, his ecrippoetics "allow[s] things to get dirty," which is how objects (including life-forms) emit time. For Morton, this means accepting Einstein's explanation of the relativity of time instead of Newtonian physics, seeing the curve in space-time rather than the grid that straightens it into time and space. "No God could be omniscient in such a world," he writes, "where time is an irreducible property of things, part of the liquid that jets out of a thing, undulating." Morton emphasizes, "You should find this idea extremely comforting. It means you cannot be omnipresent or omniscient. It means you cannot look down on the poor suffering beings of the universe from a position outside time."[80]

Eigner's early ecrippoetics thought about what it means to experience this space-time. The concluding lines of a poem dated "c. 1952–53" are a good place to end this introduction; the next chapter will pick up with Eigner in the 1950s. The poem begins with some questions, "Is it serious, or funny? / Merely?" but by the end of the poem, the question marks are gone, and we are left with Eigner's questioning-ness:

```
I am omnipresent to some extent,
but how should I direct my attention

sufficiently to what I desire, to
stop, to
what is charging on the roadbed, what
         going away, the
fire-gong, people and busses

    and even in my room, as
I know
             the waving sun
```

```
                              the

 constant ephemerals
```

(*CP* 1:76)

Eigner's wry self-assessment of his omnipresence acknowledges the limits of the imagination's ability to be omniscient, yet the "constant ephemerals" still present themselves for assaying; time takes place in the space between words (objects), outside becomes inside, the sun waves and the gongs ring in a swirl of ambience calligraphically typed on a material page.

CHAPTER ONE

From Sustaining Swampscott

Eigner's Environs

> *Two* themes generally: space, landscape, the neighborhood; and the sad state of society.
>
> LARRY EIGNER TO JONATHAN WILLIAMS, December 1957

THERE ARE MANY good reasons to consider Larry Eigner a preeminent poet of place, and for some fifty years of his life that place was Swampscott, Massachusetts—specifically, Twenty-Three Bates Road, Swampscott, Massachusetts. This fact also means that Eigner is a poet of New England, a resident of a geographic region and a participant in a literary tradition. Consider the other poets in Eigner's "neighborhood." Robert Grenier observes that Charles Olson's "principal domicile lay a mere fifteen miles to the north and east" of Eigner's Swampscott.[1] From Swampscott to Concord, Massachusetts, the distance is twenty-eight miles, and it is 105 miles to Amherst, Massachusetts. Eigner's neighbors are Ralph Waldo Emerson, Henry David Thoreau, and Emily Dickinson, as well as his immediate contemporaries such as Olson, and other early contacts such as Robert Creeley and Cid Corman, whose Boston-based radio program *This Is Poetry* introduced Eigner to the modernist and postmodernist poets of this tradition. Eigner himself often quoted Robert Frost's definitions of poetry, and he recalled his mother reading to him from "Robert Louis Stevenson's *A Child's Garden of Verses*, besides Longfellow and Poe."[2] The New England tradition is largely a Protestant one because it stems from Puritanism, but in the twentieth century it came to include the Catholic Olson and the Jewish Eigner.

The version of the Emersonian–New England tradition that is most relevant to Eigner is described by two important studies that link Emerson and Thoreau to twentieth-century poetics. In *The Grounding of American Poetry*, Stephen Fredman argues that the purpose of poetic communities such as the transcendentalists, modernists, and projectivists is to create a ground for poets to occupy in the absence of an established tradition. Fredman quotes

Creeley's assertion that American poets "had to *realize* the world anew," and he asks, "How does one, in the absence of a grounding tradition, 'realize the world anew'?" His answer: "To realize something means both seeing what is there and making that recognition apparent. We must 'realize the world anew' because we do not trust the realizations handed down by tradition." Fredman further emphasizes, "Ultimately, this is an issue of language, for language contains our realizations of the world. American poetic cults from the Puritans to the present have given allegiance to the broad doctrine we have called 'picture-writing,' the doctrine stating that words for things also signify inward reality."[3] Language must be connected to the world, yet also remain self-sufficient, and one of the main ways of achieving this in the Emersonian tradition is to attend to place. Fredman points out that "some of the most extended treatments of the grounding ability of picture-writing occur in texts whose central grounding strategy is the exploration of a place. Preeminently, three books illustrate how place can function as ground for American poetry: *Walden*, *Paterson*, and *The Maximus Poems*."[4]

These three works (by Thoreau, William Carlos Williams, and Olson, respectively) meant a lot to Eigner, and he studied *Paterson* and *The Maximus Poems* with particular interest during the 1950s.[5] Living in the increasingly suburbanized Swampscott was not a problem—Fredman notes that Thoreau, Williams, and Olson "situated themselves in locales that make no pretense to cultural centrality"—but the methods for grounding in this tradition do present potential obstacles for Eigner. As Fredman writes, "In the course of writing whole books about placement, Thoreau, Williams, and Olson move through three levels of engagement with the place: a pacing of the actual ground; a gauging of the human activities that occur upon on it; and a posing of principles consonant with the lessons learned by extended attention to place."[6]

For a poet with physical disabilities, "a pacing of the actual ground" is not so easy to do. As I have discussed elsewhere, Eigner tropes walking as poetry just as Thoreau, Williams, and Olson do, but his disability perspective turns an ableist rhetoric and "upright" poetics into an ecopoetics that accommodates disability and moving by other means.[7] As I will argue here, this is a substantial contribution to Emersonian poetics in that it more fully connects language to the world by emphasizing its embodiment. The implications for a poetics of place are significant. Too often ecocriticism reads Thoreauvian practice as establishing a sacred space, a transformation of the mundane and common into a holy site. Eigner's practice does not produce sacred space or fetishize place. And this, in fact, makes him more significantly a New England poet.[8] It is easy to forget that "Thoreau's island / of woods," as Eigner calls it in one poem, was chosen for its availability and convenience more than its particular importance as a place (*CP* 2:702). Geographer J. B. Jackson describes the disruptions in landscape order precipitated by the Great Awakening in eighteenth-century New England: "the movement abolished the idea that there were different kinds of space of varying sanctity. It decreed that all spaces—whether in the church or elsewhere—were of equal value, undifferentiated and even interchangeable."[9] In its awareness of both space and place, Eigner's ecrippoetics realizes a necessary corrective to the investment of the sacred and the sublime in particular landscapes that is still, today, a hallmark of environmentalist politics and rhetoric. His ecrippoetics acknowledges that being environed is the significant experience, one that can (and does) happen anywhere. I will examine this aspect of Eigner's ecrippoetics as a form of what is called "veer ecology" later in this chapter.

H. Daniel Peck's classic study *Thoreau's Morning Work* also offers a meaningful context for Eigner's place in this tradition. For Peck, Thoreau's "morning work" is combining memory and sensory perception in order to create a sense of the cosmos as home. This endeavor is what links Thoreau to certain twentieth-century writers: "Thoreau is a writer who, because of a unique mixture of predilection and ideas, stands at the threshold of an objectivist, process-oriented philosophy, even though he did not fully comprehend the radical implications of his morning work." Eigner does not share Thoreau's transcendental idealism, but, as Peck notes, this tradition, despite its roots in Emersonian idealism, is not truly an idealist one: "Philosophical idealism was inevitably [Thoreau's] legacy. But what makes him so interesting to us is that he inherited idealism not as a faith but as a problem. His intense love of the sentient world of things, his profound reluctance to leave things behind even as he tried to view them symbolically, drove him toward strategies of perception and language that anticipate twentieth-century poetry and thought. In the living practice of his Journal, he stands on the threshold of an objectivist, process-oriented philosophy."[10] So, according to Peck, we can trace a line from Thoreau straight through to Williams and Olson, an antipoetry tradition that emphasizes process (poetics) over product (poem).

Peck, picking up on Thoreau's statement that "wherever I sat, there I might live, and the landscape radiated from me accordingly," also contributes an apt phrase with which to think about Eigner: "Everything that enters this radius, by definition, belongs to a proximate world, a world of 'the nearest bough.'"[11] This idea of "a proximate world" is right for Eigner's sense of space and place not because it focuses on the nearest tree or smallest circle, but because it allows for those radiating concentric circles to accumulate: "At Walden, the 'interval' between the near and the far (between the proximate world of Thoreau's hut and the more distant world inhabited by the loon) disappears. . . . And when space becomes extension, everything is proximate;

we are at home in the universe."[12] Compare this to Eigner's "calculus of everyday life experience": "Well, how does (some of) the forest go together with the trees. How might it, maybe. Forest of possibilities (in language anyway)—ways in and ways out. Near and far—wide and narrow (circles). Your neighborhood and how much of the world otherwise."[13] Eigner's ecrippoetics asks these questions, but it does not have definitive answers. This chapter will examine Eigner's proximate world in the 1950s, how he begins this process of grounding, as Fredman calls it, and how he develops his ecrippoetics in order to figure out how far his neighborhood extends.

Your neighborhood and how much of the world otherwise

Let's now take a more detailed look at Larry Eigner's proximate world and the way that his ecrippoetics begins to reveal it in the 1950s. His autobiographical story "What A Time Distance" (1968–69), which describes his childhood in the 1930s, is a remarkable account of Eigner's early disability experience.[14] An expanding description of his house, family, street, neighborhood, neighbors, relatives, and town—the places and people that constituted his proximate world—it is a total evocation of a childhood in Swampscott, Massachusetts. His attention is in part determined by his nonambulatory condition most of the time. As he describes it elsewhere: "I'm nosy in all directions, curious, what with enough things beyond sight and/or hearing, out of reach."[15] The struggle to satisfy his curiosity begins "What A Time Distance": "Hard to open and look inside the paper, after the front page of course. Amount of curiosity killed the cat"; and he gives us this view of his curiosity in action: "Upholstery. Wall-paper. High surfaces. Immediate. Tipping. Chinese Checkerboard. Checkers. Dominoes. Parchesi. Anagrams. Relentless gravity."[16] These particulars reveal the lived experience that informs Eigner's projectivist poetics and creates his sense of place in the world and on the page.

Consider the phenomenological detail of Eigner's recollection of his neighborhood in an extended passage from this autobiographical story. Describing himself and his younger brother playing in the yard and driveway when his grandfather came to visit in his pickup truck, Eigner recalls,

> There was always a cigar box or two outside and some cigarette packs variously crumpled, straightened out, to look at, the heels, colors, brands and near maxims, living around the curb or the sewer next door that swung around inches to the middle one of the three side streets, or under or midway in the hedges, their own or the other peoples', between grass and dirt sidewalk. Weedy. A facing sewer between gutter and other side of the road, along by the field, usually dense and high with nettle and plantain, which some years was plowed up and was put to corn, a mass of walls, 2 or 3 odd

> lots besides Atrescas' deep wide flower and vegetable garden extending a full quiet space to their driveway under the grapevine on pipes and their house, rose-bush backed by the flag-pole with captured German helmet and in a foot or so farther the bird-bath, the field reaching almost past the side-street to an underground stream that ran between banks a little way somewhere back of the manhole with its cover in the road just before a thin isolated part of the woods, small, until another house past the third side-street at the foot of the big hill the road went up, to continue after a path through a stretch of wood a neat paved way to around a bend at width where it met another large-spaced road. Shadows of a dog, or a single one. Woof. Cat. Unaccepted streets. The land out back of them, on either side of the back street, was filled with dandelion, daisy, timothy, ragweed too, goldenrod, filled-in swamp, sunk down, the football field beyond Damani's vine-covered driveway and summer place and across all, from Demprey, oblong wide sunk basin.[17]

The point of view is almost ground level because the narrator and his brother sit in the driveway; Eigner didn't use a "walker" or wheelchair until he returned from the Massachusetts Hospital School, which he attended from 1939 to 1941.[18] His attention is focused not only on the bits of trash he and his brother play with, but also on the street, the gutter, and the sewer, how they are all connected, what they connect, and how other objects, including German helmets, rosebushes, flagpoles, dogs, and neighbors, compose the environment around them.

Eigner's prose pieces were mostly written during the first years of the decade (he dates them 1950–56), and some of the descriptive passages provide revealing context for the poems as well.[19] His first published story, "Act," narrates the day a cow was brought to that plowed field across from his house: "At the same time I did imagine this cow of mine under the circumstances had about as great a field of vision as I had myself; that is, she could see as much building, houses, mine and the man's next door, as well as the road and my driveway, as I could see the pasture." The narrator thinks about how there seems to be fewer children in the neighborhood, but soon some boys happen across the cow, and the description continues: "And on the other hand there do seem to be a couple of blooming toughs that I know of and so maybe more, even, lately moved in to the side-street two lots down from me, which stretches way out back of me, recently built up with sunny and not-too-low-lying cottages." The boys play a game of catch circulating around the cow, and, inevitably, throw a rock at the poor animal: "It dashed behind the garage that is there fronting the road which is a block north from here, and went down the driveway, mooing, and up that street, of which I can't see much, but I got glimpses of it for a few seconds while it was still not too far up."[20] And, confirming Eigner's sense of the changes in the neighborhood, he writes in another story: "No woods or void lots here any more of course. The old houses. The one next door is being changed around, the old insides tossed out, boards, an easy chair heeled in the yard again even today, after they've already moved some of the windows by now, maybe end up with a different number. Work beginning to slow as they remount the inside walls, at least because I don't follow."[21] Here, then, is the prose account of Eigner's proximate world, a portrait that includes both space and time, the near and the distant, inside and outside, the familiar and the strange.

Unlike his prose, Eigner's poetry is not descriptive or narrative, but once a reader is alerted to the changes that Eigner witnesses from sitting in his position on the porch, or moving through the neighborhood in his wheelchair, we can see how often these incremental changes happen day to day. Occasionally, a poem will present a direct account of the building going on in the neighborhood, as at the beginning of a poem called "A WEEKDAY":

```
the foundation waits  (will rise)
between morning and afternoon
for a 2nd load of dirt

the trucks move

eyelessness, uncovered
windows, the outdoors
                toothless,
        the garage
 open like a grave
```

(*CP* 1:162)

The ongoing construction is just something to watch throughout the day, and, day to day, Eigner sees foundations and walls rise into his field of vision. Is the house "eyeless" because it doesn't have windows yet? Are the "uncovered / windows" unframed openings awaiting installation? It is easy to see how questions of space arise here, with the open garage door mirroring the "eyelessness" of the windows and evoking an open grave. In other poems of this period, brief glimpses of the construction appear. For example, "the plumbed lawn / beginning a house clean," and, "similar truck and so it is the same / dump / turf and grass" (*CP* 1:156, 1:159). It is not surprising that walls are prominently featured in the work of a poet who spent a lot of time indoors, and Eigner does see walls as barriers and obstacles to his perceptions, but they are also porous and permeable, and they group things together and contain them. And once a roof is installed, there is not only a new house in the neighborhood, but also new interiors that are hidden from sight. But, then again, the outside still relates to the inside. A brief poem documents the entire cycle from empty field to new house:

```
          O l d  M a n


 two big pigeons on the new roof
 below which he grew corn
                              ten years back, one year .
```

(*CP* 1:193)

The cornfield now only exists in memory, but the pigeons have immediately put the new roof to their own use: in blending memory and perception, Eigner is doing his own Thoreauvian "morning work." Throughout the 1950s, as Eigner grounded his ecrippoetics in Swampscott, questions about space and place, time and eternity, part and whole, inside and outside, become constant concerns in the poems.

we must be animate, and walk // turn abruptly // the lines are irregular

It is in this neighborhood that Eigner's ecrippoetics is grounded, and it is here that we can see that Eigner's ideas of place and space emerge from his embodied experience.[22] How do all of these *things* add up to Eigner's proximate world? In this section, I contend that Eigner's ecrippoetics is the prototype of what has been recently called *veer ecology*. Veer ecology emerges out of Nicholas Royle's theory of literature as presented in *Veering*. Royle proposes a theory of veering that is "concerned with a sort of *détournement* (as Guy Debord termed it)—with a twisting or turnabout that pivots on the veering in 'environment.'" Royle contends that "in order to apprehend the meaning of 'environment,' it is first of all necessary to reckon with veering. Analysis of the latter discloses new perspectives on the former. Above all, the theory of veering [seeks] to interrogate and displace all thinking of an environment in straightforwardly anthropocentric terms: if an environment environs, it does not merely environ the human. The human animal is not at the centre of the world."[23] In the introduction to *Veer Ecology*, editors Jeffrey Jerome Cohen and Lowell Duckert expand on Royle's theory: "An actively contemplative response to contemporary and historical states of emergency, *Veer Ecology* attempts to complicate understandings of human entanglement within a never-separable nature, emphasizing a material enmeshment perceived long before the Anthropocene arrived."[24] The Anthropocene had indeed arrived in Swampscott by the 1950s, as it had everywhere. Eigner's embodiment is what allows him to perceive the material enmeshment that *veers*.

One of Eigner's great early poems demonstrates how his ecrippoetics is a form of veer ecology.[25] The poem was first published in 1954 in Cid Corman's *Origin*, and it was later included in Donald Allen's *The New American Poetry*:

```
E n v i r o n  s

Many shapes of wings
on the sky and the table;
and large men carefully at dusk
lengthened by lights  watering their lawns

turn, paterfamilias

  and the sweet hay as I go
  from one leg to the other
more so than I might
mingled with barber's tonic
from the morning's shops
  of papers and bright rag
         as if we could
         take time out for life

 and the afternoon's seas,  like yards


At some smell of smoke
I found a spray behind me
and the two on my right gone
  tending the grass, all night
 everyone beautifully
   (by themselves   the same thing

time     for the surroundings

        against the strip of hill
      ending low, a space
      on this side, but for clouds
```

(*CP* 1:117)

Eigner often indicates titles by inserting extra spaces between the letters (to avoid having to use the shift key to produce quotation marks, perhaps), and the additional extra space between the last two letters makes the title a play on the word as both noun and verb: the *environs* is one's surroundings; to *environ* is to encircle or surround something. The movement of the poem is predicated on the verb form's roots in the French word *virer*, to turn. Twice, a person's turning emphasizes the surroundings: the male neighbors turn as they water their lawns, and then the poet turns in the course of his exercise. Veering can be both physical and mental, and it is also what writing, especially poetry, does (verse, like *virer*, is related to the Latin *vertere*, to turn). As Jim Ferris observes, "body metaphors abound in discourse about poetry. From the basic unit of meter to discussions of language and form, from the long, skinny finger of the dactyl to the poem's beating heart and loping flesh, the body is not just an important image *in* poetry, it is also an important image *of* poetry."[26] Of course, "the basic unit of meter" is the foot, and poetry and walking have a long association in these bodily metaphors. As we saw in the first part of this chapter, Fredman's grounding involves the "pacing of the actual ground" to bring place into language, and Eigner's walking would certainly look like movement by veering. Eigner describes the physical therapy he underwent to learn how to walk: "Then trying to walk, to let go, mother or a therapist in front holding him by the wrists, the other person closing just behind, lift to step forward, now curve to go back, but left knee and hip jumpy, and there was an edge, ankle his shoe hurt unlikely to go down, heel in the air, everybody helping out right except him."[27] In "Environs," Eigner is likely exercising by using a bar or railing on the outside of the house, so he can walk "more so than I might."

I want to go deeper into this poem with veer ecology. Cohen and Duckert's anthology is organized in chapters that focus on a key term related to veering, and two of these chapters have specific resonance in Eigner's poem: Anne F. Harris's "Tend" and Timothy Morton's "Attune." Consider the basic subject matter and context of this poem: postwar suburbia. It is about the end of a summer day, after the speaker has gotten a haircut that morning and is engaging in his exercise that evening. As he exercises, he observes his neighbors "tending the grass," watering and cutting their lawns. What could be more mundane than this? Now, take Harris's account of the verb *to tend*: "To tend to someone (your love), to something (your garden); to look after it and worry about it troubles the anthropocentric georgic mode: tend is not control, it does not yield predictably. Tend strives, seeking to draw one thing closer to another, to bring itself nearer to not-itself. Tend unfurls to tendency and intention and pushes to rethink agency. Fire tends toward burning, the seed tends toward becoming a tree, humans tend to complicate things."[28] In watering their lawns, the householders "carefully" tend to the surroundings, and theirs is the first turn in the poem: "turn, paterfamilias." After each of the three blocklike stanzas, a single line stands as a pivot to the next stanza; as the fathers turn around, so does the speaker as he smells their smoke behind him. The speaker wonders at such activity, whether it is taking the time to tend to life, to the long afternoons of summer that have a spatial feel to them, "like yards." In thinking about how we *attune* to the things that environ us, Morton writes, "an environment is not a neutral empty box but an ocean filled with currents and surges. It environs. It veers around, making me giddy."[29] The veerings in "Environs" turn from the neighborhood fathers "carefully" tending lawns to "everyone beautifully" doing "the same thing," "by themselves," all night long. Everyone takes "time [out] for the surroundings."

In the afterword to *Veer Ecology*, Royle remarks, "veer ecology entails, perhaps first and foremost, what Jeffrey Cohen and Lowell Duckert call the *disanthropocentric*, acknowledging that what the environment environs, what veers in it, never was, never is, and never will be merely or primarily the human."[30] The dislocation of the anthropocentric position by veering described here can help us see the significance of the poem's enigmatic last stanza. In its tendency to veer, Eigner's ecrippoetics is a disanthropocentric practice, a method of realizing the other things that are environed with us and that environ us. From his perspective in the neighborhood, the surrounding hills environ the clouds, forming a protective shelter for them, a "hut for clouds." This environing space also protected Eigner, his family, and their neighborhood in the hurricane of 1938. The autobiographical story "What A Time Distance" ends with a description of the hurricane: "Branches went crazy. The small maple tree in front just right, it bent flexibly in the wind and didn't blow over. They were in a valley between two hills."[31]

Eigner's early ecrippoetics veers into a dynamic environs in which human and nonhuman activity constantly create and modify space. In a review of Walter Gropius's *Scope of Total Architecture*, composed a few years after "Environs," Eigner writes, "Anyway, man modifies, adds to, even creates, space, temporarily, let's say, by 'framing' it, by performing various actions. Trees modify space by growing together, animals create it just by moving, therefore touching and seeing (a doubt arises concerning smell, which is the predominant sense except in man), and all fauna, as well as climate, which also has its effect, is, by tautology, an evolvement of space."[32] Eigner titled this review essay "Participation in Space," and he signals that he might not be entirely sure of his conclusion in the sentence that follows the quote above: "Though maybe I should go back to 'in space' and let it go at that." But Eigner's reading and thinking about architecture (the citations in the essay indicate he was also reading Frank Lloyd Wright's *The Natural House* and Lewis Mumford's *The Culture of Cities*) at this point yields the insight that the environment is not an inert space containing raw materials for human use; rather, it is actively co-constituted by the human and nonhuman, the animate and the inanimate, the still and the moving. In *Meeting the Universe Halfway*, physicist-philosopher Karen Barad expresses it this way: "Bodies do not simply take their places in the world. They are not simply situated in, or located in, particular environments. Rather, 'environments' and 'bodies' are intra-actively co-constituted. Bodies ('human,' 'environmental,' or otherwise) are an integral 'part' of, or dynamic reconfigurings of, what is."[33] To be part *of* rather than just participate *in* marks a significant distinction for a veer ecology, and, as we will see in the next chapter, it is coexistence, which Morton calls *the mesh*. Eigner captures the veering of the environs in the review essay as well: "Man, the being who is most nakedly in space, if he survives must embrace the variety of impinging things. The world is more various than monolithic."[34] To be "various" rather than "monolithic" means that the relationship of part to whole also becomes a question for Eigner's ecrippoetics as the various things of the world impinge on his environs.

and commonly parts of the world / are more than the absolute whole

Ecological thinking has long relied on a version of holism in which the whole transcends its parts (it is "more than the sum of its parts").[35] Such a holism supports theories of the Earth as a superorganism, what James Lovelock called the Gaia theory, in which the value of a part is subordinate to the value of the whole. Since this kind of ecological thinking can also be a form of ecofascism, Morton proposes that "how we think wholes needs to change."[36] Morton calls for an "implosive holism" in which the parts are more real than the whole, and in which the goal is to "subscend" down into the parts rather than to transcend the parts, uniting them in an abstract whole. In a 1955 poem Eigner considers such synecdochal relations in the experience of time:

```
       W h o l e s

For a while a year is a long time
as things increase in their number
   and walls break
familiarity comes

familiarity of life, which sinks
to a level of sorts,  space

        (empty except for
        the rabbit's-hat of things
```

```
Before crumbling, the walls streak
with some tangent of minutes

and life takes on a size
```

(*CP* 1:176)[37]

The poem presents a year as a bounded container in which things accumulate, and so, in one way, a year is a whole made up of individual parts. But years themselves accumulate in life, so are they wholes (as the title would have it) or just more parts? Things occupy space as they occur in time, and as they accumulate the container expands or breaks. The walls could be literal—the building and remodeling going on in the neighborhood—or they could be metaphorical, a way of conceiving the expanding concentric circles of experience, which brings familiarity. Things, however, are as mysterious as space, the result of the magician's trick of pulling a rabbit out of a seemingly empty top hat. The "tangent of minutes," the digressions and sidetracks of life, seems to dissolve the walls, and life grows to a new size. The concentric circles are indeed increased as minutes turn into hours that turn into days and add up to a year. But the plural of the title keeps the question about the relation of these parts to wholes open.

Eigner's discovery in these early poems is that one can't experience space without experiencing time, and the relation between the two is, in experience, never absolute (Henri Lefebvre's thoughts on space-time were discussed in the introduction). In his poetry of the 1950s, Eigner is constantly aware of the difference between constructed, clock time and the "natural" temporality he experienced watching the day unfold. Although he was always *occupied* with writing, reading, watching, and listening, he himself had no paid *occupation*: Eigner never had a "job" so he never "punched the clock" in the economic sense. As Lefebvre observes, life "loses its form" when modernity erases natural temporality from experience. The goal of Eigner's poems can be seen as making this time visible to us again, giving it form again, or at least pointing out its traces to us. Nature was never "*localized* in underdevelopment" for Eigner; that is, he never posited it as a wild realm apart from the human, even though he might have been better able to see it in Swampscott before the town was fully suburbanized. In Eigner's poems, time is made visible by being "apprehended within space."[38]

An uncollected poem held in the Paul Blackburn Papers at the University of California, San Diego, makes a major statement about these characteristics of space and time. Eigner tagged this poem "m3," which indicates this is also a 1955 poem ("Wholes," quoted above, is tagged "m7," so it is closely related to this unpublished poem). The poem begins with a couple of notes or observations, seen in the reproduced original (figure 2). The first, fully capitalized, reads "SPACE IS SHAPELESS, AND DIVISIBLE [. . .] SO THERE ARE NO LIMITS TO IT, BUT ONLY INTERFACES." The second, all in lower case, speaks about what happens "when people go into separate houses, they lose track of one another."[39]

I cannot say for certain whether the epigraphs are quotations or Eigner's own notations. The word *interface* was used as a noun in the late nineteenth century, but apparently only as a specialized, scientific term. According to the *OED*, the first general use of the word as noun denoting "a means or place of interaction between two systems" was by Marshall McLuhan in *The Gutenberg Galaxy* (1962). One wonders where Eigner came across this word in 1955, but it is plain to see how the first brief note applies to his work of trying to delimit his surroundings. The second epigraph introduces time into the equation and seems to modify the preceding statement. Houses give shape to space in a neighborhood, they divide in a "relative sense," and their walls with windows and doors are the "interface" between inside and outside. From his perspective from the front porch, the poet sees people disappear into their houses, thereby interfering with the interface. The time frame here is wide; the people may emerge from their houses, or they may not. An entirely new person might appear if a birth has taken place. Do these thoughts lead to the rest of the poem? The speaker mentions his own "light illness" at the beginning of the poem; did that prompt these thoughts? Is the "mountainous tunnel" that remains after he has fallen asleep time or space? If the people in the houses are different when they emerge, is the speaker different every morning when he emerges from the "mountainous tunnel" of sleep?

Eigner is beginning to think about interconnectedness. As the poem unfolds, the poet describes what Morton calls "interobjectivity." Morton observes, "intersubjectivity is just a local, anthropocentric instance of a much more widespread phenomenon, namely interobjectivity." He offers a mundane example: "The wiring in my house is an interobjective system." "Likewise," he says, "the houses in my street form an interobjective system with the street itself and vehicles, stray dogs, and bouncing basketballs. We may scale up like this as far as we like. We will find that all entities whatsoever are interconnected in an interobjective system that . . . I call *the mesh*." This is an excellent description of Eigner's environs. Consider this comment by Morton in light of the epigraphs to the poem: "To be born and to die, as well as to persist, is for the mesh to undergo some distortion that might be felt throughout the mesh if the instruments were sensitive enough."[40] In this poem, Eigner proves to be a pretty sensitive instrument.

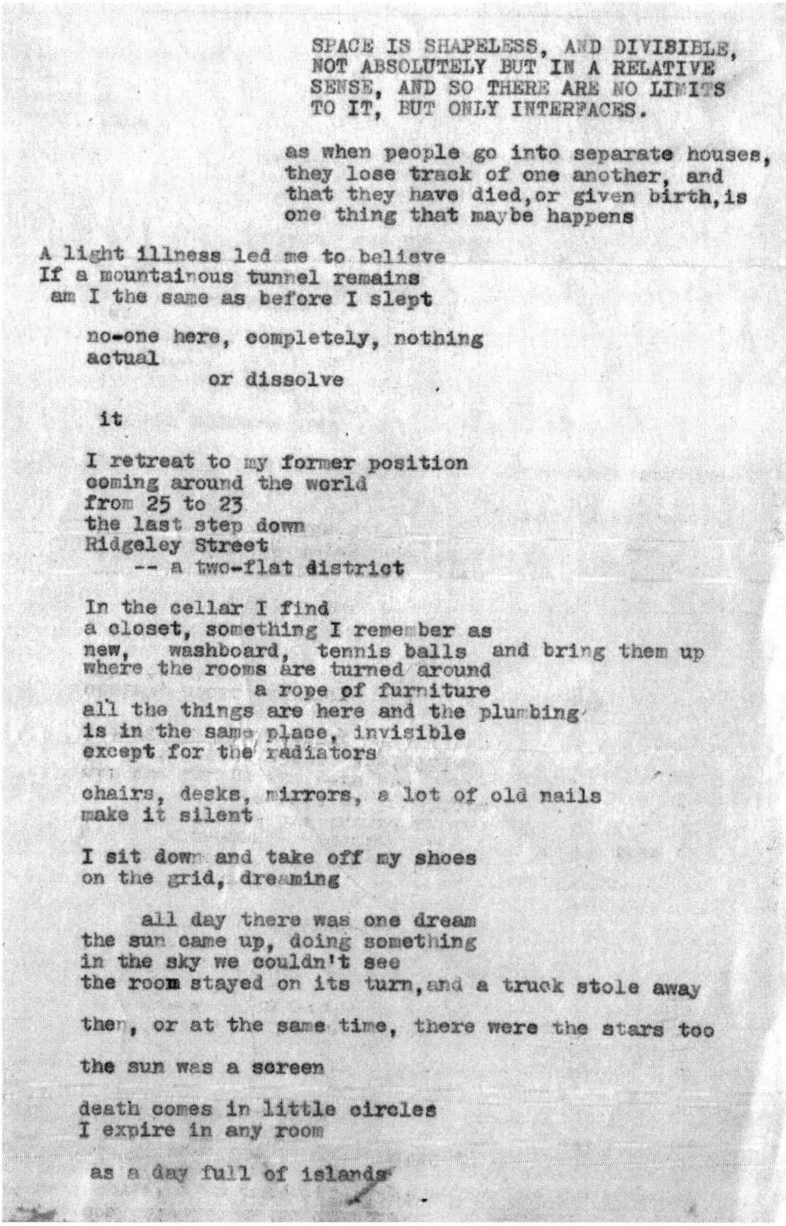
SPACE IS SHAPELESS, AND DIVISIBLE,
NOT ABSOLUTELY BUT IN A RELATIVE
SENSE, AND SO THERE ARE NO LIMITS
TO IT, BUT ONLY INTERFACES.

as when people go into separate houses,
they lose track of one another, and
that they have died,or given birth,is
one thing that maybe happens

A light illness led me to believe
If a mountainous tunnel remains
am I the same as before I slept

no-one here, completely, nothing
actual
or dissolve

it

I retreat to my former position
coming around the world
from 25 to 23
the last step down
Ridgeley Street
-- a two-flat district

In the cellar I find
a closet, something I remember as
new, washboard, tennis balls and bring them up
where the rooms are turned around
a rope of furniture
all the things are here and the plumbing
is in the same place, invisible
except for the radiators

chairs, desks, mirrors, a lot of old nails
make it silent

I sit down and take off my shoes
on the grid, dreaming

all day there was one dream
the sun came up, doing something
in the sky we couldn't see
the room stayed on its turn,and a truck stole away

then, or at the same time, there were the stars too

the sun was a screen

death comes in little circles
I expire in any room

as a day full of islands

Figure 2. "A light illness . . ." Letter from Eigner to Paul Blackburn, Paul Blackburn Papers (MSS 4), box 37, folder 34, Special Collections and Archives, University of California, San Diego. Eigner's return address and his tag "((m3))" have been cropped from the upper-left corner.

and how to make pictures of the weather

In our daily lives, we experience one slice of the space-time continuum as weather. As in Thoreau's morning work at Walden Pond, one of Eigner's daily activities is responding to the weather and atmospheric conditions; Eigner's ecrippoetics reveals the mesh by attending to diurnal and seasonal patterns. Climate and weather—which can be considered as binaries such as general/particular, abstract/concrete, theory/experience, impersonal/personal, long-term/immediate—introduce new issues for developing a sense of space and place.[41] Three poems from his first chapbook (whose title, *From the Sustaining Air* [1953], directly refers to climate), demonstrate Eigner's early explorations of space through his notations of the weather. The punnily titled "De Limits" is a poem that wonders about what "the limits" of space are, how one might go about delimiting such boundaries, and how one can connect the individual instance with longer-term patterns.

```
D e  L i m i t s

and how to make pictures of the weather
Nobody can tell  We stumble
beyond the impossible cyclone and woods
 into familiar streets by the coast

or diminutive lakesides,through their trees
at the bottom of the hill, different from the sky
and staple shades like winged land

and while the orchestras still are present in my mind
the forecaster does well speaking of fronts
              I live in continual air

Which might round my self  burst
       volumes of noise and
thick slopes blurring the smoky chimneys

                         like
                    ancient and foreign horses

and even when conditions are ideal and there are
still scheduled
                  as many as thirty games
```

```
in the middle of the year you dread the fall
waiting for what follows, when animals must retreat
and the winter must be got through

  then, Then, you occasionally see
                     the snow sharpen

          through certain windows and

memories looked forward to
```

(*CP* 1:75)

Relaying his impression of this poem after seeing it in *From the Sustaining Air*, Eigner writes to Robert Creeley (the pamphlet's publisher) in August 1953: "Then, you cant tell abt things too much. As, DE LIMITS, now, seems to get ornery, so to speak, after 1st 7 lines, and, especially, whiney in the last 4 stanzas."[42] The poet's "whining" about the end of baseball season and the diminished opportunity to watch animals during winter notwithstanding, "De Limits" offers us a view of Eigner's daily concerns and his morning work of making pictures of the weather. In this veering, environing space, there is no way to know where the limits are. Stumbling through the shortcut to the beach, or driving through the countryside, one finds that the familiar and the strange mix and mingle. Consciousness and memory further disturb the limits. The poet can recall the music he just heard as the weather forecast is announced, so past and future also exist simultaneously: the radio waves arriving through the air, the fronts of high or low pressure moving the air around and bringing the change in seasons ("I live in continual air"). As Eigner looks toward winter, he already thinks of it as the past, "memories looked forward to."

The two other poems of the trio are the first and last in *From the Sustaining Air*. Perhaps indicating Eigner's "wariness about beginnings and endings," the first poem is simply called "B." Maybe B stands for *beginning*, but it is also a *beta* following an absent *alpha*. (Indeed, there was an alpha prior to "B." *The Collected Poems* includes a poem titled, "A, Is it Serious" [*CP* 1:73], and the first lines of "B" are "Is it serious, or funny? / Merely?" [*CP* 1:76].) What is Eigner wondering about? In the poem called "A" he seems to be trying to determine whether a book he is reading is any good or not, so here perhaps this leads him to thinking about art in general. "B" continues:

```
        Miasma of art
                     The
```

```
more the merrier is my view

seeing the levels of the world

and how easily emptied space

                                     is
```

Once one sees "how easily emptied space // is," one need not worry about having too much to read or look at. The question of limits arises again at the end of the poem: "I am omnipresent to some extent, / but how should I direct my attention // sufficiently to what I desire, to / stop." How much art should he observe, how much history should he keep in mind? The paradox of the last line is the best he can do: "and even in my room, as / I know / the waving sun / the // constant ephemerals" (*CP* 1:76).

The last poem in the chapbook is the title poem, and it brings to a temporary close the twin issues of embodiment and environs that are central to the early poems. Its concern with weather and climate solidify its links to the other two poems:

```
from the sustaining air

fresh air

There is the clarity of shore
And shadow,  mostly,  brilliance

summer
        the billows of August

When, wandering, I look from my page

I say nothing

   when asked

I am, finally, an incompetent, after all
```

(*CP* 1:87)

Although this poem is dated "February 53" in *The Collected Poems*, it was likely written the year before, possibly during Eigner's birth month of August. Writing to Creeley on June 18, 1952, Eigner indicates what his incompetence may be: "I look very odd with a tray piled with books already—people ask me if I'm studying; this kidding at best, and I enjoy it. But if I had unlimited library facilities, and tried using them, I'd be flabbergasted and wd take a spill; blocked, I wdnt do anything."[43] Eigner has been dutifully reading the recommendations made by Creeley and his other correspondents, his brother Richard bringing books from the Harvard Library when necessary, but his disability restricts how much deep research he can do in the time before the Americans with Disabilities Act. So, his incompetence is in part related to his disability (the *American Heritage Dictionary* lists the synonyms for *competence* under the entry for *ability*). But his incompetence is also the failure that any poet faces in trying to capture the world and his or her experience in it. A final line, deleted by Eigner, demonstrates this poem's genetic relation to "De Limits" and "B."

Before becoming the title poem for his first chapbook, "From the Sustaining Air" was published in Raymond Souster's Canadian journal *Contact*. In a letter to Creeley dated February 7, 1953, Eigner included a copy of the poem, explaining,

> Wd you believe it, no copy of the 2nd version here, tho I thought I'd sent you one. And so this attempted reconstruction. If this isnt what Souster has, it's better, in all probability. I remember an additional word "tree" but that i didn't work it in. This gives a shade more weight and makes it easier to drop that last line, which is a headache: It ~~takes~~ took some alignment of what went before to see that preceding line as end. Only slight considerable doubt i have is whether the line was flush, or what? but yt cdnt be any other way.[44]

In the version included with the letter to Creeley, Eigner has struck out this line: "how should I record this weather?" His incompetence is therefore that of anyone who sets out to "record" or, as in "De Limits," "to make pictures of the weather." The fresh air that sustains us also allows us to see the clouds above the ocean, the light and shadows playing along the shore, the clarity and brilliance of an August day.[45]

Upper-left/lower-right

By the late 1950s, Eigner's ecrippoetics began to produce poems with a distinctive appearance, a fluid, sinuous shape that extends across and down the page in single lines and words, or clusters of lines that operate as stanzas. Robert Grenier explains,

> In the tradition of Wordsworth's "The Excursion," during this time Larry wanted to see *how long he could go on/how far he could get* on the typewriter page (and over onto the second and third page!)—"like going for a walk" was how he (later) translates that "Romantic imperative" (!)—the reader must

> understand that this means an extraordinary/exploratory/"expeditionary" setting forth from the upper left toward (*blank space*, with its initially seemingly endless/*inviting possibilities* & dark/"box canyons") the lower right *of the typewriter page*—making a ("magic") World-of-its-Own ("because" he couldn't easily walk otherwise?—much too easy!) ! Upper-left/lower-right.[46]

Eigner's poems have shed their superficial Olsonian characteristics, such as blocklike stanzas that are indented but retain a standard left margin, unclosed parentheticals, and so on. Paul Christensen graphs the projective-verse page as a set of quadrants that provide an orientation for Olson's themes and methods, but Eigner's page is better described in Grenier's account here as an open space with multiple directions and dimensions.[47] This expanding sense of space on the page allowed Eigner to expand his concentric circles of experience while at the same time continuing to ground his ecrippoetics in Swampscott. A poem from 1959 provides an example of this process and will serve as the culmination of his apprentice work as we follow Eigner into one of his most productive decades. Here is the poem:

That the neighborhood might be covered
by one roof, occurred
this morning,   Snow on the ground
phonepoles, flagpoles,
windows,   so many chimneys,

even up the hill

grass smoking out west
the tides, clouds from the past
vanishing rain
the base

beaten out,

death when you don't want it   what you like
is a plain object

the long-trunked clouds
a weltered event

shale   fish broken off

```
                a spiderweb hitched the dictionary
               overnight, I left it out there, well

screens in summer to keep the flies out

                           into the dark sea

the open garage doors
              under the vine which in autumn
               looks as if it still might hold

            shingles, encroached saw, horses
  somebody's back yard
                         angling out

you want the hills to rise

  twigs
       levelled on against the sky

                        After 3 days  the air
                            empty from the rain
```

(*CP* 2:305)

It begins with Eigner's familiar way of conceptualizing place (the neighborhood), and then the poem expands across and drifts down the space of the page and in the poet's imagination, encompassing ecological disasters out West, changing weather patterns, and, perhaps, an atomic blast. Then, it returns—it *veers*—to the immediate environs and the connections that hold the poet to things, that keep him grounded against such possible "weltered event[s]."

The snowfall makes the neighborhood itself a house, under one roof, including the hill. Perhaps this sense of security encourages the poet to look farther, perhaps news reports of wildfires bring the faraway closer to home. The natural base on which the superstructure of human culture depends might be exhausted, but its end might come in the form of a nuclear holocaust before that—"the long-trunked" mushroom cloud. From this ultimate fragmentation, the "weltered event" of splitting the atom (even fish in the ocean are "broken off"), the poet's attention hinges on a small connection that is part of his environs, the spiderweb "hitched" to his dictionary. Various connections and boundaries are then observed: screens create a barrier, the open garage doors make a space like the sea, the vine still holds. From Eigner's perspective here, he wants the hills to be higher—to see them, or perhaps to have their protective shelter as before—and he takes a bead on them, leveling his vision on the twigs. The final couplet points out the clearing of space, perhaps the air out West clearing from the grass fires after three days. It is also the clearing of the space of the page, clearing the decks for the next poem as it were. As we have seen above, in the first poem in his first book, Eigner remarked, "how easily emptied space // is" (*CP* 1:76).

Eigner's conception of space and place changed over the years, revealing how fully he had achieved a sense of place on his material page and in his consciousness: "A few years back I could feel in things a lot more than I've been able to since I moved to Berkeley (from Massachusetts Bay), it seems, I felt the world a neighborhood, or two dozen square miles of it anyway, (home) township neighborhood."[48] Geographer Yi-Fu Tuan writes, "The street where one lives is part of one's intimate experience. The larger unit, the neighborhood, is a concept. . . . The larger unit acquires visibility through an effort of the mind."[49] Eigner's poetry of the 1950s gave Swampscott visibility and created this sense of place on the page using projectivist poetics; Swampscott, in turn, emerged from a compositional practice that is an ecrippoetics. It is a more particular and humble evocation of place than is either Olson's Gloucester or Williams's Paterson, beginning with Eigner's curiosity of those things just out of reach, and extending out, stopping anywhere.

CHAPTER TWO

In the Silence of Spring and All

Eigner's Mesh

> Find, if you can, a point where there is no thread of connection. Our life is consentaneous and far-related. This knot of nature is so well tied that nobody was ever cunning enough to find the two ends. Nature is intricate, overlapped, interweaved and endless.
>
> RALPH WALDO EMERSON, "Fate"

UPON THE FIFTIETH anniversary of the publication of Rachel Carson's *Silent Spring*, the *New York Times Magazine* explained to its readers "how *Silent Spring* ignited the environmental movement."[1] When the book was published in September 1962, preceded by three extensive excerpts in a June 1962 issue of the *New Yorker*, its impact was immediately compared to that of Harriet Beecher Stowe's *Uncle Tom's Cabin*. If the atomic bombs that ended World War II inaugurated the age of ecology, according to environmental historian Donald Worster, then *Silent Spring* can be said to have initiated the age of activism. In bringing public attention to the dangers of pesticide use, Carson demonstrated to the world the validity of the first principle of ecology, the notion that "everything is connected to everything else," in Barry Commoner's phrase. Joshua Schuster observes, "Carson materializes the ecological mantra that all life is interconnected not just by indicating how one species is inextricably linked with another but also by showing how pollution in location gets distributed across many places on the planet. Interconnection is also about how industries are inseparable from science, the lives of animals are inseparable from human consumer habits, and ecosystem dynamics are inseparable from cross-species affective webs of sympathy and disregard, well-being and disability, outrage and fear."[2] *Interconnectedness* is the lesson of *Silent Spring*, and it so profoundly seized the popular imagination that Carson's book led to major policy changes and the creation of the Environmental Protection Agency. Furthermore, again according to Schuster, it changed what it meant to be "ecological": "For Carson, becoming ecological means working through crisis and critique, rather than longing for an untouched wilderness or a pristine, pure past existence."[3]

With this context in mind, consider the following poem as an index to Larry Eigner's ecrippoetics in the early 1960s:

in the silence of Spring
and all

i explore

inner space

at the Baker Memorial

the room within the rooms

like any other, with
the bed

then the other wing, so

all the walls
hold it up

(*CP* 2:531)

The reference to *Silent Spring* indicates Eigner's encounter with the advent of the contemporary environmental movement, and the fusion of Carson's environmental reportage with William Carlos Williams's high modernism (in the allusion to his modernist masterpiece *Spring and All*) reveals Eigner's willingness to dissolve boundaries between the discursive and the poetic.[4] Although *Silent Spring* deals with the "outer" space of the environment, it documented the invisible dangers that pollution and pesticides posed for human health, so Eigner's turn to "inner space" may be prompted by his thoughts on Carson's book. But he is also writing about a hospital stay in September 1962, during which he underwent an operation that "froze" part of his thalamus in order to reduce muscle spasms on the left side of his body. So, the "inner space" is not just the hospital's interior but also Eigner's brain and body. Exploring the hospital's interior, the poet finds that rooms are connected to or contained within other rooms and that the entire structure, supporting the roof, creates the space in which he finds himself. Writing to Cid Corman before his surgery, Eigner describes the curiosity that prompted the poem:

"Up on the 8th flr ther, Boston doesnt look like much, easily dismissed, then elsewhere hosp. sms enormous labyrinth, corridors streets, office on office, Gd Central Station .. Dont know what to try and take in."[5] This brief reading shows that Eigner's ecrippoetics, like Carson's environmentalism, begins with the fact that everything is connected to everything else, or, as we saw in the previous chapter, it reveals what Timothy Morton calls *the mesh*.

Eigner's correspondence provides further details that reveal how fully this poem indexes his ecrippoetics. Writing to Denise Levertov in October, Eigner tells her about an article he read on the "space race": "The March 63 Harpers lead article has it that the moon cant be reached in isolationist way, but we must find a way to collaborate with Russia, for it'd be niggardly not to use at least some of our unused potential, we might find life elsewhere."[6] Eigner quotes a passage from the article "Martyrs on the Moon?" by Carl Dreher, which argues for the vicarious adventure that space exploration would provide for those who agree to fund and support it, and he continues, "This has seemed much like poetry to me, most of the time, however it is. Fleurs des Mal in the silence of Spring, and all. I sent *Harper's* an awful 2100-word letter art[icle] on it. . O well. In same issue was an attack on a Congressman trying to encroach on conservation. So it goes." Thus, Eigner's "inner space" exploration is also a correlative to the nation's exploration of outer space. In this letter he also provides the context for "in the silence of Spring": "Last August in back bay Baker Memorial i was in this big room looking over the Charles and happened to turn to your quote fr *The Bostonians* i think at sunset, late afternoon, another thing." By referencing the quote from Henry James's *The Bostonians* that Levertov included in her preface to Eigner's 1960 collection *On My Eyes*, Eigner puts his poem in the context of an almost ten-year history with Levertov. She and Robert Duncan shared their encounters with Eigner's poetry, as well as his person, in their correspondence throughout the 1950s and early 1960s. In 1957, writing to Duncan from Mexico, Levertov explained that she thought that minor poets (or a "poet of feminine intellect"), though they clearly see details and particulars, don't have a sense of the larger whole or the way the parts relate to that whole. Then, she says of this idea,

> thinking I was generalizing, I was really only expressing my own feeling about myself, connected with my being shortsighted, as I feel Eigner's "nervous line" as they say of drawings often, and his "broken" content, are connected with his physical condition. Here by the way is a quote from Henry James (*The Bostonians*) which I copied into a notebook in 1954 with the comment "Quality of Eigner's poems": ". . . and wandered to the windows at back, where there was a view of the water; Miss Chancellor having the good

> fortune to dwell on that side of Charles St. toward which, in the rear, the afternoon sun slants redly, from an horizon indented at empty intervals with wooden spires, the masts of lonely boats, the chimneys of dirty 'works,' over a brackish expanse of anomalous character . . ."
>
> No doubt, going back, it was, tho' not directly short sight, still a combination, a complex, of that & my sense of being of strictly limited capacities, that caused me indeed to fall off my bicycle on the afternoon I last wrote.[7]

In their letters, both Levertov and Duncan associate Eigner's disability with his poetic line. While this is perhaps a crude form of the disability studies interest in embodiment, what is important is the seriousness with which they study his work for clues to their own embodied poetics.[8] In associating himself and his ecrippoetics with Levertov, Eigner confirms her sense of the "wander[ing]" attention of his poems, the way they register and recognize the "anomalous character" of the environs.

Thus, by the 1960s, Eigner's ecrippoetics is robust and the poet is hitting his stride, but, thinking of Carson's *Silent Spring* and the problems that it diagnosed, he wonders whether all this writing comes at the expense of action. In the October 1963 letter to Levertov, he writes:

> Dilemma: Living seems as good as doing (writing for instance) after a while Or the dilemma is you must get more or less specialized in order to make big heap snow (Beethoven , Conrad ..), but what is it doing, that particular size, not to mention snowballing, on top of your two feet of ground? As much as you can chew At different times though
>
> Sometimes it seems like ransacking, exploiting so much of everything to write And material is the most immediate and or constant thing, however transformed or muted or sublimate or whatever—"Jacob's Ladder," heh? - to be left alone a good part of the time, perhaps, at this point in history at least. It gives pause. It's real, hard. Would Dr Williams have spawned more interest in ecology if he had not doctored at all and spent more time on writing, cd Ginsburg now be an ecology columnist for the newspapers, a poet being by this time a good deal of a legislator? Well, I'm getting there, cannot on the other hand imagine myself not bogging down in job at the water dep.t, keeping the stuff clean, going kazy, drop in the bucket, only one life to "lead"?[9]

Then, on November 20, he encapsulated the same idea in a letter to Donald Allen: "I have promptings to for instance join the water department and try to keep the air fresh, but meanwhile I consider it wd have to be a drop in the bucket."[10] Eigner's disability perspective revealed early on dilemmas of the environmental crisis that are only now coming clear: How much is one personally responsible? How much should one do to contribute? How do we even know what the right thing to do is? In registering interconnectedness, Eigner's ecrippoetics encounters the issues involved when we discover that we live in the mesh: "The ecological thought stirs because the mesh appears in our social, psychic, and scientific domains. Since everything is interconnected, there is no definite background and therefore no definite foreground."[11] Eigner's poem about Baker Memorial Hospital exhibits his ecrippoetics, then, not simply because it alludes to *Silent Spring*, but more because it thinks the ecological thought and writes the mesh. The "inner space" that Eigner explores is not distinct from the social and built environment surrounding it, and the core insight of Carson's exposé—that what we think is external and outside of us cannot be separated from the internal and the inside—is confirmed. As Schuster points out, the dissolution of the boundary between inside and outside creates all sorts of positions that might appear paradoxical or contradictory from the nature essentialist point of view: "To think contemporary ecology involves admitting that there is no clear line now between natural and artificial components of ecosystems, and that both can be sources of uncertainty and irreversible change."[12] The machine is no longer in the garden—it *is* the garden.

my old machine / new like strange

Eigner's ecrippoetics is highly responsive to Carson's modern ecology because it is dependent on a machine.[13] Eigner does not so much write the mesh as he *types* it. In using the common idiom of referring to a typewriter as a machine, Eigner highlights the very thing that Martin Heidegger hated about the typewriter: "In the typewriter we find the irruption of the mechanism in the realm of the word."[14] The objectivist-projectivist tradition that grounds Eigner's ecrippoetics features many such references to typewriters as machines. For example, this is how William Carlos Williams described writing at his office: "I had my typewriter in my office desk. All I needed to do was to pull up the leaf to which it was fastened and I was ready to go. . . . If a patient came in at the door while I was in the middle of a sentence, bang would go the machine. . . . When the patient left, up would come the machine."[15] And, perhaps thinking of his typewriter, Williams turns the poem produced by the machine into a machine itself in his introduction to *The Wedge*: "There's nothing sentimental about a machine, and: A poem is a small (or large) machine made of words. When I say there's nothing sentimental about a poem I mean that there can be no part, as in any other machine, that is redundant."[16]

As opposed to Heidegger, Friedrich Nietzsche loved his typewriter, and therefore he is the antithesis to Heidegger's anti-technic philosophy. Friedrich A. Kittler observes,

> Writing in Nietzsche is no longer a natural extension of humans who bring forth their voice, soul, individuality through their handwriting. On the contrary . . . humans change their position—they turn from the agency of writing to become an inscription surface. . . . Nietzsche's notion of inscription, which has degenerated into a poststructuralist catch-all metaphor, has validity only within the framework of the history of the typewriter. It designates the turning point at which communications technologies can no longer be related back to humans. Instead, the former have formed the latter.[17]

This is precisely the reason that Heidegger—along with many ecocritics (for example, J. Scott Bryson, who defines ecopoetry as anti-technological)—rejects the "irruption" of the machine into the word.[18] However, Morton's ecotheory, although it draws on Heidegger's phenomenology, agrees with Nietzsche. In "Ecology as Text, Text as Ecology," Morton writes, "Life forms consist of all sorts of structures that are not very organic. . . . Humans keep trying to distinguish rigorously between the living and machinic. . . . Darwinism and genomics . . . show that not only is the distinction untenable, but life as such is a machinic, algorithmic functioning, and that what we call 'life' and 'consciousness' are emergent effects of more fundamental machine-like processes."[19] The fear of the living machine, the human robot, then, is not an outgrowth of a value system aligned with nature that privileges the organic over the mechanical; rather, it is a form of ecophobia.

In this light, we can see early criticisms of projective verse's utilization of the typewriter not as organicist rejections of the machine but as ecophobic reactions against "the irruption of the mechanism in the realm of the word." In his review of Donald Allen's *The New American Poetry*, X. J. Kennedy mocked Olson's proposal for the typewriter as a method of scoring a poem: "Who would have thought his Corona portable an instrument of such sensitivity?"[20] And, Galway Kinnell, reviewing Eigner's first major collection in *Poetry* magazine, writes, "The real value of getting rid of rhyme and meter, I had supposed, was in order to throw the responsibility for the poem wholly on speech itself. Here this is not done. The laying out of a kind of score by typewriter-spacing only supplants those old devices with a newer one, which is, this time, not even integral with the words."[21]

In the early 1960s, Eigner himself had reason to think about how integrated words and their medium were. Writing to fellow poet Paul Blackburn in 1961, Eigner describes a journal he received in the mail:

> I had a few things lined up, of course, out on the porch here. Eg the same day of your letter or 2 days later came from Germany (place called Itzehoe) this mag Rhinozeros mit drawings and calligraphically done poems—most of em

> broken up on wavy lines but one of the two in English, by Ginsberg, sort of walled and held in as well as clogged up by tall steeple A's (solid triangles) and towering I's, as long as lines above and below permit, and the e's just 3 horizontals of varying lengths.[22]

Rhinozeros was a small-press journal published between 1960 and 1965 by the brothers Rolf-Gunther and Klaus-Peter Dienst.[23] The text of each issue was rendered in calligraphy by Klaus-Peter, in varying styles and formats. Responding to the richly illustrated journal, Eigner continues:

> Which shook me out of a fine idea I'd bn entertaining lately thats come in course of my stuff, that it gets to a mesh effect, and might be a manifestation of my wariness of beginnings and ends as liable to be kind of stentorian and meretricious. Well, it's hard to tell in abstract what you want—in this case what to make of calligraphy, how intrinsic to poem (speech? weighed words) can it be? (I got this idea of *mesh* from one comment on Eyes, reader considered sense of eternity "a hesitation in the flow")[24]

Morton adopts the term *mesh* to express the core concept of ecology, interconnectedness, and here Eigner finds the same meanings that Morton invests in the word. Eigner says that his work produces "a mesh effect," which gets Morton's idea just right. Reflecting further on the mesh in *Hyperobjects*, Morton writes, "The mesh is an emergent property of the things that coexist, and not the other way around."[25] So, in writing poetry that is an attempt to realize things as they are, in coexistence, Eigner detects the mesh. His "wariness of beginnings and ends" also engages another aspect of the ecological thought: "The ecological thought has no center and no edge."[26] With no origin and no terminus, no distinction between foreground and background, the ecological thought is a key way to think about Eigner's poetry. As Eigner developed his ecrippoetics, he was thinking the ecological thought.

It's not just that Eigner proleptically picks up Morton's term in the letter to Blackburn, but also that he sees the mesh as an emergent effect in his poetry: the coexistence of words (things) on the page effects the mesh. What is more, he turns Kinnell's doubts about typewriter scoring back onto speech-based poetics, wondering whether the medium of a poem informs its meaning.[27] Does the outside affect the inside? Can calligraphy be intrinsic to the poem? Here, Eigner is not certain, but his ecrippoetics answers affirmatively. In relying on his typewriter as his primary means of production and, in fact, sometimes allowing the machine itself to determine his margins, spacings, and arrangements, Eigner has no need "to distinguish rigorously between the living and machinic." The visual layout of his poems, whether in the Courier font of his Royal typewriter or in other typefaces, is indeed integral to his words as they are weighed on his material page.

These ideas prompted by receiving a copy of *Rhinozeros* must have lingered in Eigner's mind. Almost twenty years later, on January 3, 1979, when his old typewriter was brought to his new residence in Berkeley (commemorated by the two-line poem that serves as this section's title), he wrote the poem that begins "calligraphy / typewriters," mentioned in the introduction. The juxtaposition of "calligraphy / typewriters" contrasts the organic inscription of "beautiful writing" by hand with the mechanical form of the typewriter. Consider how calligraphy was used by Eigner's contemporaries Philip Whalen and Gary Snyder, as described by Whalen's biographer David Schneider:

> Whalen and Snyder shared calligraphy mind. . . . They shared the mind that exists in the hand. Calligraphic mind leads and follows black ink around on white paper; it understands how black marks, even simple ones, as well as the white spaces described by them, convey meaning in a way that precedes and interrupts discursive mind. . . . Chinese and Japanese masters . . . produced works admired as much for the way they were handwritten as for their meaning. Strictly speaking, it's impossible to separate these. Whalen complained bitterly about how "dead" he felt his poems looked set in type and crowded on book pages.[28]

According to Schneider, for Whalen and Snyder, calligraphy joins the mind and the body, it produces positive and negative space on the page, it melds meaning and appearance, and it distinguishes between living and dead poems.

Eigner's juxtaposition of "calligraphy / typewriters" forces us to recognize the machine in the words—the words as machine-made—and, as in Morton's ecological thought, it destabilizes the boundary between living and dead, organic and inorganic. So, just as Eigner wondered whether the calligraphy of *Rhinozeros* magazine was integral to the poetry, here he proposes that his machine's typeface is integral to his words. If the ecological thought blurs the distinction between cause and sign, essence and appearance, thereby revealing the mesh to us, so do Eigner's poems. They are the mesh.

As we saw in the introduction, the "missing X" in an Eigner poem might be another part of the poem itself. This poem reads in full:

```
calligraphy
   typewriters


       my hat
```

```
(bureau)

    the world

       inside

          spins
```

(*CP* 4:1359)

We can fill in one of Eigner's ellipses here with a silent "is" to find one of these missing Xs. In declaring that "calligraphy / typewriters // [is] my hat," Eigner uses "hat" as a metonymy for one's job ("a head covering . . . worn as a symbol of office"), and Eigner indicates this with his parenthetical clarification: one's bureau determines one's duties, and a bureau is a part of a larger whole ("an office, usually of a large organization, that is responsible for a specific duty").[29] And then Eigner tells us what the duties of his office entail. With the newly supplied verb, we can read the poem as two sentences, or, now that we have reached the poem's only verb, we can reorder the lines to produce a complete statement: the world spins inside my bureau of calligraphy typewriters. Or, translated into Morton's terms: the mesh appears in my typewriter calligraphy. That Eigner identifies this as his job is significant; as we saw in his comments to Levertov and Allen, Eigner always wanted to make a contribution, to help fix problems with practical solutions, maybe through a job in the water department. By 1979, he realized he had been employed the whole time because, in the 1960s, he started his job typing the mesh. It is the interface between ecology and textuality that defines Eigner's ecrippoetics at this time, and as he continued to refine his practice in the tumultuous 1960s, his typewriter played a central role in what Curtis Faville describes as "the key 'prosthetic' link between Larry's disabled body and the universe of print media, facilitating his participation in it, while gratifying his hunger for contact and intellectual discourse" (*CP* 4:xxxii). As the following sections of this chapter will show, Eigner's ecrippoetics reveals the mesh because it is open to information from any source—from phenomenological perception to any sort of media.[30]

it takes imagination / to supplement / the water

Jonathan Skinner observes that "the air (or the wind) is the body of the soundscape, and Eigner . . . is always ready to give himself up to the wind, tunes in to it like his radio, adjusts himself to the news it brings. In this sense, he is the most 'environmental' of poets, our best listener, stenograph of the soundscape."[31] Skinner's examination of Eigner's soundscape blends music theory with acoustic ecology to demonstrate the importance of sound in his poetry and to make a case for his "ambient poetics." The closest parallel in music would be John Cage, who concluded that there is no silence and used compositions such as *4'33"* (which consisted of a pianist not playing a piano for four minutes and thirty-three seconds) to integrate random, ambient sound into music (or to make "silence" into music). Although he finds no direct connection between Eigner and Cage, Skinner writes that juxtaposing them "is justified . . . by what they share: a period in which the new technologies (radio, television, magnetic tape) were beginning to shape and extend the human relationship to acoustic environment."[32] So, considering Eigner's soundscape means we must listen for both motivated (human or animal) and unmotivated (ambient or accidental) sound—whatever is present in the sensible surround. Skinner is exactly right that Eigner is a recording device, in the sense that his goal is to hear what is there without discrimination or selection, or in that his typewriter is also a machine for listening. But this is only a partial account of how Eigner responds to sound because sometimes the sound he hears is in his mind (as a memory, a sound described in something he is reading, or an abstraction). The examples that Skinner provides are mostly drawn from Eigner's later collections, which contain many more short poems that are even more rigorously minimalist than the work of the 1960s, and in which sounds largely do come in from outside the poem in identifiable patterns. I would like to bring Skinner's ecological interest in Eigner's soundscape back into the 1960s in order to gauge how sound—especially the combination of motivated and unmotivated sound, or classical music and the sound that Eigner hears around him—is one of the ways that Eigner types the mesh.

This section proposes to trace the ecrippoetics of Eigner's reading and listening from November 1964 to April 1965. During these months, he's been listening to classical music (often compositions involving water as a thematic element), reading chapters on diving and shorebirds in a field guide, and thinking about environmental issues such as overpopulation, food shortages, and pollution. The great culmination of these themes is "the music, the rooms," which is one of the most significant 1960s poems of ecology, on par with such canonical "ecopoems" as A. R. Ammons's "Corsons Inlet."[33] In his examination of Eigner's "soundscape," Skinner observes that "'Silence' is most readily associated with John Cage" because of his *4'33"* composition, and the word *silence* is repeated four times at the beginning of "the music, the rooms."[34] As the poem about Baker Memorial Hospital shows us, after 1962, the word *silence* should always be heard with an environmental resonance. However, it is Rachel Carson the oceanographic nature writer who informs the poems written over the fall, winter, and spring of 1964–65, rather than

Carson the activist and investigative reporter. Eigner was reading, among other books at the time, Carson's *Under the Sea Wind* and *The Sea around Us*.

But let's start with the music. If there is a latent sequence of poems involving music, water, and environmental issues, this poem dated December 8, 1964, might serve as its introduction:

```
IN APPRECIATION

            ridiculous  that's
              all I do

            but, on the piano
              to repeat
                the work

            as the trout for instance

            it takes imagination
                  to supplement
                       the water
                      wings hollowed in earth
```

(*CP* 2:611)

At first, the speaker bemoans the fact that all he does is listen to music and appreciate it. Then, he reconsiders: perhaps, in performing the piece of music, in repeating it, something is added to it, a Derridean supplement that is both optional and required. If Franz Schubert's goal was to supplement the water in his piano quintet (which Eigner mentions in a poem written the following March), to give listeners a sense of a trout moving through a stream, then the products of imagination do something more than mere appreciation, whether these products are quintets or poems. In the later poem, Schubert's quintet is described: "or the Trout a / change of wing floors the earth" (*CP* 2:625).

Writing to his friend and publisher Jonathan Williams in December 1964, Eigner mentions reading Carson's *The Sea around Us* and Thoreau's *Cape Cod* and *A Week on the Concord and Merrimack Rivers*.[35] The first poem of my proposed sequence (Eigner himself never suggested that these poems were a sequence), written a week or so prior to "In Appreciation," is drawn extensively from a chapter in *The Sea around Us* titled "The Birth of an Island." It is, perhaps, one of the first poems that self-consciously takes anthropogenically caused species extinction as its topic:

Small, flightless birds
the voice far, tinkling bells

museum

of sorts, the rats destroyed

moving ashore, M i d w a y

s l o w i s flat wall of the sea
t h e
p o e m and sky

each island
rose

farther than any whale

fins

breathing above the waves
the mirrors

heat

past sunshine

vibrations of air
spiders, then birds, settle

reflexive
man
bringing what he can

interest

in

the quickening run-through

one thing at a time

```
                        tides, a large motion

                         small waves give boats

                      menageries
                        from the bottom

                          rock crumbles to earth
                                  under rain
                               the seas

                         clouds mulct the moon
                                     flats

                               the whale is still hunted
                                     in certain parts

                                    prodigal
                                      the deep light
```

(*CP* 2:609)

Michael Davidson provides a brief but significant reading of this poem in *Concerto for the Left Hand*. Because his concern is with disability experience as it is recorded in various mediums, he uses this poem as an example of how Eigner's physical limitations, even when not introduced into the poem thematically, condition his graphing of the poem on the page, thereby producing rhythmic and stylistic effects particular to his defamiliar body. Davidson notes the seascape and the oceanographic content of the poem, but he draws no specific environmentalist statement from it. He cites the poem from Eigner's 1968 collection *Air the Trees*, which seems to be a version or alternate draft of the poem as it appears in *The Collected Poems* (which was not available at the time *Concerto* was published), so he was most likely unaware of the references to Carson's *The Sea around Us* or the supposedly definitive version of the poem. However, I don't think this matters much: Davidson is concerned with disability experience, not ecology and environmentalism, and his sense of the poem's meaning is in line with its ecological thinking. It is, he writes, "less a score for the voice than a map of intensities whose subject is 'a large motion' of global, geological forces."[36] Nonetheless, if we read this poem along with *The Sea around Us*, we can see how fully Eigner is thinking the ecological thought and typing the mesh. What he gains from Carson is not only an understanding of the geological, atmospheric, and hydrologic processes that control the ocean, but also a conservationist message that indicts humanity for its part in species extinctions. Davidson's is some of the best criticism on Eigner, and his emphasis on disability is not an imposition on the poem, but I hope the interpretation that follows demonstrates that reading for the mesh is just as productive as reading for disability, and that Eigner is always practicing his ecrippoetics.

The idea of human-caused species extinction is extracted, as I noted, from Carson's chapter "The Birth of an Island." The major portion of the chapter describes how islands are formed in the ocean by volcanoes, and then it turns to what would now be called island biogeography, an explanation of the evolution of flora and fauna in these isolated and remote locations. Eigner takes his beginning from the end of the chapter, where Carson introduces the Laysan rail, "a charming, gnomelike creature no more than six inches high, with wings that seemed too small (and were never used as wings) . . . and a voice like distant, tinkling bells."[37] Carson is not shy about expressing her conservationist ire in this chapter: "man, unhappily, has written one of his blackest records as a destroyer on the oceanic islands," she writes, and she later observes, "in a reasonable world men would have treated these islands as precious possessions, as natural museums filled with beautiful and curious works of creation."[38] With the mention of Midway Atoll, Eigner makes the idea of species extinction brought about by "reflexive / man" the main subject of the poem's first part. Carson explains that the Laysan rail died out after rabbits were introduced to the island in the late nineteenth century. A ship's captain had fortuitously moved a group of the rails to Midway Atoll around the same time, but, as Carson notes, "during the war in the Pacific, rats . . . invaded Midway . . . [and] the world's last Laysan rail was seen in 1944."[39] In light of this, the lines "reflexive / man / bringing what he can," which are about dead center in the poem, have a couple of meanings. Humans regard only their own well-being—they always only refer back to themselves—or they react to things automatically, unconsciously following their own impulses or interests. In his reading, Davidson proposes "reflexive / man" as a figure for the poet, regarding himself in relation to the ocean, certainly another possible meaning for these lines, but in the context of Carson's chapter it is clear that Eigner is also thinking in terms of species. In *Imagining Extinction*, Ursula Heise observes, "Extinction narratives allow their readers or viewers to reflect on turning points of cultural history as the loss of a particular species comes to stand in for the broader perception that human relationships to the natural world have changed for the worse."[40]

The lines "reflexive / man / bringing what he can" also serve as a pivot for the poem, turning away from the specific topic of island biogeography to a more general response to Carson's account of oceanic process and natural history. Eigner, like any of Carson's readers, has an "interest / in / the quickening run-through," which can be a reference to Carson's writing as well as to extinction. *The Sea around Us* is basically composed of "run-throughs"—encapsulations of millions of years of geological processes, explanations of how waves form and tides work, accounts of the evolution of species, and so on—and the conclusion of "The Birth of an Island" (itself a run-through) shows how extinction can be sped along by "reflexive / man" (the Laysan rails meet their demise less than a hundred years after invasive species arrive on their island homes). This is not the kind of "quickening run-through" conservation-minded readers would enjoy reading. Is that the import of the next line? It can be read either as an acknowledgment that we lose these things one at a time but that they add up, or as an admonition from the poet: rather than conducting a quick run-through, we should slow down and take one thing at time. This would be familiar advice coming from Eigner, and could also gloss the poem's paratextual note, "slow is the poem," which might be an acknowledgment of how long it takes to type a poem with one finger.

The remaining lines appear to incorporate random details from other parts of *The Sea around Us*, for example, "tides, a large motion // small waves give boats // menageries / from the bottom." The first line quoted here seems to encapsulate Carson's chapter "The Moving Tides," in which she writes, "the tides present a striking paradox, and the essence of it is this: the force that sets them in motion is cosmic . . . but the nature of the tide at any particular place is a local matter," which would certainly intrigue Eigner, who is always interested in the relation of the near and the distant, the global and the local, the parts and the whole.[41] Perhaps the following line, "small waves give boats," contrasts the larger tides with the smaller phenomena of waves—to which Carson dedicates a whole chapter as well—but I think this line is more likely connected to the next two, "menageries / from the bottom." In this case, the small waves would be the sound waves of fathometers used by ships to record water depth. Carson writes, "probably no one suspected that it [the fathometer] would also provide a means of learning something about deepsea life. . . . Answering echoes were returned from intermediate depths, presumably from schools of fish, whales, or submarines."[42] Eigner might have had this discussion in mind in the final lines of the poem. Carson points out that "the existence of an abundant deep-sea fauna was discovered, probably millions of years ago, by certain whales," and she describes the effect the deep sea has on light and color a few pages later. So, the prodigality Eigner names might refer to this abundance, rather than to the waywardness of the whale, and "the deep light" might then be an image of "the blackness of the deep sea."[43]

Thus, "Small, flightless birds" is an encounter with the mesh in which a textual sea in the imagination coexists with the actual sea just beyond the woods behind Eigner's house. Carson's science-based writing, itself supplemented by the imagination as she attempts to bring the facts to life, is also supplemented by Eigner's imagination through his retextualization-by-collage of these fragments from her book. Eigner absorbs and extends Carson's environmentalist critique of human irresponsibility and neglect, but he does so by letting the details that he has selected speak for themselves on his material page. This poem is distinct from the others in this 1964–65 sequence in drawing so heavily from one source, but it also constitutes a proving ground for these techniques of collage, quotation, and citation, which allow the real and the imagined to intermingle in the mesh. The music theme is not prominent in "Small, flightless birds" (though we will hear those "tinkling bells" again), but classical music on the theme of water appears in a poem written the following day:

```
the sea wall
    ending
  the Moldau

 merged
      in music

   the past which is remembered
                         a force rises

      in the ears, innocent
        clarity
            having time
```

(*CP* 2:610)

Listening to Bedřich Smetana's "tone painting" *The Moldau*, which follows the Moldau, or Vltava, River as it forms its main current from two separate springs—one hot and one cold—and runs to the sea, Eigner thinks of time and the past. The two springs are merged into one river just as the river itself is turned into music ("merged / in music"), and the past—which exists in the present through the imagination—merges with the present moment of listening, both memory and music being forces, one rising in the mind and one rising "in the ears." If we have time to listen and remember, we can experience the "innocent / clarity" of Smetana's composition.

A poem dated December 20, 1964, integrates the music theme with more quotation collages, this time drawn primarily from Thoreau's *A Week on the Concord and Merrimack Rivers*. The poem is drawn mostly from the

"Saturday" chapter, which concludes with a description of the sounds the Thoreau brothers hear as they camp by the river: "As we sat up, kept awake by the novelty of our situation, we heard at intervals foxes stepping about over the dead leaves, and brushing the dewy grass close to our tent."[44] Eigner begins his poem by condensing this sentence into the first two lines:

```
foxes stepping
   about the tent

      g-bird
        to make music around

   sound beyond the leaves
      other than the rain

      darkness we might imagine
        coming down

         firefighters' grim
        object
           a bulkhead  past the horizon

         as of tinkling music

      the dogs  the cocks
             the fishes
           cries in the water
          sealed off   from us

      let eyes be
         no torrent  slight
            tilt of this river
             reflecting also
           what is rooted along
        its banks
                and opens quickly enough to
             the sun but
           with no increasing weight

                a dreaming sparrow
                 makes song a way
```

```
no fire
bright from the moon
```

(*CP* 2:613)[45]

The next two lines obliquely refer to a "mountain fiddling tape on radio awhile back," as Eigner indicated to Jonathan Williams: the phrase "g-bird" is not clear, but the lines suggest a human-made music in response to birdsong.[46] Thoreau mentions the day beginning with rain; however, there is no rain in this nighttime passage, and there would be no leaves on the trees in December, so Eigner appears to be "imagin[ing]" the night "coming down" as the brothers camp by the river. Thoreau uses musical figures throughout the passage that Eigner picks up for his poem: "we were serenaded by the song of a dreaming sparrow"; "there was a fire in Lowell, as we judged, this night, and we saw the horizon blazing, and heard the distant alarm-bells, as it were a faint tinkling music borne to these woods"; "the most constant and memorable sound . . . was the barking of the house-dogs . . . it was a sufficiency of sound for the ear of night, and more impressive than any music."[47] And, at the center of the poem, Eigner blends his reading of Thoreau and Carson into a consideration of which animal sounds we can hear and which ones we can't—"the dogs the cocks / the fishes / cries in the water / sealed off from us"—which adds Carson's ocean world to Thoreau's riparian setting. The "Saturday" chapter's conclusion reads in part, "All of these sounds, the crowing of cocks, the baying of dogs . . . are the evidence of nature's health or *sound* state."[48] As Eigner knows from reading Carson, the state of nature is not as sound as it was in Thoreau's day, and her figure for this ill state is silence. Although he seems ready to stop reading and go to sleep himself, or at least stop trying to see what is going on outside—"let eyes be"—the poem concludes on a visual image rather than a description of sound. There is no fire outside Eigner's window illuminating the horizon; rather, it is light from the moon, which was full the night before.[49]

These poems, with their matter drawn from various sources (what he is reading, what he hears on the radio or in the neighborhood, what he sees on television or out his window, what he "sees" or "hears" in his imagination or memory), emphasize interconnectedness in extremis. Eigner attempts to get as much as he can into a poem, to figure out the relationships between these things without imposing an order on them or interpreting them for his reader. At the same time, these poems are unmistakably "Eignerian"; in their appearance on the page, they are like no other poems being written at this time. The "form" of the poem, as it takes shape from the interplay of Eigner's right index finger and the mechanics of his typewriter, becomes the frame through which we "see" the subject matter. Although I have tracked down some of Eigner's sources and sifted some of the quotations from the rest of the poem's language, the point is that these things cannot be separated. The poem that culminates this sequence, "the music, the rooms," demonstrates Eigner's ecrippoetics working at full strength.

Writing to Cid Corman on April 19, 1965, Eigner describes the context for the composition of "the music, the rooms," which is dated April 10–17:

> Getting into Rachel Carson's *Under the Sea Wind*, though, some wks ago - Disneyish in spots of course and hardly a gripping opus, scenes like habitat displays at the Museum - I've bn going to sleep off from it, practically, or into a big bk here *Birds of America*, in which maybe, at last, like they say, I have found my level, that is I've bn roaming around in and coming back to it rather comfortably for a few wks (well, getting out of mind, now, sure enough, and the size irksome last few days, to my lap), the 106 color plates for instance I can connect with better than ever with fine art, for all sorts of sundry reasons, and reading abt for instance nests with both young and eggs in em, and the warmest blood in the world, and different powers of flight and migration distances and routes (aeronautics, physics, et al, satisfies a more spectacular, sensational *kind* of curiosity, anyway it brings hardness to the mind, hard subject, hard surfaces, hard drivin narcissistic achievement, while the ultimate inaccessibility of animal life, where dog eats dogs any old time, makes the irrelevancy of the anthromorphism stay more steadily in view, and allays its prplexing quality somewhat perhaps)[50]

Eigner tried out the same citation technique with *Birds of America* that he used to integrate Carson's *The Sea around Us* in the earlier poems. One example is "the water is the sky" (*CP* 2:633), the poem just prior to "the music, the rooms" in *The Collected Poems*. In this poem, Eigner incorporates information about loons, grebes, and other waterbirds from the bird book, with a particular interest in their feeding and nesting habits. This interest in feeding habits is also evident in "the music, the rooms," but the references here appear to be gleaned not only from *Birds of America* but also from Carson's *Under the Sea Wind* and, most likely, from *The Sea around Us* as well. The poem begins,

```
  the music,   the rooms

silence silence silence silence sound
          on the walls

  the beach raveling
   times advance
```

```
or back up
     around earth
   electric poles

 the sun a reflected color
    tropic
     how distance is to some birds

              in the wind

        fishing

             pinpoint

         the circling air

              food

            the power

           with desperate ease

       food for me hits the water
        without break, the cries

         the meaning of change
```

(*CP* 2:634)

The reader is not told where the action of the poem is occurring. We seem to be inside and outside at the same time: there is music, there are rooms and walls, but there's also the beach, birds, wind, and water. There are four walls of "silence" that sound seems to penetrate or occur upon. But whether the speaker has left his house and headed to the beach—Eigner's house in Swampscott, Massachusetts, was less than half a mile from the ocean—readers are not told. Eigner tries to see this activity from the birds' point of view ("how distance is to some birds"), and perhaps the cycles of feeding, breeding, and migrating are "the meaning of change." Then again, maybe not. The following lines of the poem read:

```
information shifted,  player piano
   on the screen,   the swimming moon
```

```
     enters eclipse
    out the window, and other station

   none of us is watching

 the cabinet

                 instrument forgotten

     the clock shakes out

    head bent from the wing

               in a live broadcast

        a case for various things

               dry grassy fields

                 the blank sky

             wampum gulls broke shells

              such eyes
                directed
```

(*CP* 2:634–35)

"The meaning of change" may be the act of changing the channel ("information shifted")—to a show with a player piano in it, evidently—so there still seems to be an inside here, but the outside is also present, and lines about the birds feeding and diving are interpolated with the "live broadcast." Their eyes, unlike those of the distracted viewers of the television, are directed toward the particulars of the world in order to survive. The last lines of the poem read:

```
   a malnutrition
         Kenya

    straightens hair it turns blond

     scurvy is wiped out
```

```
 the dogs come, the group
             on bikes

   the street comes

    the North Sea

      studio on a ship

         pivot   spun

            dark life
           rises
               leaving the island

             the dim expanding miles

          a steady white light
              they might drive headlong into
                 the mist like a magnet

            blows   lost bearings

              nest in fisherman's pocket

                        the wash
```

(*CP* 2:635)

The hunger of the birds feeding makes Eigner think of food shortages in Africa (a manifestation of the mesh), the interconnected issues of food shortages, population growth, resource extraction, and consumption, as well as the media that makes one aware of these things. I have not been able to identify the source of the "nest in fisherman's pocket," but it returns to the idea of enclosure and containment in the four walls of silence that began the poem, and it places a natural container inside of a human-made one. "The wash," then, completes the restatement of the poem's opening: it is the "music" that is the context for the "rooms" of the nest and the pocket. The poem closes with a quotation—a kind of inverted epigraph—that extends this interconnectedness into the past and textuality. Immediately after "the wash," Eigner types out this quote:

" ... distant thunder ... Nearer and nearer came the strange commingling sound of sleigh bells, mixed with the rumbling of an approaching storm ... I gazed in wonder and astonishment ... They passed like a cloud through the branches of the high trees, through the underbrush and over the ground ... They fluttered all about me; gently I caught two in my hands and carefully concealed them under my blanket.

I now began to realize they were mating ... "

-- Chief Pokagan, describing an onset of the now extinct passenger pigeon, in Michigan, May 1850

(*CP* 2:635)[51]

Without a distinction between inside and outside, text and context, Eigner's poem is radically open to all aspects of experience: perception, memory, and bodily sensation, as well as reading, watching television, listening to music, daydreaming, observing birds, and so forth. But, as Eigner indicates to Corman, his poem is a sort of walking nonetheless. He has been "roaming around in" *Birds of America* and Carson's *Under the Sea Wind*, and this roaming reflects not just perceptions of his surroundings but also his reading, wondering, and remembering. Dogs and bikes come down his street and blend with what he is seeing on television and learning about the ocean from Carson; there are no lines, no boundaries drawn.

In his letter to Corman, Eigner admits that writing a longer poem is an example of "hard drivin narcissistic achievement" even as he wants to critique the human centeredness of such achievement. *Under the Sea Wind* and *Birds of America* give him some understanding of the natural processes and cycles of the poem's environmental content, but they also give him a sense of "the ultimate inaccessibility of animal life." In a poem that is concerned with sound as much as sight, Eigner might be thinking of passages from Carson's book such as: "The mackerel are voiceless and they make no sound. . . . As the mackerel hurry shoreward they swim in tier above tier. Throughout those weeks when the fish are rolling in from the open sea the scattered shoals between the edge of the continent and the shore are often darkened as the earth was once dimmed by the passing of another living cloud—the flights of passenger pigeons."[52] By juxtaposing the quotation from *Birds of America* (Chief Pokagan's description is included in the entry on the passenger pigeon in volume 2) with the "dark life . . . leaving the island" and the "wash" of the sea, Eigner imagines how one "living cloud" in the ocean mirrors another "living cloud" that once filled the air.[53] What is more, the quote from Chief Pokagan highlights the sound of the passenger pigeons, and this seems to be another reason Eigner tacks the quote to the end of a poem that hasn't mentioned these birds.[54] By repeating the word "silence" four times in a row at the beginning, and concluding with a description of an animal sound that will never again be heard, "the music, the rooms" embodies the meaning of the title of Carson's *Silent Spring*. Attempting to get as much into his poem as he can, and to find the interrelations among these things, Eigner types the textual and extratextual weave of things as they appear in the mesh.

But if you don't fly, you can't come to a value of the earth

Although Eigner often indicated his poems' sources (usually radio or television programs) in paratextual notes on his typescripts, the extent to which his poems of the early and mid-1960s are intertextual collages is not widely recognized.[55] As a student of Charles Olson's poetic methods, Eigner was aware of projective verse's emphasis on research, historical documents, and archival materials, a legacy of the modernist methods of Ezra Pound's *Cantos* and William Carlos Williams's *Paterson*, but he was also sensitive to his own limitations in this area. Olson's investigation into the history of Gloucester, Massachusetts, is prominently featured in *The Maximus Poems*, and his advice on working with "PRIMARY DOCUMENTS," in "A Bibliography on America for Ed Dorn," was "*to dig one thing or place or man* until you know more abt that than is possible to any other man. It doesn't matter whether it's Barbed Wire or Pemmican or Paterson or Iowa. But *exhaust* it. Saturate it. Beat it."[56] For Eigner, whose disability made holding books and papers difficult—and also limited his access to archives and repositories in the era before the Americans with Disabilities Act—such a method was not feasible.[57] Nonetheless, in the early 1960s Eigner was giving Olson's historical poetics a shot, reading about the South during the Civil War and writing a sequence of poems about it.[58] Sending Cid Corman poems in February 1960, Eigner wrote, "some of them evidence of my reading up the Civil War during January—THIS HALLOWED GROUND, by Br Catton, for a general acct ((pedestrian, eh?)), a bk of Brady photos et al, and most of vol. i de Freemans *Lee's Lieutenants*."[59] Eigner stuck with it, and by January 1965 he sent Corman the "foxes stepping" poem discussed above, calling it "My 1st quotation-style poem," though, he admitted, it was "not my styl."[60] Nonetheless, as he continued his reading and research, citations from nineteenth-century American writers circulated in his poems throughout the mid-1960s. Eigner had earlier sent some of the Civil War poems to LeRoi Jones (Amiri Baraka), who edited the journal *Yugen* with his partner, Hettie Cohen. Writing to her, on April 29, 1966, Eigner informed her that "the 'Frederick Douglass' thing sort of an unexpected grand climax to th CWar pieces, for the likes of me (I'm carrying on as if the series was 50 pp. long!), getting T Roosevelt, remote vertebrate cousins and all in there. One of my best, I guess."[61] If "quotation-style" poems weren't his forte, why would he consider the "Frederick Douglass" poem "one of [his] best"? Because it again demonstrates how textuality and ecology are entangled in the mesh, and it includes one of Eigner's most exciting personal experiences, his first time flying in an airplane.

His first flight—a trip to visit his brother Joe's family in Saint Louis—was an exciting prospect for Eigner because he would obtain his first view of the earth from above. In June 1964, a few months prior to his trip in October of that year, these lines appear in a poem: "elude the 4 walls / tenuous I've / wanted to fly / for the view," and he commemorated the actual event in a poem written on October 20, 1964, which begins, "Last day on earth / for a while at least" (*CP* 2:573, 2:603). The poem with Douglass is dated January 31, 1965, the same day that Douglass was featured on the PBS show *Profiles in Courage*, which Eigner viewed. Eigner's experience of air travel, his ongoing historical research, and his viewing of this broadcast all combine in what is one of Eigner's best poems indeed:

```
   Frederick Douglass
 took his chances  like
   when we fly?

  I don't know   the landing gear
      far from my mind I
     was trying to see
    where there was anything but

            a large ship only
           that appeared small


     Do you love Maryland that
      state there  how
       would you like to go back
      where you didn't come from  Most

         have something they can
       take shame from   withdraw it   fish

          life lurks in the sea
         we eat it,what
               is germane
```

the St.Louis slave mart

something to remember is
still there   days
after the War--
of the Rugged Individual when

man was man the
head of the family and so on we
couldn't have gotten along

why risk your shirt no
hands to pick the cotton no
gin

in a man's thoughts

Faneuil
Hall after what happened

the slave likes
what's in the air

the free wonders
as well what
there might have been

don't often lose sight of the ground

a cruise is expensive

no tall dark face in the air
no porter   what

have I to do with
what I don't see

(*CP* 2:620–21)

The opening juxtaposes Eigner's airplane flight with Douglass's "flight to freedom," both, as the poet sees them, risky endeavors.[62] His ability to see things is raised in the next stanza, and getting his first view of things from above takes precedence over his fears about the functioning of the landing gear, though he can't see much at all. His thoughts turn back to Douglass, who was fleeing from slavery in Maryland, and perhaps to the African repatriation movement in the Reconstruction Era ("would you like to go back / where you didn't come from"). As he thinks about the history of slavery, racism, and civil rights, Eigner determines that most states "have something they can / take shame from" in their past. Considering these issues as he recalls his first time in the air, Eigner thinks about what is "in the sea," the life that he cannot see but that is consumed by humans. This thought may be prompted by his reading of Rachel Carson's *The Sea around Us* the previous fall. In asking "what is / germane," Eigner poses an ecological rather than historical question. The word *germane* is derived from the Middle English *germain*, which means having the same parents or being closely connected, so asking what is germane is to inquire about interconnectedness. What is the connection between all these things and the poet who sees or thinks of them? Missouri is connected to Maryland by "the St.Louis slave mart," the something it "can / take shame from," and remembering slavery and the Civil War means remembering what came after: Reconstruction, Roosevelt's notion of rugged individualism (which asserted a direct link between "Manhood and Statehood," as he announced in his address at the quarter-centennial celebration of Colorado in 1901), and so on. For Eigner, as he himself took his first trip west, this frontier thesis is unworkable ("we / couldn't have gotten along") and offers no solution to the issue of slavery and freedom. The lines "the slave likes / what's in the air" appear to refer to the "freedom songs" of the civil rights movement, which were slave spirituals with updated lyrics, such as "Freedom in the Air."[63] Eigner thinks of himself "in the air"—"don't often lose sight of the ground"—and the fact that airlines did not have African American porters as cruise ships and trains would have. The concluding implied question returns to the point about visibility and invisibility, what can be seen and what can't. What does the poet, the perceiver, "have . . . to do with" what he cannot see? If we are connected to the life under the surface of the sea, through consumption but also through evolution (as he wrote to Hettie Cohen, he was happy to get our "remote vertebrate cousins" into the poem), then even if we cannot see it, we are responsible for it. If Eigner cannot see the ground, or a "tall dark face," while he is in flight, does that mean he is not connected to such things? Eigner's ecrippoetics finds endless interconnectedness, so the implied answer to this question is no. In "los[ing] sight of the ground" that he was on for so long, Eigner gains a deeper sense of coexistence, not just in space but also through time.

Eigner's reading in nineteenth-century American literature becomes directly connected to his ecological concerns as the decade continues. In a letter dated April 16, 1966, Eigner writes about India, “where reportedly 1,000,000 slowly starving people bed down in the streets of Calcutta at night.”[64] A poem called “CALCUTTA” begins “Night // prone / bodies” and includes the lines, “how much // food / is brought in // what to do with / heaps of it” (*CP* 2:708). Another “quotation-style” poem follows “CALCUTTA” in *The Collected Poems*, and it draws from Eigner’s reading of Walt Whitman’s *Specimen Days*, specifically Whitman’s memories of the Civil War:

```
Whitman's cry at starvation
  in a land of plenty


       prison camps  the mean
                South


                  six ways
                          of saying it
         the big problem is


           consumption and conservation and population


             population consumption conservation


               conservation population consumption


                 population conservation consumption


            or what about
              bringing others in


                  conservation consumption population


                   consumption population conservation
```

(*CP* 2:709)

Eigner’s opening lines quote from Whitman’s “Releas’d Union Prisoners from South”: “over 50,000 have been compell’d to die the death of starvation—reader, did you ever try to realize what *starvation* actually is?—in those prisons—and in a land of plenty.”[65] The letter of April 16 and this poem demonstrate how Olson’s historical method is integrated into Eigner’s own projective verse ecrippoetics. Rather than uncovering the history of a place through research and fieldwork, as Olson would have it, Eigner's ecrippoetics reveals the interconnectedness of ecology throughout time and space.

Trying to find a balance between thought and action in the April 16 letter, Eigner writes, "There are times for living, or let's say purposeful action . . . and times for contemplation of the world, which includes the self," and later he includes a long quotation from George Santayana's *Character and Opinion in the United States* that makes the case for reflection as the most intense form of action even though nothing physical is being done.[66] "But," Eigner continues, "we have to live not only in the present (in enough of it, which is impossible if we're too personal or anyway introvert or perhaps selfish, egotistical or hard-up), but also the past and (least of all, it had better be, probably—or how fast does life go?) future, and different times come together in memory, all sorts of times."[67] To live in the past, present, and future means that Union soldiers dying of starvation in the 1860s is connected to Indians starving to death in the 1960s. The unheard cries of the fishes is manifest in "Whitman's cry at starvation," and our "vertebrate cousins" are "germane" because the expanding population will further diminish them as a food source. Eigner's first time leaving the ground is connected to Frederick Douglass's risky escape from slavery, and whether or not the poet sees a Black face in the air he is connected to those who fight for civil rights in the present. And "consumption and conservation and population" are problems of the future as well as the past and present, even in a "land of plenty."

Eigner's mesh—the intertextual weave of sight, sound, information, literature, history, science, everything—directly encounters the environmental crises that gained national (and global) attention at the end of the 1960s. As we will see in the next chapter, as poets and writers became aware of such problems, they wanted to provide solutions, to encourage and take part in "social action." So did Eigner, and the next chapter examines the ethics that accompanies his ecrippoetics as his work gained a wider and younger readership.

CHAPTER THREE

Enough Defined

Eigner's Ethics

> Human life is made up of two elements, power and form, and the proportion must be invariably kept, if we would have it sweet and sound.
>
> Ralph Waldo Emerson, "Experience"

If, as Larry Eigner had determined by 1966, "the big problem is / consumption and conservation and population"—and if there is more than one way of seeing this problem—then what should be done? (*CP* 2:709). Conservation has its roots in the nineteenth century as a form of enlightened resource management, but it was not until the mid-twentieth century that a conservation ethics was formulated, by Aldo Leopold in *A Sand County Almanac* (1949). Leopold's "Land Ethic" proposed that human interaction with the environment is ethical when it "tends to preserve the stability, integrity, and beauty" of an ecosystem.[1] Leopold was thinking mainly in terms of agriculture, game management, wilderness recreation, and urban development—that is, his ethics is intended to guide land owners and government officials to think and act with an "ecological conscience"—but as the populist protest movements of the 1960s developed, writers were also wondering how their art could contribute to social change. Of course, taking direct action and presenting oneself as a spokesperson for the movement were ways that poets and writers could make a contribution, and Eigner's compatriots in the New American poetry movement—most prominently Denise Levertov, Robert Duncan, Allen Ginsberg, Michael McClure, LeRoi Jones (Amiri Baraka), Jackson Mac Low, and Gary Snyder—participated in antiwar and civil rights marches, read their work at demonstrations, and expressed their political positions in interviews.

The poetry reading itself became the site of possible transformation, as Raphael Allison's *Bodies on the Line* demonstrates: "A skeptical humanism was born out of the crucible of 1960s culture, when presence meant literally 'putting your body on the line,' a defining personal and political gesture that resonated throughout American life. The importance of presence in poetry readings can be linked, for example, to the sit-in, a mode of nonviolent resistance to white power pioneered by southern blacks. . . . merely occupying public space with one's body could constitute an act of social awareness and political commitment."[2] Although Eigner began reading his work publicly in the late 1960s, and he had been attending readings since the late 1950s, his disability made his speech difficult to understand and his style certainly didn't lend itself to rhetorical strategies and political pronouncements. Eigner was never "housebound," but prior to the Americans with Disabilities Act it would have also been difficult to gain access to certain kinds of demonstrations. In other words, public protest and activism were not viable options for Eigner to express his environmentalist views, but he nevertheless wanted to contribute to the cause, raise awareness, and make a difference, and he had to find a way to accommodate environmentalist politics to his defamiliar body.

Eigner thought of the balance of more and less, of what's *enough*, both in terms of his writing and in terms of the environment, especially production and consumption. "Enough" is the figure that combines disability, ecology, and ethics in Eigner's projective-verse ecrippoetics. In a 1978 interview, Eigner was asked, "does it ever bother you that your experience is so different from other people's, because of your infirmities?" He responded, "No," and continued: "I took to aiming for normalcy—of course, being self-sufficient is good. Long time though since I've been keen on a job, even work, except if and when I get into a thing. Aside from ecological problems, which I for one am increasingly aware of—fatiguing the earth, clogging it up with extras—it seems quixotic to work when you've enough and more."[3] Enough is a matter of balance, finding, as Eigner phrases it, the "optimum mix," yet that balance is not always self-evident: "You can't tell what an optimum mix is, the pleasantest proportions, or can hardly tell enough—it can't be achieved or predicted anyway, it just happens."[4] As Benjamin Friedlander points out, seeking this balance is a matter of poetics as well as ecology for Eigner: "His goal was always to strike the right balance—Larry's poetics in a nutshell, and politics too. (His deeply felt response to the ecology movement is a rarely noted key to the work)."[5] Eigner's ethics is the continual search for a balance between more and less, and, through his disability perspective, a transformation of more and less into an accommodating *enough*. In one poem from the 1960s, he refers to Walden Pond as "enough defined," a phrase that can stand as the motto for Eigner's ethics (*CP* 2:702).

The constant search for balance that is Eigner's ecrippoetics and ethics demonstrates the importance of his work not only to disability studies but also to ecocriticism. In *Enough*, Bill McKibben explores sufficiency as an environmental trope, approaching it from the other end of the spectrum of disability, posthumanism. The promise of the posthuman, for McKibben, is an excessive compensation; we trade the "less" of being human for the "more" of the cyborg. McKibben argues for limits—a classic environmentalist position—and his goal is to replace a compensatory more with an accommodating enough. For McKibben, "the choice [is] between Enough and More."[6] Adequacy and excess are also distinctively Emersonian categories, but, again, when do we know that we have enough and have not just settled for less? According to McKibben, posthumanists consider the human mind to be an inadequate machine for performing high-speed, accurate cognitive functions, "but," he writes, "the human mind may nonetheless be the apex of thinking machinery, simply because it is able to hold things in balance. To weigh desires. To say no."[7] Eigner's embodiment was such that he always thought of things in terms of balance, and he discovered how to weigh things in language in order to arrive at a definition of enough.

This chapter will track the development of the ethics that follows from Eigner's ecrippoetics. In seeking the form of his work—as each of his projectivist compatriots did in her or his own way—Eigner was working out the Emersonian ratio of power to form. Leopold's environmental ethics acknowledges that ethical behavior entails a sense of aesthetics; *beauty* is one of three essential terms of the Land Ethic, and the foreword to *A Sand County Almanac* emphasizes what can be called Leopold's "three E's": ecology, ethics, and esthetics (in his spelling of the word). Ecology, ethics, and aesthetics also merge in Timothy Morton's ecological thought, which "compels us to recalibrate our sense of justice."[8] How does our—both poet's and reader's—encounter with words and space on the page inform and lead to decisions about justice?

Eigner's limits, perhaps, made the decisions we all face more stark, but they also reduced them to essential terms. As his experience came to include air travel, visits from younger poets, publication in the journals and magazines that these poets edited, road trips to attend and give readings, and an ever-wider correspondence with family, friends, and fellow poets, he was constantly linking his work in poetic form with his ecological concerns. A surprising array of contacts, connections, and sources combine in Eigner's environmental ethics: from the moon landings to the death of Charles Olson, from visits to his brothers and their families in San Francisco and Saint Louis to the media coverage of the civil rights and antiwar movements, from family celebrations of Jewish traditions to *Newsweek* and *Scientific American*, nothing was excluded from consideration in decisions about how much is enough. Eigner was thinking the ecological thought as his ecrippoetics developed, and his search for balance is one of the first consistent responses to the need for environmental ethics in postmodernist poetry. One of the primary things that occupied Eigner's attention in the mid to late 1960s, which is also directly related to thinking the ecological thought, was the opening of a repository for his papers at the University of Kansas.

Copies will flood me frm Kansas maybe in no time

Eigner had reason to reflect on his writing as a whole in the mid-1960s and early 1970s, and it is this notion of an oeuvre—a term that refers both to an individual work of art and to a writer's lifework—that makes him think of his own poetry in terms of *enough*.[9] In 1965, a cousin, Edwin M. Eigner, who was a professor of English at the University of Kansas, established a repository for the poet's typescripts and correspondence at the Kenneth Spencer Research Library.[10] Because Eigner's papers often suffered rough treatment due to his lack of coordination and dexterity, the repository was set up to preserve his original typescripts, and an arrangement was made to provide him with copies of the typescripts after they were deposited. It was also an attempt to establish a chronological order and definitive versions of the poems. As Eigner informed Robert Duncan in December 1969, his first bibliographer, Andrea Wyatt, had just visited Swampscott after working with the typescripts in Kansas, where she "looked over mss of mine there and took xeroxes of all (wow!), in order to put them in order."[11]

The idea of organizing and dating his entire life's work prompted Eigner to wonder about how his poems added up to a whole, and as he, his brothers and cousin, his bibliographer, and the librarians in Kansas worked to establish the collection his concerns about ecology and other subjects became entangled in his thinking about his oeuvre. In a letter to Alexandra Mason, the special collections librarian who took over from Terrence Williams, with whom Edwin Eigner opened the repository, Eigner writes,

> I'm farther and farther away from brown study, e.g. new things piling up here every day (fine memories of that I have) and bibliophilic scholarship. And some kind of study there'll always be. But Rbt Frost, for instance, who was metrical throughout, as he could be, and rhymed, spoke of "The Figure A Poem Makes," and then there's Charles Olson, his "Projective Verse" (you start from yourself, where you are, go into the world from there, the individual is the source, constantly, of motivation and purpose, goals, priorities - like recently I learned that Elohim, God the Creator/Commander/ Judge, means mighty powerful, able, which I guess may imply will and ability too) and field theory of writing, writing from the field of experience (motive, goals, purposes, are made of many things, and synthesized by however many or few, and being, other than as beginning, if it doesn't in fact include

> this, seems a compound, the thick or middle of things, or the conscious individual, being involved - and the Name for God the Merciful, Careful, Caring, Loving, Jhvh, the one maybe to be reticent about,* is closely related to the hebrew for "to be"). Anyway it seems pretty clear that the more there is at hand, within reach or at your fingertips rather than at arm's-length, the more is improvisation, adaptation, invention, combustion spontaneous, whatever the specific details of such a process (Newton said he was able to see farther because he stood on the shoulders of giants, for instance, but I didn't realize this fully till someone sent me *Future Shock* 10 months ago and I saw Toffler's 2 or 3 pages on invention/production/diffusion/invention/. . . , faster and faster, like a nuclear reaction, say). The various densities of matter in space, if this can include anyone's head or mind as well as artifacts ‡see ##539, 540‡ and "raw material," might be a valid and simple explanation, of writing and revision, for example, which are about the same. While how much to go into any details is anybody's day-to-day option, and what details, at least as long as how to lessen the disadvantanges of abundance, an explosive situation, is such a riddle.
>
> *which may be one way of containment of your being, to preserve and continue it, as in Hinduism (and in past ages no part of the world was considered inanimate - all kind of dependent on man, i guess)[12]

This remarkable passage documents the big thinking Eigner was doing in order to find an ethics of enough. He encapsulates his sense of Olson's "composition by field" poetics and associates it with Robert Frost's antimodernist theory of organic form, moving seamlessly to Judaic scripture and Hebrew etymology. Eigner's source for the Hebrew etymologies is the Hertz Chumash, a translation with commentary of the Pentateuch and Haftorahs, edited by J. H. Hertz, chief rabbi of the British Empire. Writing to the poet, designer, and publisher Ian Tyson on November 19, 1970, Eigner says,

> Gitin passed som bks onto me - wow - and gave me Olson's Black Mountain Lectures, *A Special View of History*, which in the last 4 wks has sent me into 3 of the 200-odd bks a former nhbor brght over 4½ yrs ago before moving to Dixie, 2 of em by Paul Tillich, and into a "chumesh," a hbrw/English torah haftorah with notes (ed. 1936-7 London by a J H Hertz, Chf Rabbi) dropped in my lap at a cousin's bar m. . 2½ wks ago, where i found a clue to Olson's sense, such as it may be, so i took it home[13]

Something in Olson's lectures on history connected with the discussion of the terms for God in Genesis. In the notes on the origin story, Hertz explains, "The two most important Names of the Deity are here used. 'Lord' is the usual English translation of *Adonay*. *Adonay* is the prescribed traditional reading of the Divine Name expressed in the four Hebrew letters YHWH—which is never pronounced as written." The etymology Eigner then cites is also in this note: "The Heb[rew] root of that Divine Name means 'to be.'" Hertz continues, "The other and more general Divine Name is *Elohim*. . . . *Elohim* denotes God as the Creator and Moral Governor of the Universe. . . . *Adonay* (Lord) describes the deity stressing His lovingkindness, His acts of mercy and condescension and revelation to mankind . . . while *Elohim* (God) emphasizes His justice and rulership."[14] And an earlier note on Elohim presented Eigner with the idea of power or strength: "*Elohim* is a plural form, which is often used in Hebrew to denote plenitude of might. Here it indicates that God comprehends and unifies all the forces of eternity and infinity."[15]

Eigner, who expressed his confusion about many of Olson's writings but was also awed by his learnedness, assumes that Olson would be familiar with the etymologies he finds in the Hertz Chumash. Writing to George Butterick, Olson's literary executor, a few years later, Eigner remarks, "Kind of hard to imagine Charles didn't know Hebrew, as well as Greek and Latin etc etc., forwards and backwards, nor the elohim/yahyeh etymology, but for quite a while I thought maybe he didn't, for instance till yesterday it scarcely looked like there was anything much in Walter Kaufmann's *Critique Of Religion and Philosophy* [. . .] of what I came across in *Pentateuch and Haftorahs* [. . .] on being taken to a cousin's son's Bar Mitzvah in September 1970."[16] In a marginal note, Eigner adds, "theres no dire danger I guess of Charles being taken for a savior very much, in Chaos and the humptydumpty (grassroots) world we're in (?), seem to be irrevocably, while he sure was/is a saint in it. (Is guru holy or wise or both ???)." (In a postscript, Eigner confirms: "Guru - Sanskrit for venerable one.") Realizing that his interest in Olson may be taken as hagiographic, Eigner nonetheless pushes his notion of Olson as savior as he discusses "the call of Moses" in Exodus. Eigner is still interested in the various names for God and their meanings:

> Hertz on "*Ehyeh asher Ehyeh*" "I am that I am . . ." ascribes an identical interpretation to the Midrash, maybe - quotes it but doesnt translate evidently, anyhow not literally, and says "Most moderns follow Rashi in rendering '*I will be what I will be*,'" i.e., ...
>
> 'I shall save in the way that I shall save.' . . .
>
> "Around the bend/ of the next second"

Eigner refers here to Hertz's commentary: "The answer which Moses receives in these words is thus the equivalent to, 'I shall save in the way that I shall save.' It is to reassure the Israelites of the *fact* of deliverance, but does not disclose the *manner*. It must suffice the Israelites to learn that, 'Ehyeh, I will be (with you), hath sent me unto you.'"[17]

What Eigner intends by juxtaposing Hertz's interpretation of God's "Ehyeh asher Ehyeh" with lines from Olson's "I, Maximus of Gloucester, to You" ("Around the bend/ of the next second") is not entirely clear, but the implication is that his predecessor is in the God position.[18] Eigner may be applying the unquoted first line, "the thing you're after," to himself in his search for etymologies and meanings, but he may also have in mind the poem's title in relation to Martin Buber's theology. In a marginal note, Eigner writes, "So it seems Buber might have got his 'I/Thou' most directly from this ch. as 10 verses before Moses when called says 'I'm here.'" Maximus's prophetic declamation can be abbreviated "I . . . to You," a vernacular I/Thou. Is it merely a whimsical way to think about his recently deceased mentor, or does Eigner, who answered the call of projective verse early on, really consider himself Moses to Olson's YHWH?

In either case, Eigner drops the notion of Olson as savior, and continues writing to Butterick about his research:

> Anyway at sundry times as I picked up on things on my own [. . .] I imagined Charles getting a kick out of them. Hertz says somewhere that "the ancient Rabbis" considered Elohim and YHWH [YHVH and Elohim typed above these terms respectively] inseparable [. . .], which fits in with purpose/ involvement (or i../p.. from the human viewpoint), to my mind, as you cant have one without more or less (always there's the rub or one of the Unanswered Questions in the increasingly humptydumpty and/or grassroots universe nowadays), and so, further, with Greek Justice (might be for one thing self-restraining in being fairly blind?), due proportion [. . .], as well as with the Trimurti, Creation/Destruction, and Preservation (besides Brahma, the whole), i.e. beginning/ending/continuing, though I have that only from the dictionary, M-Webster's Collegiate.[19]

Here is Eigner's environmental ethics in embryonic form. His "bibliophilic scholarship," as he characterized it to Mason, reveals how he located the elements of his environmental ethics as it emerges from the mesh of language, religion, science, news, and the texts in which Eigner finds himself. In establishing an ethics of enough, Eigner will use anything that comes to hand—a pragmatism not unlike Frost's, which Eigner associates with Olson in the letter to Mason—and his ethics is always a matter of finding the right balance. In another marginal note in the letter to Butterick, Eigner continues his thinking on the etymology of Elohim after the discussion of Buber's I/Thou: "Well, so the primary meaning of Elohim isnt 'very mighty' but for instance I've been helped to some gd poems." He then types the following poem at the bottom of the page:

```
    justice or purpose among things


i try balance and
          time slips
```

(*CP* 3:1020)

Certainly Eigner himself slipped many times in trying to maintain *his* balance, and here the instability of his stance extends out into time and space, reminding the reader that any balancing act is only temporary and improvised. Furthermore, in seeking to weigh things in the scales of justice, time is a factor: How far to go back in the past for reparations? How far to go into the future to sustain life on the planet?

In the 1971 letter to Alexandra Mason quoted above, another element of Eigner's ethics can be found in his reference to Alvin Toffler's *Future Shock* (1970). As I noted, Eigner applied his ethics of enough to his own writing and wondered how much publishing contributed to the environmental degradation he was worried about. In Toffler's best-selling account of the ever-increasing rate of technological change, Eigner found confirmation for this concern. His phrase "invention/production/diffusion/invention/. . . , faster and faster" echoes Toffler: "The stepped-up pace of invention, exploitation, and diffusion . . . accelerates the whole cycle still further."[20] One example that Toffler uses for this process is, in fact, publishing: "Prior to 1500 . . . Europe was producing books at a rate of 1000 titles per year. This means, give or take a bit, that it would take a full century to produce a library of 100,000 titles. By 1950 . . . the rate had accelerated so sharply that Europe was producing 120,000 titles a year. . . . By the mid-sixties, the output of books on a world scale, Europe included, approached the prodigious figure of 1000 titles per *day*."[21] In his letter to Mason, after this citation of Toffler, Eigner writes,

> Waste, the idea of it, or actually what it is, has become paradoxical, at that, by now. Once something is more or less done, there's letting pile up with others, circulating or recycling it which may in not too long a time amount to putting too much in many heads and pairs of hands, though these comprise a larger system than one does, or else, throwing it away, casting it however far back to raw material, what I've heard is done (yearly?) with sculpture in Bali. [. . .] Our over-all system is a closed or finite one now - we know the earth is our space ship. (At that, the Creator ordered Noah into the Ark, and the Careful shut him up in it, making all watertight, or making the hatch so.) . . . Well, the whole business is a merrygoround bush at that.[22]

Eigner's letter to Mason is dated July 20, 1971; a week later he wrote a poem that begins:

```
The closed system
  Of earth
    Of the Ark

            Love

  Mercy

         shut him up carefully
   in it
```

(*CP* 3:1032)

As Eigner informed Butterick later, the Torah passage for his cousin's bar mitzvah was Noah and the ark, and he would have found this note in the Hertz Chumash: "*The Lord shut him in*. This means . . . God fastened the door so that it withstood the violence of the storm. . . . Hence the employment of the term Lord, *Adonay*, for this act of Divine mercy."[23] In another gloss, Hertz writes, "The Midrash says, 'Thus spake the Holy One, blessed be He: If I create the world by Mercy alone, sin will abound; if by Justice alone, how can the world endure? I will create it by both.'"[24] Eigner finds his own dilemma in the scriptural passage and etymologies: in creating the world, the Divine itself must find a balance between justice and mercy. This applies not only to the biblical flood and cosmogony, but also to the copies of typescripts that "flood" him from Kansas. A passage in the middle of "The closed system" reads:

```
 creation

   and the floods

the more there is the more

   begins

            a kind of chain

               firecrackers or

                  burning woods
```

(*CP* 3:1032)

Creation—of the world or of a poem—produces a "chain" reaction of beginnings, thereby threatening to fill up and overflow the "closed system."

Publishing poems in books and journals uses material resources—paper and ink, but also the energy required for printing and distribution—and Eigner was obsessed with saving paper, filling letters to the margins with text, typing multiple poems on a single sheet, using the backs of envelopes and scraps of paper for notes and drafts. Moreover, because interconnectedness—or Morton's *mesh*—is the primary element of his ecrippoetics, Eigner was sensitive to the "externalities" of the publishing process. On September 11, 1970, writing to Douglas Calhoun, Eigner observes, "(Like, 5 yrs ago i read the NYT uses up 5.500.000 trees a year, and lately I read that, aftr coal-mines or mines in general, papermlls are, together w.steelmills et) al, the unhlthiest for wrkers."[25] The mimeo revolution of the 1960s—the second great period of underground publishing, after modernism's "little" magazines of the 1910s and 1920s—was coming into full bloom in the 1970s, and Eigner's prolific output was well served by young editors who favored the New American poetry. Calhoun was the editor of the small journal *Athanor*, and Eigner was also corresponding with Allen De Loach, editor of *Intrepid* magazine, at this time. On August 25, 1970, he writes to De Loach, "I've always wondered about optimum quantity, how much it wd be good to approximate it more or less, for instance how much or then *what* should see print or even be written down or thought about, some years anyway longer ago thn 5, when I rd the N Y Times consumes 5½ millions trees annually, and of course wrote a page-long poem about it."[26] And, a little more than a week after the letter to Calhoun quoted above, he followed up with the *Athanor* editor: "Of crs all the quarterlies this cent. . , I'll bet, have consumed but 1/nth of the trees consumed by 1 wk of the daily press, I'll bet. And how short- or long-range is a difference between frugal or pennypinching and calculating habits, seeing how close you can well come to overloading the earth and juggling too many things."[27] The new technologies of photocopies, mimeographs, and other cheap and accessible printing processes meant an increase in the journals and magazines that were publishing poetry. (Eigner himself contemplated buying a portable copier the size of a suitcase, designed for executives who travel, to avoid the necessity of retyping his poems or using carbon paper to make copies for submission to journals.)[28] But, for Eigner, such abundance always raises the question of how much is too much, how do we know when we have *enough*? In order to make any decisions about what is adequate as opposed to overabundant, one must have a sense of proportion and scale, and one must be able to determine how the parts add up to a whole, whether that whole is one's lifework or the planet.

Towards the whole earth in time and space While its always bn humptydumpty enough, in fact mostly

Eigner's interest in etymology began before the Hertz Chumash appeared in his lap at a bar mitzvah, spurring his fascination with the names for God in Hebrew.[29] In the letter to Butterick, Eigner writes, "'Health,' 'holy,' 'whole' - anyway what Duncan quotes Charles as saying, wanting a Dr who'd 'attend him in "holy things". . .' (a homeopath is somewhat a specialist, at that, I guess, compared to a 'family Doctor' orin however many of few cases a clergyman), prompts me to show you the enclosed #792," which begins: "health / holy / wholesome / hole."[30] Eigner had discovered this etymology a few years before July 1973, when he wrote this poem, and he also draws on Judaic tradition and ceremony for context when he reports his discovery to Robert Duncan in December 1969: "Was about to say above, a few months ago i saw in Webster's Collegate that holy, whole and health all go back to the sam AS word meaning whole, maybe - i forget - to make hole, (holw) heal, anyway to make whole."[31] Eigner is also thinking in terms of his work as it is being archived and organized, and he has been rereading Duncan's collection of early poems, *The Years as Catches*. He tells Duncan, "Oh yes, you do say on p.1 of the intro to *Years As Catches*, you dont know what makes a whole except 'a working feeling' Yes, and there may be no very definable order, or 'syntax of things.' Gestalt. With any arrangement you have a shape, anyway pattern." Eigner, like his friend, admits he can only know what a whole is by "a working feeling," and he depends on gestalt, or serendipity, to know it when he sees it. This observation prompts a poem to emerge in the letter. Eigner continues in an unclosed parenthetical: "(Noticed this back when I encountered the game of jackstones at that school in Canton, Mass. Whatever way the stones fell when tossed - to be picked up, the ten or so of them, between bounces of a ball, by twos, threes, fours - it was in a design. Topology, eh?" A draft of the poem "formations in the / blue" begins immediately after this last sentence. Here is the final version:

```
formations in the

          blue

                          considerations

                    life

                        jackstones
```

windfalls

hordes

(*CP* 3:935)

What shape will his life and his lifework take? Will the random formation it makes add up to a whole? Are the copies of poems arriving from Kansas "windfalls" to be celebrated or "hordes" to be avoided? After drafting the poem, Eigner closes the letter with another association he had while reading Duncan's poem "The Years as Catches," which was written in the early 1940s:

Reading the line
Lift, untimely joy in "The Years As Catches" late last
night , crossed my mind

V'yishkas, . . .Lift up His
v'yishkadahl Countenance Upon Thee
something And Give Thee
something Peace
something
. . . shalom but,
Guess i picked up a dozen words you're not supposed to see God
in five or six years . . .* and Live

‡as a kid might put in as responsive reading, say - but that benediction was always the last word , . . . shalom was . A queer time it did seem, back there in the Temple. Contradictions. With decurum and unction. Then in High School the ridiculously jumbled jurisdictions of the Greek and Roman - heathen - gods)

*of hebrew school afternoons and week [added in pencil]

If Eigner presented himself to Butterick as Moses answering YHWH/Olson's call, here he turns the tables on Duncan, whom he usually considered the older and wiser in the friendship, and plays the rabbi, offering the traditional Aaronic benediction: "The Lord bless thee, and keep thee; The Lord make His face to shine upon thee, and be gracious unto thee; The Lord lift up His countenance upon thee, and give thee peace."[32] Eigner's rabbinical blessing seems to be a response to Duncan's own search for the structure of his life and work, which he says "was to emerge in a series of trials, a problematic identity. A magpie's nest or a collage, a construct of disparate elements drawn into the play they have excited, a syncretic religion."[33] Eigner responds with his thoughts on such bricolage:

> Read some more of your *Years* . . . vol.. last night , yr speaking of among various improvisations "a syncretic religion". Considerable talk in these parts of "the Jewish tradition," one of the phrases that keep people constantly on their beam or in their (circular) tracks, e.g. it's a prime concept of my cousin the boyscout zionist Economist (Ph.D. Harvard) who's been with RAND and now with MITRE; and when last over at his place in September i remarked a tradition has to be assembled from day to day, nowadays, and think i may have quoted that Chinese Emperor on his bathtub. Well, in a tribe, small group, religion unabstracted or undistinguished from the rest of culture, or life, whereas this cousin of mine follows baseball and football some, has his own sailboat or it cd be small yacht in which he makes excursions out from M..head Harbor, has a color set. Ah the Departments! I figure if there was something Jewish about the Wright Brothers or Abner Doubleday life wd be that much more colorful, a little more. (Just a propriorty attitude actually - the guy keeps saying " our .. our our ", and I'd be surprised if he knows much abt Xtnity or anything abt Islam or Buddhism)[34]

Eigner's "syncretic religion" begins at home, in the context of his extended Jewish family. Explaining the circumstances of the discussion with his cousin to his brother Joe and sister-in-law Janet, Eigner, in October 1969, writes,

> Tongue-tied in retrospect. I guess if there's "Jewish value" in sports, boating, driving, . . . beethoven . . . the Gregorian Calendar . . . —so much the more whoopee! Ed's paw was down heah a wk ago talking abt preserving "the tradition", too, although "I don't believe in a personal God," one that prefers the jews or shows anything but indifference to mankind. "It's a tradition that should be preserved." Possessiveness.
>
> Such airy and careless talk, notions, frm so many, as if a tradition was *the* thing in danger. One listener who recently phoned this late and lamented radio program said a woman died on a nyc street not long ago and the diagnosis was air pollution (wonder if thats true) Well, the earth is flat, isn't it? That's what we do/ believe or how
>
> If i find a text for conservation and moderation in buddhism , great . . . Judaism . . . fine thoreau, yeh . . . cherokee proverb, sho nuf. Precedent and historical interest makes thing less grim and technical.[35]

In other words, his environmental ethics is intentionally pragmatic as well as syncretic. Not unlike his fellow New American poet Gary Snyder, Eigner synthesizes his ethics from various sources—world religions, Indigenous wisdom, science, and literature. A magpie's nest, indeed.

In the December 1969 letter to Duncan, Eigner also recaps some of his biblical research:

Got to look in The New Testament Friday night - after a reference. Something I'll never get to read through. In ACTS, crowds, quite a cast of individuals, besides proselytizing. Corinthians, Hebrews - fine-spun argument, polemic, as well as attempted advice (Paul caught rather off-base when asked abt marriage, or of course in process). O T simple, dogmatically codied . . . it hit me; no such argumentation there, as I'll bet. The world or mid-east world before Alexander. After him quite a few regions flowing gether. (Towards the whole earth in time and space   While its always bn humptydumpty enough, in fact mostly

MAXIMUS   IV   V   VI came this morn - got by Andrea W in NYC.
Wow!   Ouch!   Wow!

Three primary elements of this excerpt are significant in this context, and each one has something to do with understanding how parts add up to wholes. In thinking about the difference between the Old and New Testaments, Eigner wonders about the shift in culture and values—from the "dogmatic" codes of the Old Testament to the argumentation and "proselytizing" of the New—and especially the way that the various "regions" of the Middle East "flow[ed] [to]gether" to form a whole. Eigner then pans wide to consider "the whole earth in time and space"; getting a sense of how the biblical Middle East took shape might gain him an understanding of the whole planet. Eigner here uses a phrase that runs throughout the letters I have been quoting but have left unnoted until now: "humptydumpty." The world is a whole, yet it is broken. Invoking the nursery rhyme as a metonym for the environmental crisis, Eigner both captures and questions one of the central tenets of environmental ethics, holism. He realizes that humans mostly see and handle things in pieces, yet to have an ethics that addresses global environmental degradation they also need to have a sense of the whole. Just as Eigner cannot quite pin down what the whole shape of his work is, he acknowledges that it is hard to conceptualize the whole earth. The idea of the earth as singular entity is directly associated with the image of the planet from outer space (the subject of this chapter's next section), and Eigner may have had Stewart Brand's *Whole Earth Catalog*—which was first published in 1968, with such an image for its cover—in mind in using this phrase in his letter to Duncan. But he also had another cover image of the whole earth at hand.

Eigner tells Duncan that his bibliographer, Andrea Wyatt, has just sent him Olson's *Maximus Poems IV, V, VI* from New York City. This would be the Jonathan Cape / Goliard Press edition, published in England, which bears on its cover a rendering of Gondwanaland, described by Olson in a note as "the Earth (and Ocean) before Earth started coming apart at the seams."[36] Although the idea of continental drift developed in the early twentieth century, it wasn't until the 1950s and 1960s that plate tectonics was scientifically accepted. Olson's note indicates that his awareness of Gondwanaland comes from Alfred Wegener's theory of continental drift, which was first proposed in 1915, and a 1966 article published in *Nature*, so this is both a new and an old image of the whole earth. It is another "humptydumpty"—the earth put back together after its fall (at least in terms of scientific theory). This idea of a whole earth circulates through Eigner's research into Hebrew scripture, his reading of *The Maximus Poems*, and the organizing of his archive in Kansas, and it was a key component of early environmental awareness.

other earth now // small one

Throughout the 1960s, the American public was fascinated by NASA's ongoing missions, which would culminate in a human being stepping onto the moon's surface on July 21, 1969. The spectacle of the moon landing was one of the most watched television broadcasts in the twentieth century, and the pictures of earth from space sent back by earlier missions became iconic representations of our terrestrial home. Poets, of course, were not immune to the excitement, and by 1970 there were enough poems about outer space by American poets to produce a 350-page paperback anthology, *Inside Outer Space: New Poems of the Space Age*, edited by Robert Vas Dias. In his introduction, Vas Dias remarks that "this is not a collection of poems *about* space," but rather a collection of poems "in which space associations act as a force in the making of the poem." He continues, "The space-derived image, for example, is the unifying element of many of these poems; a number utilize the language and terms of astrophysics and astroengineering, or depend on information that has become available as a result of space-age science and technology; a few go beyond this sort of dependency to employ a construct that stems from mathematics, statistical probability, and relativity theory."[37] Vas Dias's selection of poets and poems is remarkably diverse, including traditionalist and academic poets, such as W. H. Auden and Adrienne Rich, alongside many of the New American poets, including Eigner, Olson, Robert Creeley, and Allen Ginsberg, as well as William Carlos Williams, Louis Zukofsky, and A. R. Ammons, among many others. Nonetheless, Vas Dias draws heavily on the objectivist-projectivist line of modern poetics in his introduction, citing Williams's "The Poem as a Field of Action" and Olson's "Projective Verse," as well as quoting Richard Grossinger on the Hopi conception of space and time (which prompted Eigner to write his own space-time poem, "on the face of" [*CP* 3:966]). Vas Dias also includes concrete poetry by Raymond Roseliep and Mary Ellen Solt, as well as Jackson Mac Low's chance-based poems for performance, and excerpts from David Antin's "The Black Plague," based in the math of physics and astronomy. For Vas Dias, these intersections of art and science model the formal innovations of the objectivist-projectivist poem. Solt's "Moonshot Sonnet," for example, is an Italian sonnet represented by abstract grid lines "made by copying the scientists' symbols on the first photos of the moon in *The New York Times*"—a text that might have been the inspiration for the anthology's epigraph, a two-page block of capitalized terms that Vas Dias adapted from a National Geographic Society map, "The Earth's Moon."[38] As he notes in the introduction, "what is involved here is basically the recognition that the material of poetry exists in sources heretofore considered unsuitable, even 'anti-poetic.'"[39] Although poems about space exploration and moon landings can be written in any form, open or closed, Vas Dias finds the poetics of the New American poetry the most productive of new forms and perceptions.

A central insight would be of particular interest to Eigner, a poet of the antipoetic whose work was dependent on the prosthetic extension of his body through machine age technology (the typewriter) and modern communications (radio, television, film, and the postal system). Vas Dias observes,

> As man perfects his technology to enter the environment of outer space, technology itself becomes a means to discover the human. . . . Beyond the extension of manual or observational abilities that even a simple instrument provides, there is a more intimate relation arising from the fact that in bio-space technology, one's life functions are monitored and supported by an inorganic "neurological" system: one's life depends on these circuits. Colonel Borman wrote in his report on the Apollo 8 flight: "My personal feelings on this flight in many ways centered on the hardware, and I was deeply interested in vindicating our Apollo hardware." On the other hand, the poet uses hardware as a means of revealing the shape, the eidolon, of himself in his time: thus *techne* inevitably becomes a shaping force in the process of art.[40]

On July 21, 1969, the day Neil Armstrong stepped onto the lunar surface, Eigner wrote this moon-landing poem:

```
The moon is cold

   a background by

  all hardware  more and more to

     go to a heavier place

       more miles
```

in little pieces

poor restless imagination

buoyant motion awhile
in stillness

(*CP* 3:919)

As Buzz Aldrin, the second astronaut to leave the capsule, stepped off the ladder and bounced due to the lighter gravity, Walter Cronkite commented, "like walking on a trampoline"; this moment is likely what Eigner's "buoyant motion" evokes (Vas Dias refers to "Aldrin's instinctive moon caper").[41] The hardware is foremost on Eigner's mind as he watches the moon landing, and it is perhaps the media's emphasis on the technological feat that it represented, rather than on the knowledge that might be gained, that he critiques here. The moon, the object of our fascination and the goal of the mission, becomes mere background for the technological display. Thinking about the moon landing a few days later, Eigner writes,

Wanting everything real
Materialize the moon
Bring it in good and close
Beat it down again to a pulp

(*CP* 3:919)

In "materializ[ing] the moon," NASA brings it into consciousness in a new way, a way that the "poor restless imagination" cannot. When the moon is brought "in good and close," when it is made "real" in a way that gazing at it in the night sky cannot make it seem, then it can be exploited, consumed, destroyed. Bringing back "moon rocks" for experiments was one of the primary purposes of the mission (in another poem Eigner writes, "picking up rocks and / dancing," and he wonders about "a highway on the moon"; *CP* 3:928).

Along with the televised landing, Apollo 11, and Apollo 8 before it, captured the first images of the earth from space, particularly the Earthrise photos, in which a small blue earth is seen "rising" over the lunar surface. Vas Dias recognizes the underlying idea of interconnectedness in the space-age poems in his anthology, and he captures the paradox of the whole earth images that were being relayed back to earth: "against the agate swirl of the blue planet seen from the port of the command module 30,000 miles away is set the image of dark pollution hovering over our megalopolises."[42] Vas Dias may have had one of Eigner's poems from the anthology in mind when he made this comment: "in all the smog / instruments of the stars," it begins (*CP* 3:904). Eigner reflected on the blue-planet images in another poem later that fall:

```
  other earth now

       small one

   imagined tides

 illusion of ease  from

     improved communications
```

(*CP* 3:929)

Indeed, the video cameras that were used to record and transmit the moon landing were cutting-edge technology, and Eigner picks up on the sense that "improved communications" make the planet smaller as the signal comes from the farthest place a human has ever reached (thus making our "world" larger). Eigner's response to the Apollo missions, and the complex mix of technology, politics, and science that produced them, is a key manifestation of his ecrippoetics and, as we can see from Vas Dias's anthology, a key component of the environmental imagination of American poets. Poetry engaging with the whole-earth image and space-age technology, in fact, has a central place in the environmental imagination.

In *Sense of Place and Sense of Planet*, Ursula Heise observes, "From its beginnings in the 1960s, one of the founding impulses of the modern environmentalist movement was its attempt to drive home to scientists, politicians, and the population at large the urgency of developing a holistic understanding of ecological connectedness, as well as of the risks that have emerged from human manipulations of such connected systems. This concern to engage with the 'Whole Earth' took several different forms that sometimes intertwined and sometimes conflicted with each other." Among these forms was the image of the earth from space, and the notion of holism was immediately popularized when Brand's *Whole Earth Catalog* used the picture on its cover. As Heise points out, "in spite of their technological—indeed, to some extent, military—origin, images of Earth in space were quickly appropriated by the environmentalist movement and prominently displayed at the first Earth Day in 1970."[43]

Timothy Clark provides some probing analysis of this image in *Ecocriticism on the Edge*. He writes, "the Apollo images have usually been read in terms of humanity's conception of itself," readings that either emphasize the unity of the image (we are "one earth" now) or its fragility (the "whole earth" is small and isolated in a vast, inhospitable universe, so we must protect and preserve it). Clark continues, "both readings assimilate in given cultural terms (conceptions of a shared humanity, or of the human as Earth's failing steward and manager) an image whose initial force is to dislocate given frames of meaning-making and scale."[44] Scale is one of the central ecocritical concepts in Clark's book, and his attention to the scale effects of the Earthrise images reveals how much Eigner was thinking in the same terms. "The earth is not 'one' in the sense of an entity we can see, understand or read as a whole," Clark writes. "No matter from how far away or 'high up' it is perceived or imagined, or in what different contexts—of cosmology or physics—it is always something we remain 'inside' and cannot genuinely perceive from elsewhere." The problem, as Clark sees it, is that "the Earth is both an object *in* the picture, but also the frame and ground of picturability."[45] Eigner was especially prescient in thinking this way; in 1964, a few years before the images from space were widely available, Eigner begins a poem: "if the earth were an eye / disembodied or not / there would still be frames" (*CP* 2:574). The reason that Eigner is already thinking in Clark's terms is his defamiliar body and what Clark calls *terrestriality*: "*Terrestriality*, defined as that 'normal' prereflective sense of scale inherent to embodied human life on the Earth's surface, forms a kind of transcendental, one that both underlies and exceeds any view that it is merely our social context that determines our understanding of ourselves."[46] From the perspective of disability, terrestriality cannot be taken for granted. To be a norm by which things are judged, terrestriality assumes a normate body—in other words, it is ableist. Just as disability theory must always recognize the constructedness of the body through social practice and policy, so must ecocriticism recognize that terrestriality is an anthropocentric and ableist concept. Again, Clark: "If consideration of literary and cultural criticism in the Anthropocene involves the need newly to think on differing and conflicting scales, then the default scale of human terrestriality will have to be kept constantly in mind, often now as an object of suspicion."[47] Indeed, along with Heise and Clark, Timothy Morton has also emphasized the contradictions and complications of the whole-earth image: "Earth magnitude is bigger than we thought, even if we have seen the NASA Earthrise photos, which now look like charming and simplistic relics of an age in which human hubris was still mostly unnoticed—relics of, precisely, a 'space age' that evaporates in the age of giant nonhuman places. . . . This uncanny sense of existing on more than one scale at once has nothing to do with the pathos of cradling a beautiful blue ball in the void."[48] Seeing the earth from space *does* paradoxically make the earth smaller, but it thereby makes the human bigger, so, for Morton, it is not thinking big enough (or at earth magnitude, as he calls it above). This, as Eigner also knows, is not just a matter of space and distance: "We live on more timescales than we can grasp."[49] Eigner's ecrippoetics brings his disability perspective to the whole-earth image at its advent. As he, with the rest of the country, watches the space race unfold and sees humans step onto the moon, Eigner captures the contradictory meanings of the Earthrise photos—this mix of smallness, fragility, and beauty, on the one hand, and vastness, durability, and survival, on the other—and the ethical implications of our new view of this "other earth" that is, in his phrase, "humptydumpty."

Grass-roots is humptydumpty, more and more it looks like

The term that Eigner pairs with "humptydumpty" as he thinks about the state of the environment at the turn of the decade is "grass-roots."[50] The phrase for a political movement arising organically from the members of a community had been around since the early twentieth century, but it gained a new currency when it was used in the preface to the *Port Huron Statement*, the Students for a Democratic Society's 1962 manifesto. Environmental and social historians point to the late 1960s as the period when the New Left's war resistance became the model for emerging environmental activism. As Adam Rome writes, "The Vietnam War contributed in a very different way to the rise of environmental protest. By the late 1960s, the news media had begun to report that U.S. forces in Vietnam were fighting a war against nature as much as a war against people"; and, he observes that "for many activists . . . the war and the environmental crisis were related causes. In 1969 the magazine of the War Resisters League devoted a special issue to the environment."[51] That magazine was called *WIN* (an acronym for Workshop in Nonviolence), and one of its editors at this time was Eigner's friend and fellow poet Jackson Mac Low. Eigner began publishing poems in *WIN* in 1969, so he likely read the August 1969 issue on the environment. In the September 1970 issue, he published this poem:

```
                    oil at st.a barbara


grass-roots
sky-high

          violence

  earth mined
```

(*CP* 3:897)

"Grass-roots" here captures and condenses Eigner's response to the advent of environmental activism; if the solution to the ecological problems of this time is to come from the "grass roots," Eigner is ready to weigh in on its effectiveness. As one of the first environmental disasters that unfolded in the media in real time, the 1969 spill that covered Central California's beaches and their marine life in viscous, black crude oil produced a worldwide reaction, and it also exposed some of the contradictions of environmental activism. Stephanie LeMenager observes, "As an originary incident, the Santa Barbara oil spill . . . points to the weaknesses of mainstream environmentalism. . . . For instance, its attraction to middle-class rhetorics of rights, consumption, and sacrifice forecloses structural critique, and its overinvestment in spectatorship troubles its relation to action."[52] As one of those spectators, watching it on television and reading about it in the paper, Eigner would have seen images of the volunteers (the "grass roots") who, along with furloughed state prisoners, swarmed the beaches trying to save seabirds and soak up the oil with straw, cat litter, and talcum powder.[53] If the cleanup happens at ground level, as it must, can it really address the paradoxically "sky-high // violence" of drilling into the earth under the ocean's surface? Eigner may also have the violence of the other petro-engineering term for the accident, *blowout*, in mind, and LeMenager further indicates a violent impact on middle-class consciousness: "Privileged people, conscious of their happiness, witnessed the violence of the cheap energy that made it possible." Oil is much like coal as a source of energy, so "earth mined" is an apt phrase that can easily morph into "earth mind"—what is required for understanding the "slow violence" of fossil fuel production and consumption.[54]

As Eigner sought out sources and ideas for his environmental ethics, and the ways to act on such ethics, he was joining his New American poetry peers as they extended the role of the poet to include spokesperson, advocate, and activist, as well as artist. In the 1960s, poets such as Denise Levertov, Allen Ginsberg, and Gary Snyder became "acknowledged" legislators, at least within the counterculture. As Rome noted above, the late 1960s entailed a shift in activism from the radical student protests against the draft and the civil rights movement to include a focus on the environment. He writes, "For many members of the New Left, the degradation of the environment became a powerful symbol of the exploitive character of capitalism. The horrors of the Vietnam War also led many people to question 'the war against nature.' By 1970 the effort to protect the environment seemed to many activists to be part of a larger movement to affirm 'Life,' a word they often used as a shorthand for everything they valued."[55] Poets not only wrote poems of protest and resistance; they also gave speeches at rallies, took part in civil disobedience, worked on committees and with activist groups, and published manifestos and essays to express their positions and advocate for solutions.[56] One of the most prominent of these texts was "Four Changes," written by Snyder with the help of other poets, activists, and social critics. It was, Snyder tells us, "written in the summer of '69 in response to an evident need for a few practical and visionary suggestions."[57]

The essay was published in multiple broadside editions and distributed widely, free of charge. Each proposed change was broken into two main parts, and each part had further subsections. First, there was the condition that needs changing, and the group's position on that condition, how it sees the situation, and what its goal is for the change; the second part presented the proposed action to be taken at the social/political level, within the community, and in "our own heads." Writing to Mac Low in March 1970, Eigner says he has received a copy of "Four Changes" from Nick Kimberley, the editor of a UK journal called *Big Venus*. He tells Mac Low,

> Great stuff, i hope it gets wide publication although it loses a little by having so many things, going on and on some, and in a few places off, like where it puts in a plug for astrology—always the question of attending to neither too much nor too little. And I should take Gary's advocacy of soil banks up, first getting his address from somewhere. It appears untilled land should go back into production again because 80% of the excess nitrogen in the environment, ~~1948-68,~~ came from chem.. fertilizers, needed (. . .?. . .) in intensive agriculture. Maybe a good idea to have a weekly fast, as a reminder of the likelihood and values, whatever they are, of shortages, and of people with below-par living-standards, and a fund drive to have money saved from food budgets on fast days go towards getting ample supplies as long as they're in existence, and even to recompense grocers and restaurant men for lack of business. A switch from production and consumption to sharing, without which you couldn't avoid inducing widespread fear and chaos when lowering production.

Eigner also tells Mac Low that Michael McClure has "urged me to send for EARTH READ OUT, and to send Keith Lampe something, but it'll be a fluke if I ever get around to that. Information overkill here."[58]

Despite feeling overwhelmed by information, Eigner wanted to participate in the larger conversation about how to respond to the ecological crisis, and as Snyder and his friends were working on "Four Changes" in summer 1969, he was drafting one of his most sustained statements on the environment, an essay that he eventually titled "Integration Interchange," which began as a letter to the editor regarding an article on fertilizer pollution in *Scientific American*.[59] As he developed and expanded the letter into an essay, Eigner shared it with various correspondents and tried to circulate it as widely as possible. In November 1974 he sent a copy to George Butterick, explaining,

> The enclosed "Integration Interchange" [. . .] began as a March 69 letter to *Sci.. American*, wch wasnt printed there although I got word it might or wd be if space allowed, and went through 3 or versions as I recopied it. Penultimate version in a mimeoed mag from Blackburn, Lancs, England, in 70 or 71, and near- got into the *Nation* when I sent it there a little before Labor Day 70-72, at the suggestion of a cousin who with R Nader coauthored an article that was in *The Nation* abt ten months before; and before that a frnd in NYC tried to get it in the NYT, spking to frnd of hers on the *Times*. This copy is by my housepainter frnd who as I proposd sent it to his favorite newspaper, which ran it. This latest version (most likely) done abt May 70 or 71 (before I read as much as I did read of *Future Shock*, on hearing of Earth Day at Harvard (teah-in to be brdcast frm Sanders Theatre), where I sent it to address given on th radio though uncertain in memory[60]

Hoping to reach as wide an audience as Snyder's manifesto (or wider, with his attempts at the *New York Times* and the *Nation*), Eigner wants to offer his own "practical and visionary suggestions," with perhaps a little more emphasis on the practical. Three of the four issues that concern Eigner are the same that worried Snyder: population, consumption, and pollution.[61] In trying to reduce the "so many things" that were discussed in "Four Changes" down to a practical suggestion, Eigner proposes a simple solution to all three problems. If a weekly day of fasting was adopted as a national (or global) practice, less fertilizer would be needed, more food would be available even if the population increased, and the ritual itself would be a reminder of the limits of the earth's carrying capacity and the need for sharing resources. As Eigner relates in the original letter to *Scientific American*, "Barry Commoner's 'painful dilemma' between insufficient food production and pollution reminds me of an idea that came to me last Fall, of a Weekly Fast—to include Thanksgiving in the U.S.—as a reminder to ourselves of the likelihood . . . of inadequate harvests, and of how great food is." Eigner also directly links this idea with religious ritual: "Community and participatory democracy in general of course. That day devoted with much heart to public living. If the thing didn't broaden to this it would in some little time be a routine fad instead of an earth- and life-oriented religious element."[62] As a Jew, Eigner had a model for days of fasting and feasting—the holiday of Passover and its ritual meal, the Seder—and he links feasts and fasting in the letter: "Frugal days come to think of it used to alternate, or be relieved by (rather), plentiful ones, which they outnumbered. Fasts and feasts—the two words have the same source—were closely connected." He also incorporates such rituals in the "Integration Interchange" essay: "it's like Dante had lonesome, selfish gluttony below and the Convivio, banquet, symposium, Seder, Last Supper, Love-Feast . . . above."[63] Eigner's use of Jewish tradition here is apt. Ruth Gruber Fredman explains that "one ceremony in particular suggests the ambivalent but optimistic condition of the Seder: the Fast of the First-born. In Judaism, fasts are understood as self-affliction through which one manifests awareness of a state of personal or social crisis."[64] In this case, Eigner (the first born in his family) extends the idea of the "Fast of the First-born" to the ecological crisis. As Fredman indicates, the Seder, whose food is symbolic of the Jews' Exodus from Egypt and also represents the distinction of culture from nature, is in fact a good model for a ritualized fast and feast: "The Passover meal has always been a proclamation of the distinction between 'insiders' and 'outsiders.' What has changed through time is the degree to which the concept of 'insider' could be extended to include the society immediately surrounding the family group."[65] As we saw earlier in this chapter, Eigner was pragmatic about his "syncretic" ethics: "If i find a text for conservation and moderation in buddhism, great . . . Judaism . . . fine thoreau, yeh . . . cherokee proverb, sho nuf. Precedent and historical interest makes thing less grim and technical."[66] Likewise, Snyder, who was also associated with the ethnopoetics movement, is explicit about the syncretizing impulse of his "Four Changes": "It seems evident that there are throughout the world certain social and religious forces which have worked through history toward an ecologically and culturally enlightened state of affairs. Let these be encouraged: Gnostics, hip Marxists, Teilhard de Chardin Catholics, Druids, Taoists, Biologists, Witches, Yogins, Bhikkus, Quakers, Sufies, Tibetans, Zens, Shamans, Bushmen, American Indians, Polynesians, Anarchists, Alchemists . . . the list is long." In adding Jews to Snyder's list, Eigner does indeed provide a more pragmatic solution in a sense. Snyder calls for a radical reconsideration of family in his manifesto—"group marriage and polyandrous marriage"—as a means of reducing population and consumption, but certainly extending the traditional family to include the society that surrounds it, as Fredman claims the Seder does, would be more feasible for most people than Snyder's countercultural sexual mores and practices.[67]

Nonetheless, as Rome points out, one central faction of the New American poetry was the prime example of such values: "the countercultural roots of environmentalism went deepest. In the late 1950s, the beat writers began to tout the open space of nature as an antidote to the poisonous conformity of suburbia." In turn, the Beats' non- or apolitical counterculture was grafted onto the New Left's structural critique of capitalism. "By 1970," Rome continues, "several countercultural writers had begun to contemplate radical action to save the planet. In a series of 'revolutionary letters,' the poet Diane Di

Prima imagined blowing up petroleum lines and destroying Dow Chemical Company plants."[68] Eigner himself had the opportunity to consider such "ecotage," or ecological sabotage, which became a key tactic of radical environmental groups such as Earth First! in the late 1970s, after the publication of Edward Abbey's *The Monkey Wrench Gang* (1975). In a note added to a typescript of a poem titled "crossed self hand and foot re strained" (*CP* 3:949), Eigner writes,

> ‡‡ The above poem and (draft of?) letter a response to a mimeoed booklet that came one day from LA advocating sabotage such as blowing up dams to reservoirs as blackmail to extort gov.. action in re ecology. Mailed there, the poem and letter came back marked no such address. LE 1974 ‡‡

Although he feels committed to taking action as best he can, Eigner rules out violence as one option for his environmental ethics. The "draft" letter reads:

> May 11 70
>
> To be negative seem wrng and to disagree at al cnfusing. I'm a babe in th wds, and quite the sitting duck (n ahlchr [in a wheelchair]), and unprepared for anything just abt. Always bn more or less impossible to add thngs up. A gd idea abt rf grdens eg but a constant puzzle has bn, unless you're omniscient, what pro osl and how many to push and really demand. As to disagreement, anyway and my inclination towards doubts and rsrvations, h rs th qstn of how mch can man expect of himself, natural and unnatural as he is in various ways. You advocate letting nature take its crs, as i do mostly, but also of upsetting domesticity and status quo. Sabotage . . . sabotage, disruptio, upset, is violence, wch usually overflws frm that done to thngs to . . . to ple—psychologic to physical *dam*age. Revolution is spectacular reform. while the slow type does bog dwn and run to earth. Th wrld nerly all people, at lest in my experience being non-listeners who either sleep and dream of lash out when awakened. The pres.. cant be god - the caesars cd be so only in name mostly.[69]

Eigner rules out violence for practical reasons (hard to blow up a dam when you're in a wheelchair) as well as ethical ones (violence against things will "overflow" to people). The poem that accompanied these notes captures Eigner's sense of futility or frustration; "crossed self" can be taken as the conflicting impulses toward action and inaction that he cannot sort out, and his "hand and foot" are "restrained" because of his disability. And the poem also thinks in terms of what is enough:

```
crossed self  hand and foot  re strained
```

```
abstraction
   in the dark

               d
              e i
               a s
                s
                 e

          or how much to
               live

              how many
            times
                  breathe

          to decide death
            besides life at

             what time
```

(*CP* 3:949)

In the typescript, the second line ("abstraction") reads "abstention"—perhaps the better word here as the poet seems to be abstaining from the proposed violence. But what Eigner is more interested in is the question of how one would decide to take such action. In taking violent action to protect and preserve life—ecologically—one is making decisions that also lead to (possible) death.[70] In the poem's last lines, he sums up the "constant puzzle" that comes with the lack of omniscience: "how much do we / have to know // for the habit of hours." Considering any action, violent or not, Eigner always wants to know how much is too much, how much is enough.

Golden mean point between activity and in- or non-activity indeterminate, unfathomable

As more and more information about ecological degradation became available, as more and more editors and publishers sent requests for submissions, as copies flooded in from Kansas, Eigner wondered whether he had written too much, published too much, whether he was contributing to "fatiguing the earth, clogging it up with extras." "Yet," as he observed later in life, "'since feeling is first,' where to stop and put on brakes???"[71] In early 1970, Eigner put together a sequence of poems on ecological themes, which were published by the New York–based journal *Athanor* as a "microbook" that was included with its second issue (Fall–Winter 1971).[72] This microbook, *circuits*, provides an excellent example of how Eigner's ethics circulate through his poems when they are deliberately assembled as a sequence.

The idea of a microbook certainly would appeal to Eigner at this point, since he is concerned with production and consumption as an ecological issue. Smaller poems mean smaller books, which means less paper and therefore fewer trees cut down. As we saw earlier in this chapter, Eigner was corresponding with his editors with these issues on his mind. As he conferred with Douglas Calhoun about poems that *Athanor* had accepted for its first issue, Eigner responded to a request from Calhoun for material for a microbook:

> Anyway yr suggestion abt a microbook touched off ##493 and 494 - the april 18th one, #489, too, maybe - so, natural thing to do, although 2 3 or 4 requests from other places lie neglected these weeks, i show you 7 poems for a microbook (##493, 494, 460, 495, 484, 475, 489), which might be called in flight but i think circuits a better title, implying ecologic or at least planetary water, and food, cycles, as well as flight x y and z, and routes, the jet set.[73]

As we saw in the previous chapter, Eigner himself joined the "jet set" in the 1960s, taking his first flights to visit his brothers in Saint Louis and San Francisco, and he was excited to "elude the 4 walls" of the family home and see "the view" from above (*CP* 2:573). The first poem in the *circuits* sequence, however, presents a less sanguine response to being "in flight":

```
  jaggied
     potential

 abundance
 associations

   farm
    country

   seen from a plane

   lightning

     we turn away

   fuel dumped behind us
```

related speeds

we don't know

headlong   palpable

over what rooftops

roughnesses

(*CP* 3:1003)

This poem embodies Eigner's ecrippoetics and ethics not only because it comments on the environmental impact of air travel (for example, planes dumping fuel in emergencies), but also because it is literally a recycled poem. *The Collected Poems of Larry Eigner* includes an earlier version, dated "c. 1951–52":

There are many things we do not know
Say possibilities are enough and more
we don't have to know it, which is good.

Jaggied potential, when it will come
Over what house grown headlong and palpable
Descending with ultimate speed, wind in the eyes

till we turn to our shelters confused moving away

and no-one can tell if any clouds bring rain

(*CP* 1:74)

What prompted Eigner to rewrite this poem twenty years later? Did it arrive in the flood of copies from Kansas and simply present itself for revision? The question of omniscience was often raised in the early poems, how much we can know and how much we need to know, and Eigner seems to be wondering about "how to make pictures of the weather" as he put in "De Limits" (*CP* 1:75). The speaker takes comfort in merely knowing something is possible. Will those clouds bring rain? Who knows, but they have the "jaggied potential" to do so. Since he did not revise "jaggied" to "jagged," the coinage must be, as the editors of *The Collected Poems* insist, "intentional" (*CP* 1:xii). Bolt lightning from a storm cloud forms the impression of a jagged line, and perhaps the *-ied* suffix is meant to evoke verbal modifiers such as "hurried" or "harried." The mood of the poem is ominous: the approaching storm might even be evocative of Cold War fears, and perhaps "shelters" is literal rather than being another way of saying "houses." (Is there also an echo of *The Waste Land*'s "In a flash of lightning. Then a damp gust / Bringing rain"?)[74] In any case, Eigner's "revision" of this early poem is an act of recycling; indeed, it exemplifies the environmentalist slogan of reduce, reuse, recycle.

In revising this poem, Eigner deletes more than half the words (reducing a sixty-two-word poem to twenty-nine), whittling it down to its essential terms and laying it out on the page in the format of his mature style. Most significantly, Eigner's experience with air travel alters the poem's point of view. The first version is from ground level, as it must be, but the revision presents "farm / country // seen from a plane." Eigner eliminates additional words through ellipsis ("headlong and palpable" becomes "headlong palpable") and contractions ("we do not know" becomes "we don't know"), but he also makes additions. Along with the view from the plane, Eigner adds "abundance / associations," "fuel dumped behind us," and the final word, "roughnesses." The first two additions incorporate his concerns about ecology, making the poem about one of the "circuits" that are the microbook's theme, and the last one captures the idea of jaggedness that began the poem (the *American Heritage Dictionary*, third edition, includes *jagged* among the synonyms for *rough*). The fields and rooftops seen from a plane may appear to the speaker as areas of roughness that stand out from the rest of the landscape, and, because "we don't know," we may only have a rough idea of something's potential or the "abundance [of] associations" that may come with it.

The next poem in *circuits* introduces balance and sufficiency, two main elements of Eigner's environmental ethics:

```
big or small  slice up
     lines confusing

                       figure
                         areas

          great size or
             great numbers

           great sizes and

       maximum  minima  maxima
```

```
what's
 an illusion

what
     cloud
  to see so far

 dyanu



  or the maxima
    the minima
       the gold
```

(*CP* 3:1004)

Attempting to determine the proper balance between too much ("big") or too little ("small"), the maximum or the minimum, Eigner inserts a bit of Hebrew from the Passover Seder as a corrective. The poem is dated "April 28–May 1 71," and Passover that year began on April 10 and ended on April 16, so Eigner likely had recently experienced the ritual meal and was reminded of its forms and meanings. As described by Ruth Gruber Fredman, the Seder's ritual recitations and the meal itself express the central concerns of Jewish identity and tradition:

> Jewish culture, concerned as it is with creating order through distinction, is also concerned with concepts that either uphold or threaten these distinctions. Where order is perceived as divine, disorder is not only a threat to society's comprehension of its universe, but profanation as well. The more the society clarifies its distinctions, the more it simultaneously prohibits anything that would weaken them. Yet people must continually deal with the gray, ambiguous areas not totally encompassed by strict definitions: "twilight" can appear to "exist" as well as dark and light; there are hybrids and homosexuals, and the diaspora itself is conceived of as an indeterminate state.[75]

If one cannot make a clear distinction between big and small, figure and area, or the maximum and the minimum, the prospect of discovering a golden mean between them is not promising. Fredman's acknowledgment that the binary distinctions between nature and culture made during the Seder do not actually resolve the ambiguities of experience validates Eigner's skeptical questioning here. Morton's *Dark Ecology* identifies this problem with the "Law of the Excluded Middle," which he describes as "the idea that there is black and white, yes and no, with nothing in between. Very little in regular experience survives this exclusion. For instance, you can't be 'in the doorway' if you believe that you are either inside or outside a room. Motion seems to be impossible. So many ecological beings are 'Excluded Middles' and so much ecological action is in the realm of 'not quite' and 'slightly,' gradations of yes."[76] Thus, Eigner's unpunctuated question, "what's / an illusion[?]" Twilight and doorways are liminal, threshold states that produce in-between experiences that feel real but also appear to be illusory.

The cloud that appears in the next stanza seems associated with the idea of illusion, and, interestingly, Fredman finds a parallel between the Passover wine and clouds: "As an amorphous form, wine—like water, blood, clouds, and smoke—is used in Judaism to suggest 'interconnectedness' between man and man, and man and God."[77] The very idea of an "amorphous form"—a formless form—is paradoxical, and these shape-shifting entities do indeed make us question the difference between being and appearing. As Morton says, "The ecological thought gets along just fine with the Trickster."[78] For Eigner, even if he cannot determine the golden mean in absolute terms, to be able to see far enough to see clouds should be enough, and his citation of the Seder's "hymn of thanksgiving *Dayaynoo* ('It Would Have Sufficed for Us')" confirms this.[79] Dayaynoo ("dyanu") not only sounds the keynote of the microbook, it could serve as the one-word summation of Eigner's ecrippoetics and environmental ethics.

Along with the theme of air travel, *circuits* contains poems on other ecological themes. For example, Eigner's concern with overpopulation is expressed in this poem:

```
enough new
            each day
                      births

 there's enough of the old, the dying


            approach to the present
```

(*CP* 3:997)

The main contributor to the expanding human population is the number of live births outpacing the mortality rate, and as Eigner indicates here, this fact connects the past (the dying) and the future (the new births) with the present (too many people). Eigner rounds out this brief sequence by returning to air travel in the last poem:

```
taking          fuel
 the plane off
    smells presses
            the wind

   where
    to  calm

   day
       the earth brought round

        shapes
```

(*CP* 3:1000)

The economy of Eigner's arrangement is impressive. The first stanza contains possibly two complete statements ("taking off the plane presses the wind" and "fuel smells"), and it also refuses to distinguish the sense impressions as they mingle in the poet's consciousness. There is a possible question about the flight—where to?—and, despite the wind, it seems to be a calm day. Perhaps we are to hear an echo of "dayaynoo" in "day." "The earth brought round // shapes" completes the "circuit" of the sequence, bringing it back to the "roughnesses" of "farm / country // seen from a plane."

By the early 1970s, Eigner's ecrippoetics produced visually distinctive poems on the page as well as an idiosyncratic form of environmental ethics that attempted to define what is *enough*. As his connections with poets, readers, and publishers continued to grow, Eigner became one of the New American poetry's primary influences on the next generation of postmodernists, especially those known as the Language poets. The next chapter will examine how Eigner's ecrippoetics informed the advent of Language poetry and how his friends among this cohort helped him continue to develop and refine his own work. The inaugural issue of Charles Bernstein and Bruce Andrews's *L=A=N=G=U=A=G=E* newsletter opened with an essay by Eigner in which he declares his search for the golden mean ongoing: "No really perfect optimum mix, anyway among some or many thousands of distinct(ive) or distinguishable things." His ecrippoetics will continue to seek that balance, because, as he says at the end of this essay, there are "many/and/various/mixes."[80]

CHAPTER FOUR

Wild Wor(l)ds

Eigner's Language

> Breath is man's special qualification as an animal. Sound is a dimension he has extended. Language is one of his proudest acts.
>
> CHARLES OLSON, "Projective Verse"

IN A POSTCARD to the special collections librarians at the University of Kansas, dated January 2, 1986, Eigner notes that *In the American Tree*, "a big anthology of 'language writing[,]' [is] dedicated and very largely baffling to me."[1] Since the early 1970s, Eigner had been corresponding with and reading the work of younger writers who would come to be known as Language poets, and after he moved to Berkeley two poets associated with this group, Robert Grenier and Kathleen Frumkin, were his caretakers and roommates. So, his bafflement at the work contained in the anthology is telling given that he was part of this community of writers from its inception. As Robert Creeley noted in his review of *In the American Tree* for the *San Francisco Chronicle*: "The brilliance of the writers collected here is not simply literary. Their response to the world, however demanding, is intently communal. They are asking—often with great wit and heart—that we recognize that language itself is real and we must learn to live in its complex places."[2] Language as the place in which we dwell is a necessary idea for an ecopoetics, and the realness of words is a concern that stems directly from modernist and objectivist-projectivist poetry. The writing is difficult because it is experimental, as Creeley observes, but for him that simply means that these poets "enjoy thinking, they like the thingness of language." About a year later, Eigner expressed a similar view, writing to Carroll Terrell of the National Poetry Foundation, the anthology's publisher: "Hm, maybe this 'language' poetry is centered on thinking—the descendant or else the parent of speech?—rather than speech itself. Putting it up my alley. Thinking that gets man from one thing to the next. And realization, recognition or real awareness of things, may not be a different kettle of fish, much."[3] So, even if he doesn't understand much of the writing designated as "Language" poetry, Eigner feels that his ecrippoetics—thinking with things, which means realizing the realness of things in language, finding their weight in words—"may not be a different kettle of fish, much." In fact, the Language poets were responsible for Eigner's continuing presence, both in person and in print, in American poetry in the 1970s and 1980s. Eigner's Language-writing friends were not necessarily interested in the *eco* or *crip* elements of his poetics, but Language writing in general was a critique aimed at not only the postconfessional lyrical ego but also the political structures that commodify language into such things as identity and subjectivity. To the extent that a mainstream, middle-class environmentalism relies on a coherent, unified subject position not entangled in the meaning-making apparatus of language—what environmental historian Dorceta E. Taylor calls "environmental identity"—Language poetry's engagement with the issues of reference and signification has much to offer an ecopoetics that would take language to be part of the environment, if not an environment itself.[4]

Language writing shares its advent with the ethnopoetics movement, and early publications from both groups often posited language as the "environment" of poetry. For example, in 1980 Tom Beckett and Earel Neikirk began publishing *The Difficulties* in Kent, Ohio. An editors' note in the first issue proclaimed, "We are starting a new journal of the arts which is to be devoted to process-oriented, language-centered work," and it informed the reader that the contents were "gathered . . . [in] response to the following query": "Is it meaningful to you to speak of locating yourself in your work in terms of a 'language environment'? If so, please respond to what constitutes a 'language environment' and what you consider the relationship between you and it to be. If not, what sense of language would you oppose to this and why?" "Some fifty persons" received the query, and among those who responded were Cid Corman, Charles Bernstein, John Taggart, Susan Howe, Michael Davidson, Rosmarie Waldrop, and Tom Raworth, as well as Eigner himself.[5] Along with three of his poems, the first issue of *The Difficulties* included an untitled prose statement by Eigner, later called "Dilemmas by Their Horns," in which, of course, Eigner wonders about how much is enough when it comes to words, and writes, "There's enough language around (me) so listening gets harder and harder and then impossible, quite a barrier to being adequate. Yet it flows on like a river of nice clean air. Does it?"[6]

In 1979, Jerome Rothenberg published volume 2, number 7, of his journal *New Wilderness Letter*, which he began after leaving an editorial position at the ethnopoetics journal *Alcheringa*. It is also something of a collective statement about the "language environment," and its contributors indicate the overlap between Language and ethnopoetics groups. Along with Rothenberg himself, the table of contents includes, among others, Gary Snyder, Clayton Eshleman, Jackson Mac Low, Steve McCaffery, Charles Bernstein, and Eigner. Rothenberg printed his editor's notes on the inside front and back covers, and he included Eigner's poem "a monkey wrench" at the end of his note inside the back cover (*CP* 3:1127). He placed this quote on the outside back cover: "'My inventory is a wilderness.'—Larry Eigner (letter, 6/6/77, to J.R.)." In his notes, Rothenberg wrote, "the three principal arenas of 'wilderness' discussed herein are (1) the ecological, (2) the imaginal, & (3) the wilderness of language."

Thinking of language as an environment or wilderness posits it as a "wild" system that humans are a part of or exist in, something that can be used for our own purposes but that we do not own or control entirely. As the medium for poetry, it is a strange and intangible substance, but it is also the form that thought takes. Ethnopoetics and Language writing are two prominent responses to the New American poetry, extending the modernist-objectivist-projectivist-Beat poetics of Donald Allen's *The New American Poetry* anthology, through their associations with the poets published in that collection (Eigner, Mac Low, Snyder, Denise Levertov, Allen Ginsberg, Robert Duncan, and Robert Creeley), to the generation of poets coming of age in the late 1960s and 1970s. Charles Olson's death in 1970 might be considered the turning point between these generations: he was the "strong" precursor figure to be both embraced and contested. His "Projective Verse" manifesto is the dominant statement for open-form poetics after *The New American Poetry*, and the next generation defined itself by both accepting and rejecting aspects of Olson's projective verse.

The typewriter's ability to graph and score a page to indicate the breath and voice of the poet is the most notorious claim of "Projective Verse," and it underwrites the sense of poems as objects that is so important to this generation of poets. As we will see in this chapter, Eigner's "calligraphy / typewriters" extends Olson's typewriter fetish into the aesthetics of Language writing. "Typewriters were predictably important to the Language poets," Matthew Hofer observes, "perhaps most so to Bernstein, who not infrequently writes metacritically about the process of writing on a particular typewriter or even with a particular font."[7] Typewriting represents an ambiguous relation between eye and ear, as I argued in the introduction: if the font changes how a text is received, then the visual layout of the page must have a role in making meaning, in the way we see the words that we then hear in our mind. Language poets are commonly thought to be phonophobic, based on Grenier's proclamation "I HATE SPEECH" in his essay "On Speech" in the first issue of the language-oriented journal *This*.[8] The typewritten "score" appears to be a mechanization of the voice that breaks its connection to speech, and this visual emphasis is one of the main ways that Language poetry defamiliarizes speech. According to Hofer, Language poetry "is perhaps best defined as an attempt to break away from the constraints of the New American Poetics of the 1950s and 1960s, particularly with regard to speech and what 'voices' entail for ideas about presence as well as reference."[9] Grenier, however, indicates in "On Speech" that distinguishing a poem's ontological status is not as easy as pointing to its appearance on the page. He includes an epigraph by Randolph Dud that captures the ambiguity of language as a medium ("My poems exist in my head. They need not be spoken or written"), and says that "words of the poem have something to do with the forms of written spoken usage . . . in which they may be heard/seen, but there is no value in the linguistic vehicle per se, i.e., spoken noises and written letters are signs of the reality of words in the head."[10] Again, as I argued in the introduction, the distinction between a *text* and a *work* is still useful, and this is the distinction that Grenier makes here. The poem is the work that exists in the mind; its texts can be visual or sonic. Still, this does not resolve the issues of "presence as well as reference," and this chapter will use Jacques Derrida's idea of "the hinge" to examine how Eigner's ecrippoetics uses the typewriter to create meaningful space on the page.

So, Eigner fully participated in the debates these poets had about form and content, reference and meaning, speech and writing, and words and world, and this "language environment," in turn, nurtured his ecrippoetics. In a poem titled "wild wor(l)ds," dedicated to the editors of *This*, Grenier and Barrett Watten, Eigner sums up his sense of Language writing:

```
              the framework
                   of go
 the context                wherever
  of anything
      goes                   some things really come out
```

(*CP* 3:1312)

In Albert Gelpi's account of this lineage, Eigner's dual sense of "wild words" and "wild worlds" is exactly right: "The progression from Williams to Creeley to Eigner to Grenier traces a clear trajectory in American poetry, and in Grenier, orthography stands in opposition to geography. Writing / reading words is writing / reading the world; we come to know the world as words and words as world."[11] What "really come[s] out" of Language writing for Eigner is a renewed engagement of his ecrippoetics with the medium of his poetic art. Trying to find the weight of things in words, Eigner discovers that the ecological thought cannot be abstracted from the mesh of language in which meaning happens.

i // mean // at // moments

Ron Silliman, along with Grenier and Watten, was one of the first to claim Eigner as a forebear of Language writing.[12] In his 1975 note on a group of nine language-oriented writers in a special issue of the ethnopoetics journal *Alcheringa*, Silliman writes, "Beyond such 'cues' as concretism and certain tribal literatures, the work of two men ought also to be noted as fire source: Creeley and Eigner. Creeley's work, both in the poems and such essays as 'To Define' and 'Poems are a complex,' has sensitized many to the possibilities of getting at, to, in the word. Eigner, by fact of physical situation, has take[n] the logic of speech as such out of discourse, creating sequences of presences. Power to their words."[13] Finding the possibility of "getting at, to, in the word" in Creeley's essays, these poets conceive of language as a site, location, or place: one can "get to" the word as one gets to a destination. In "Poems are a complex," Creeley posits an ontological status for the poem: "There had to be an independence derived from the very fact that words are *things* too."[14] Poems are a "complex" of things, which, as Creeley indicated in his review of *In the American Tree*, means that words (their material) are the "complex places" in which we live. Acknowledging this idea, and anticipating such things as the "new wilderness" and "language environment," Silliman titled the selections from the nine poets in *Alcheringa* "The Dwelling Place."[15] If words can be things, they can be made into places. Another poet who thought about the realness of words as things stands behind Creeley and Eigner: Charles Olson.

Silliman's Promethean image ("fire source") echoes Robert Duncan in his introduction to the published version of Olson's lecture *Causal Mythology*: "For all the poets who matter to me in my generation Charles Olson has been a Big Fire Source." Silliman acknowledges Olson as the source behind his sources by using Olson's "epigraph" to this lecture as his own epigraph for "The Dwelling Place": "that which exists through itself is called meaning."[16] Creeley also identifies this quotation from Olson as a source in "Poems are a complex": "Two . . . statements of Pound's long ago attracted me: 'Only emotion endures . . .' and 'Nothing counts save the quality of the emotion. . . .' I have used that sense with respect to all instances of writing, but I would feel, as he, that poetry is that most fully charged with meaning. To that I would now add a recent emphasis of Olson's: 'That which exists through itself is what is called meaning.'"[17] Creeley links Ezra Pound's modernism with Olson's projectivism in order to express a constituent dilemma of such a materialist aesthetic: if words are things, where does meaning come from? If "poems are not referential, or at least not importantly so," then their meaning comes not from their reference to an "outside" world but from themselves (or, to follow Pound's formulation, from their *motive* force).[18] Although Eigner himself does not quote Olson's statement as Creeley and Silliman do, the question of how to find meaning when words are things is also a central issue for his ecrippoetics.

Stephen Fredman points out that Olson modifies the phrasing of his epigraph, taken from the Taoist text *The Secret of the Golden Flower*. In the original, the word is *Tao*, translated as *way*, rather than *meaning*. Fredman observes, "by suppressing the word *Tao* in his formulation . . . Olson deflects attention away from the 'exotic' quality of Taoism . . . and from theological terms in general and concentrates instead on an interpretation of 'meaning' as produced through the self-grounding existence of an object rather than through the manipulation of concepts." In locating meaning in objects rather than in concepts, Olson not only aligns himself with objectivist poetics but anticipates Morton's ecotheory to the extent it draws on object-oriented ontology to displace the subject-object binary. Fredman asserts that Olson is replacing the logos of Western metaphysics with the Tao as the ground of being; therefore, "to recognize meaning, we should not seek to compare things to one another but rather [seek] to penetrate deeply enough into each thing that we find the unending Tao within it."[19]

Around the time that Eigner was reading *Causal Mythology*, the mimeographed journal *Earth Ship*, based in Southampton, England, dedicated its eighth issue to his work. The special feature contains poems that cover themes similar to the microbook *circuits*. For example, fuel shortages and air travel come up again in "High piled / clouds," written shortly after Eigner returned to Swampscott after visiting his brother in Saint Louis: "all that fuel / stored on the ground // for which the / demand is / rising," he writes (*CP* 3:1035). *Earth Ship* 8 is also significant because Eigner wrote a preface for the issue, later titled "Arrowhead of Meaning." This statement introduces ideas about language, meaning, and poetry that relate to ecology and link Eigner with the incipient Language-writing movement that was emerging from objectivist-projectivist poetics in the 1970s.[20] "Arrowhead of Meaning" is a deliberate exploration of some of these ideas at the advent of Language writing, and it bears traces of Olson's thinking in *Causal Mythology* and other sources.

Two substantial paragraphs make up the first half of "Arrowhead of Meaning": the opening paragraph offers a definition of poetry, and the second discusses what poetry might concern. In other words, Eigner is thinking through a central issue in modern poetics, the relation between form and content. "Poetry," the essay begins, "seems to be deliberate speech." Eigner tells the reader that he gets this idea from Robert Creeley's review of Charles Olson's first chapbook, *Y&X*. "Further," he writes, "deliberate thought (though meaning may still ultimately be, by aimed words, happening between people, out of one situation and towards another which is like or more or less unlike it, a happening, a discharge), for, as Creeley put it, 'The line is the means to focus, . . . says "how" we are to weight the various *things* we are told.' Thought voiced and/or in the mind."[21] Eigner's ideas here are deconstructive—that is, speech and thought are associated with each other, as in Derrida's notion of logocentrism. Can words be "aimed" at meaning? Or are words themselves "the arrowhead of meaning" in that they make up a line at the end of which is the *point*? Eigner's thoughts on meaning also come from his reading of Creeley's review. Discussing Olson's "La Préface," Creeley writes, "Here the line is used to make the ground logic beyond the single 'senses' of the words. The poem can't be understood, lacking a comprehension of the work the line is doing here. What it does do then, is give the base pattern which pulls the poem's juxtaposition of *action* and *thing* to a common center where the reader can get to bedrock. Meaning."[22] Creeley locates meaning between "action" and "thing," the "bedrock" arrived at by assembling words into lines. And, in the line that Eigner quotes from Creeley, Creeley uses the word "weight" as a transitive verb. Does the reader make the line heavier, *adding* the meaning? Or does she *weigh* the lines themselves to determine their meaning?

Eigner concludes the first paragraph of "Arrowhead of Meaning" by reiterating his original definition of poetry: "Thought voiced and/or in the mind." For Eigner, "deliberate thought" goes together with "deliberate speech," and the line is the means by which the things thought or spoken are weighed (though he indicates that he can't say which one comes first). But thought and speech require matter to take form, and Eigner moves from his objectivist-projectivist models to the wider tradition in English as he starts to think about the subjects of thought and speech. The second paragraph begins with a quote from John Keats's "Ode to Melancholy": "Yet 'but to think is to be full of sorrow.' As true in the past as currently, an indeterminate part of the whole truth." Thinking itself brings melancholy, and the question of what to think about doesn't solve the problem. There are new "things" (a central and ambiguous term in this essay) every day, "something that could well involve you or that you could well be concerned with, like '. . . any man's death,' or life, the other side of the earth as much at your fingertips as the house across the street and what goes on in there."[23] Thinking is therefore ecological; Eigner here is thinking Morton's ecological thought by "thinking big," which means viewing things from "earth magnitude," refusing to stay at the scale of terrestriality.[24] Just as the quote from John Donne's Meditation 17 ("any man's death") invokes the shared lives of humanity, Eigner's sense of the incipient "global village" extends his concern to "the other side of the earth." Eigner puzzles over how to decide what to think about, what *things* to give weight to in a poem, if one could even have a plan for what needs to be done. He concludes by deciding that things have gotten done more often on a makeshift, pragmatic basis: "plans and *a priori* first principles have had a big share in the world. Easy to see the advantage in them, if they can be had, as well as their disadvantages. Well, it does seem that most people have always lived day to day and from hand to mouth."[25]

The next paragraph is just three sentences: "If a thing is hard enough, no one can do it. I enjoy doing things that are easy enough. If it gets to be work, physically tiring, still it's enjoyable work." What does *thing* refer to here? An activity? A job? A poem? All the above? Here is the typical conflation of physical *labor* with poetic *work* that American poets are particularly fond of —as Richard Poirier notes in *Poetry and Pragmatism*—and Eigner's embodiment was such that typing *was* intensely physical labor.[26] The next paragraph, however, makes it clear that Eigner is thinking that *things* in poetry are the same as *things* (or actions) in the world:

> I once wanted to do big things and to try of course is the only way to begin, and to quite an extent continuing depends on it too. (While now there's haiku for model, say, where before there was only the epic, the sonnet and so on—as if Greek was American or English or Biblical enough, but not Japanese.) I'm still naturally about as interested as I ever was in improving things, i.e., things in general, whatever that is. "Poetry makes nothing happen." Although in places where there are or have been shamans, a word is a deed, a right word an effective cause. Getting together enough.[27]

To have only the epic or the sonnet for a model is to be stuck with only one scale (in terms of epic, large) or one form (in terms of the sonnet, closed). Now that he has haiku for an alternative model, Eigner can do small *things* in open forms as well as large ones.[28]

Eigner now distinguishes between the "things" he does in writing and "things in general," which are in need of improvement. The quotation from W. H. Auden's elegy for William Butler Yeats ("Poetry makes nothing happen") returns him to questions about poetry's effectiveness, whether it can be "causal" like Olson's mythology. If the poet can just get *things* together enough, "a right word [can be] an effective cause." Eigner throws his lot in with Olson, theorizing that the discovery of form is poetic action that produces effects in the world. In Eigner's ecrippoetics, poetry makes *something* happen. As an example, Eigner quotes William Wordsworth, "My heart leaps up when I behold / A rainbow in the sky," and comments: "Those are two things." Are the "two things" here Wordsworth's heart and the rainbow? In getting them together, is the poet discovering the effect (elation) the rainbow has on him? Its meaning?

Eigner concludes his statement with a return to the idea of the golden mean—"I wonder about purpose, what priorities if not principles are possible, how to balance things"—and the final paragraph propounds his ethics of enough: "Enough it seems has been produced, enough writings, enough cars, enough music, enough of a lot else. Production or creation is a human quality or whatever, anthropoid, mammalian, vertebrate, proceeding through time. Contact outwards or something, besides bringing in and familiarizing. Days themselves are new. And old. But now appears a time to share. Only, to share what? All? An imposition that wd be. Too much. . . ."[29] If words can be things, if discovering form is the weighing of things in words, if poems *do* make things happen, then a poet should consider what his production contributes to "things in general." The outcome is not guaranteed to be positive, and unintended consequences can make things worse. Eigner condenses this idea in a poem a few years later:

```
so many poems

   so many cars
```

(*CP* 3:1339)[30]

The result of "so many cars" is air pollution and global warming; what might be the result of "so many poems"? Exactly the same thing if those poems take a physical form that requires carbon-based energy to produce it, which any physical form must in a carbon economy. If words are things that constitute "complex places" that are poems, then poets should consider their own production's material impact on the environment. As he had hoped do with his letter on pollution by fertilizer, Eigner was able to disseminate "Arrowhead of Meaning" a little further than its appearance in a UK-based small magazine. In May 1972, Robert Grenier invited Eigner to read at Franconia College in New Hampshire. Writing to his relatives in Saint Louis afterward, Eigner told them that "I read aloud the intro.. to EARTH SHIP 8."[31]

In Eigner's language, in a poetics of words-as-things, the visual layout on the page takes on a new significance. There were questions about spacing at the Franconia reading as well. In describing the reading to his family, Eigner writes, "I had along the booklet of which so far only one copy has come here, the one with too many blank lines and a lacuna following nearly every word, together with the perfect mock-up or dummy, ts of the publisher/printer's making - this latter one student had under his arm, having picked it up on a recent trip to London, it was one thing providing feedback and/or a good amount of distraction before the reading got underway."[32] Later in the letter, he provides more information on the conversation with this student. He relates that after the reading, "we followed Grenier and a student [. . .] to his place [. . .] and after supper with her and a boy, the one who asked the question (in re spacing) when Bob G announced the q.. period, the one who had my booklet from London, a few others dropped in and stayed pretty late. Before we got to the college Bob mentioned a couple of students told him they got my continuity - well, the fee wasnt the price of a car."

Eigner had told Grenier in a letter the previous December: "the pauses—blank lines, line breaks, and indents too, usually anyway (with me)—certainly are essential, of the substance, of deliberate speech."[33] Eigner was aware that readers could be frustrated by the distractions and disruptions that his spacing and punctuation cause in trying to determine his meaning, yet Grenier's students "got" his continuity (at a fair price, according to Eigner; that is, he didn't think it should be all that difficult to get). To be continuous is to be "uninterrupted in time, sequence, substance, or extent"; it also implies being "attached together in repeated units."[34] In what way can spacing (absences, gaps, blanks) be "essential" to a poem's meaning? How can an insubstantial element of a text—if absence can be an element at all—be part of the "substance" of a poem? How do two things that seem completely discontinuous, a mark and the absence of a mark, become an expression of continuity?

The "booklet from London" is Eigner's *What You Hear*, published by Edible Magazine in 1972. The misprinting was significant enough for Eigner's bibliographer to include a note: "Most of the poems are printed with extra spaces between each word which was not Eigner's intent when he wrote the poems."[35] If Eigner's spacing is intentional, then it has meaning (to him at least). However, the relationship between intention and meaning is not an easy issue to resolve because Eigner's spacing is also *not* intentional; it is, at times, the product of his inability to control precisely the carriage of his typewriter. In the early 1960s, Eigner wondered about his practice in the same way when a student named Jack Lorts wrote a paper on his poetry. Describing his response to Lorts's analysis, Eigner wrote to Cid Corman:

> Lorts leads one to muse on the oddity of th craft resulting frm th casual—tho its nothing very new. 1st time, however, i clearly see where th spacing may well be distracting, rather thn capture wt. of words. Problem. In effort at interpretation he reminds me of myself—casting abt, etc. In one place biog. misleads im partly. I have used my imagination at times, aftr all. I guess finding "themes" is a way in, hm.[36]

Eigner admits his spacing can be, at times, a result of being "casual." The phrase "th[e] craft resulting fr[o]m th[e] casual" evokes the title that Eigner later gave to a poetics statement he wrote for the anthology *A Controversy of*

Poets: "Method from Happenstance."[37] The active mastery implied by terms such as *craft* and *method* is diffracted through the lens of Eigner's disability into an equally significant *passivity* and *randomness*. The ambiguous relationship between intention and arbitrariness, in the case of Eigner's response to Lorts's essay, even leads to Eigner's own sense that he, too, is "casting abt" when trying to figure out what his poems mean, whether they might have "themes" at all.

how much should words / take.up.space ?

Words only take up space when they are printed on something (a page, a wall, a shirt, a sign).[38] For Derrida, the space between words is the first meaningful distinction: "Arche-writing, at first the possibility of the spoken word, then of the '*graphie*' in the narrow sense, the birthplace of 'usurpation,' denounced from Plato to Saussure, this trace is the opening of the first exteriority in general, the enigmatic relationship of the living to its other and of an inside to an outside: spacing."[39] The Language poets were fascinated by Eigner's spatial arrangements of words. Writing to Bruce Andrews, Silliman tells him, "Typing out anybody's poems is a good way to learn them, to approximate the actual act of composing them (try typing out a half dozen of Eigner's poems & see if your response isnt one of amazement at the precision & the intensity of the forces at work therein)."[40] In an essay on Eigner, Grenier wonders whether there is anywhere for a young poet to go after Eigner, who "tuned" the " 'American' language . . . to such finenesses of registration & articulation."[41] *Registration* and *articulation* are precisely chosen words here, and paying some attention to their various meanings will help us uncover the arche-writing at the heart of projective-verse poetics that makes Eigner's typewriter a hinge.

Olson begins "Projective Verse" by claiming that " 'closed' verse" is "that verse which print bred."[42] It is an odd claim in that meter and rhyme, the two main elements of "closed" verse, were originally mnemonic devices to aid the memorization and oral recitation of poetry. In proposing to return to a poetics of orality and aurality by means of the mechanical device that allows writers to produce their own *printed* (as opposed to hand*written*) texts, Olson accesses Derrida's arche-writing, and the typewriter becomes the "hinge" that both connects and separates the visual text (writing) and the invisible voice (speaking). The paradox is that projective verse produces visual texts that are meant to be heard rather than seen. Olson's manifesto is less a prescription for this kind of poetry than a description of it. "The sons [*sic*] of Pound and Williams," Olson claims, are "already" projective: "Already they are composing as though verse was to have the reading its writing involved, as though not the eye but the ear was to be its measurer, as though the intervals of its composition could be so carefully put down as to be precisely the intervals of its registration."[43] What makes this statement truly paradoxical is the deep connection that Olson's terms have to printing. One definition of *composition* related to printing is "typesetting," and *register* in printing refers to "exact alignment of the lines and margins on the opposite sides of a leaf."[44] The poem's *composition* (how it is put together) is precisely related to its *registration* (how it is positioned on the page, how it "registers" both on the eye and in the ear).

This connection to printing and typesetting is also related to Olson's embodied poetics through sexuality. Tom Clark's biography describes how Olson's extramarital affair with Frances Boldereff was the catalyst for his beginnings as a poet. Boldereff was not only a writer interested in many of the ancient and esoteric traditions that Olson studied; she was also a printer and book designer. Clark informs his reader that the "first typed version of [Olson's] ground-breaking essay" was "dated February 9 [1950], and on the following day sent off, with extensive revisions inserted by hand, to his 'mistress printer' Frances."[45] A few months later, trying to get Boldereff some work in literary publishing, Olson introduced her by letter to Robert Giroux: "She is the book designer, Mrs Frances Boldereff. . . . What impresses me, is, how grounded her work is, how her sense of printing is not type alone but a profound understanding of the space which a page is, and what breath—to speak like a writer!—leading can give. I dare say it is a clue, that she learned her trade in the hardest kind of discipline, the Jersey City house that does the N.Y. telephone books. For she knows her business (like a good writer knows syllables!)."[46] Here is projective verse in compressed form, and its essential component in this instance is the relation of type to page, of breath to space. In printing, *leading* refers to the spacing between lines, the amount of space created by inserting blank slugs of lead in between the rows of type. Breath, for Olson, is the space on the page. We can see how much spacing (*leading*) mattered to Olson in an abandoned printing of *The Maximus Poems*' second volume. The edition got "as far as the typesetting, which was not done to Olson's satisfaction. He objected to the spacing of the poems, especially the spacing between lines, insisting there was too much 'leading.'" Olson's objections were vehement: "Where in hell did anyone get the idea these *lines* are *not* as <u>*written*</u> [. . .] *SHRINK LEADING!!!!* oh God it's too much!"[47]

Articulation is as important as registration. Derrida uses "the hinge" (*la brisure*) because its double meaning—it is both a joint and a break—expresses both "difference and articulation." *La brisure* is the "hinged articulation" that allows a shutter or door to open and close. Derrida writes, "This articulation therefore permits a graphic ('visual' or 'tactile,' 'spatial') chain to be adapted, possibly in a linear fashion, to a spoken ('phonic,' 'temporal') chain."

Articulation, in the sense of the hinge, thus manifests its own double meaning and becomes a central term for Derrida. He points out that Ferdinand de Saussure was aware of this double meaning, quoting from chapter 6 of the *Course in General Linguistics*: "articulation can designate either the subdivision of a spoken chain into syllables or the subdivision of the chain of significations into significative units."[48] In other words, the hinge (of language as writing) articulates the difference between the stream of air and the stream of ink—the intangible and the tangible, the intelligible and the sensible—and in turn demonstrates that language itself is neither speech nor writing. If language can be "represented" by both speech and writing, then its *substance* is neither sound nor graphic mark. "The hinge [*brisure*] marks the impossibility that a sign, the unity of a signifier and a signified, be produced within the plenitude of a present and an absolute presence."[49] The hinge between articulation and difference, the thing that is both the joint and the break between substance and form, undermines the logocentrism of speech. Presence requires absence to make meaning. This is what Silliman means when he says Eigner is able to "take the logic of speech as such out of discourse [and] creat[e] sequences of presences," in his note to "The Dwelling Place."[50]

Eigner had been thinking about spacing and absence for a while before encountering the Language poets. In a letter to his sister-in-law written in 1963, Eigner explains the function of spacing—or his use of lacunae—in his work. For Eigner, a gap or blank is a form of punctuation: "lacuna became punctuation devices different from commas, say, which connect, lead on, are elisive rather like apostrophe, besides being a stop, a lacuna seem part way between , and . [. . .] Coordination between typing and mind's voice."[51] Eigner sees standard, grammatical punctuation as being too rigid; commas are too weak to be a stop, but periods are too unambiguous in signaling a pause. The space, like a comma, both "connect[s], lead[s] on," and it serves as a break or stop: it is a *hinge* that opens and closes possibilities in a poem. And, most significantly, lacunae demonstrate the "coordination between typing and mind's voice." That is, typing is the best way to create meaningful space on the page, to connect the substance of expression (paper and ink) to its form (language). Like an apostrophe in a contraction, blanks and gaps, in their in-between status, indicate both presence and absence: instead of a mark, there is a blank, but the reader is meant to hear or see that something was elided. Just as a reader or listener can "fill in" the elided letters in a contraction, Eigner expects his readers to experience his blank space as both presence and absence, to feel the gap and to fill it in at the same time. These explanations indicate that long before encountering Language writing, Eigner had thought about spacing as a means of weighing words—or weighting them, as Creeley would have it—in order to determine their meaning. In being both an active choice and a passive result, Eigner's spacing becomes a kind of deconstructive practice.[52] His spacing is what Derrida calls the "hinge of language as writing."[53]

exact reproduction of my momentous layouts

Eigner's Black Mountain contemporaries and Language-writing followers have been accused of "orthographic essentialism" and "page fetishism" by Raphael Allison, who also argues that the editors of *The Collected Poems* "make a virtual fetish out of the typewriter's centrality to Eigner's work."[54] As I explained in the introduction, Allison offers an alternative approach to Eigner through listening to sound recordings of his readings rather than reading poems on the page, and his emphasis on aurality and voice over textuality and signifier presents a compelling case for Eigner's "cripping" of lyric poetry in performance. However, as the continuity-discontinuity dynamic of his poetry is not resolved by flipping the binary, so does the spoken-written, sound-mark binary need to be understood in differential relation rather than opposition. Eigner himself never privileged speech over writing, or vice versa, but was always interested in the differential relationship between the two. Although he was willing to work with Grenier and others, notably Benjamin Friedlander in the 1980s, to establish "definitive" typescripts for the texts of his poems, he was also gently skeptical of their "orthographic essentialism." Writing to Charles Bernstein in September 1989, Eigner tells him:

> Last night I finished going over Ben's notes for the book and likewise revised your ts of the four I sent you - the two latest, done 1 month ago on Aug 15, occasioned by your invitation (all the indentation discrepancies betwen your ts and mine what I have here now can be ignored, but I've indicated these "corrections" een though it's a bit possible I miscopied myself, since you might be as much onto exact reproduction of my momentous layouts as Ben, Bob and 1 or 2 othrs; the dates are ok, an explicit reference to the occasional or ephemeral, but the numbers aret opera numbers or anythg, just tags to record things by [. . .]).[55]

The sardonic reference to his "momentous layouts" and the admission that he might miscopy his own texts indicate that Eigner still appreciates how much contingency and serendipity are at work in his compositional practices. The relationship between Eigner's "voice" on the page, manifested in his spacing, punctuation, and spelling, as well as diction, tone, and mood, and his speaking voice at readings and in conversation, is ambiguous and central to his ecrippoetics.

Nonetheless, Eigner experienced some bad typesetting himself over the years. One example is the book he had with him at the Franconia College

the children what
knot to no cry

life something
begins as will

to
what you have see
quiet chairs

the clock the same anything

with its insides

as
well say as
breezy days

stars or the sun, the moon
pour up

Figure 3. Eigner's "the children what" as it appears in *The Collected Poems*, with its intended spacing.

reading, *What You Hear*, "the one with too many blank lines and a lacuna following nearly every word." A few years prior, the Mexico City–based journal *El corno emplumado* (The Plumed Horn) printed some of Eigner's poems with too little spacing. Writing to the editors, Eigner observes, "(my pieces, lacking the blank lines and most of the lacunae I had there, much like a nuclear pile with all controls pulled out, seemingly—fttt!—but a man in Heidelburg wrote that he liked em) . . . ? . . ."[56] So, we have two examples of poems with incorrect spacing, according to Eigner's intentions: one with too much, and one with too little. Does this change their meaning?

the children what
knot to no cry

life something
begins as will

to
what you have see
quiet chairs

the clock the same anything
with its insides

as
well say as
breezy days

stars or the sun, the moon
pour up

Figure 4. Eigner's "the children what" as it appears in *What You Hear*, with additional spacing.

In Eigner's way of composing a poem, a stanza has a double space before and after it, whether that stanza is a single line or a group of lines. Taken from the Italian, *stanza* means a "stopping place," therefore removing spacing speeds the poem up, and adding spacing slows it down, making more stopping places (or, in Olson's sense of *leading*, creating more breath). The poem "the children what" in its "intended" layout is a seven-stanza poem (figure 3; *CP* 2:724). If an Eigner poem is an aggregate dispersion pattern rather than a random or uniform one, then the stanzas—a line or a group of lines with space around them—are the primary means of weighing the

the fuselage

a present

length of moon

turn one corner

in the neighborhood

now here too number
in night

where a branch settles

is it the same
bolted light

square of the eye the

shadow slipping of tides

an armchair in more than one

these cellars

when you travel by

familiar way

Figure 5. Eigner's "the fuselage" as it appears in *The Collected Poems*, with its intended spacing.

things in the poem and indicating their relationships. By adding space between the lines that constitute stanzas, the *What You Hear* version causes the blanks to lose some of their importance by overwhelming the marks, dispersing them farther apart than intended and thus altering the aggregate pattern, which is largely a function of the stanzas (figure 4). With the additional space, even though the printer did insert extra leading to indicate Eigner's intended double-spacing, each line looks like a stanza, thereby having more weight as an individual line than was intended.[57] So, if we are reading the *What You Hear* text, we will get a different sense of how things are being weighed in this poem. However, paradoxically, too much space decreases the

LARRY EIGNER

the fuselage
a present
length of moon
turn one corner
in the neighborhood
now here too number
in night
where a branch settles
is it the same
bolted light
square of eye the
shadow slipping of tides
an armchair in more than one
these cellars
when you travel by
familiar way

Figure 6. Eigner's "the fuselage" as it appears in *El corno emplumado* 20, without intended spacing.

weight of the things in the poem: some poems need multiple-line stanzas in order to establish their aggregate patterns, but others require single-line stanzas. The groupings are indicators of significance, with the spacing acting as the hinge between "stanzas" to differentiate them while at the same time joining them together (difference and articulation is the nature of the hinge). The more-spaced text makes certain words feel lighter, less connected, or more discontinuous than they are. For example, "what" in the first line of the *What You Hear* text seems suspended on the page, hanging in space in a way that feels isolated rather than related to the other words on the page. Or, consider the stanza "as / well say as / breezy days," which loses the condensed feel of the singe-spaced version, and being spread farther apart on the page disperses the force that condensation adds to its visual impact. Are these just two variant texts for one poem, or does the additional space change the poem's meaning?

If meaning is the paraphrasable content, "the children what" might be about how things come to be in the world. "Children" are the result of the lover's "knot" ("the children what / knot to no cry"); they are not the answer to a "cry," as in a demand or complaint. These might be the same children that appear in the following poem, written on the same day, also included in *What You Hear*: "love children / poams [*sic*] / the unexpected // in a noisy world" (*CP* 2:725). The first poem seems to comment on this more directly expressed correlation: poems unexpectedly come into being, like "love" children that are unplanned, so one can never know what to expect from the noise of the world. If we fill in some of Eigner's lacunae, the second and third stanzas of "the children what" might be rendered: life [is when] something begins as will to what you have [to] see. The force of will comes from the inside, and the remaining images in the first half of the poem characterize this internal state as "quiet," with the other things inside sharing this quality; they are "the same." Eigner then compares this quiet, homogenous inside with a noisy, heterogeneous outside. The "something" that began, the "anything // with its insides," have their same motions "as / well say as / breezy days." The "quiet chairs" inside are parallel to the "breezy days" outside; the "as will" of the first part becomes the "as well" of the second part. The markers of natural time—sun, stars, moon—provide the same function as the clock inside, and if inside and outside are no longer distinguishable, then neither are up and down. The light from the sun, stars, and moon "pour[s] up," perhaps an effect of seeing the light through the breeze-blown leaves. Or maybe it is a way of imagining the effect of being at or on one of these celestial bodies; the light would "pour up" from the surface. In dispersing the measure more widely, the *What You Hear* text does not change the meaning of individual words and phrases, but it certainly makes it more difficult to find the continuity within the discontinuity of the spacing. The "form" of the poem contributes to its meaning.

If too much spacing makes the individual words lighter, less weighty, and makes the clustering of the aggregate pattern harder to discern, what happens when spacing is removed? Writing to the *El corno emplumado* editors Eigner compares his misprinted poem to a failed nuclear reactor: "like a nuclear pile with all controls pulled out, seemingly—fttt!" The spacing allows Eigner to control the "reaction" that produces the energy of the poem. Nuclear energy is produced by splitting an atom's nucleus (fission) or combining nuclei (fusion), so "the children what" fizzles because there was too much "fission," and "the fuselage" goes "fttt!" because there was too much fusion. In its intended arrangement, "the fuselage" is a fourteen-stanza poem, with twelve single-line stanzas and two two-line stanzas (figure 5). In the more densely packed text, in contrast, the two-line stanzas are elided, and the poem itself is turned into a single-verse paragraph (figure 6). If the weight of words is determined by spacing, and weighing is how Eigner discovers meaning, then the texts as printed in both *What You Hear* and *El corno emplumado* alter the way Eigner's poems make meaning, thereby the meaning itself.

what kind of poetry is / a horizontal line

As we saw above, Eigner quotes Creeley's statement that the "line is the means to focus, . . . says 'how' we are to weight the various *things* we are told" in "Arrowhead of Meaning."[58] Open-form poets are especially concerned with the line—what it is, how it works—because they don't work with preset metrical patterns that would determine what a line is in a particular poem. The way that meter makes meaning is already a form of disruption. Guides to prosody and scansion tell us that it is when a poet alters the dominant metrical pattern that the poem's rhythm signifies.[59] Most listeners or readers will be quickly bored or irritated by a poem that is perfectly metrical from beginning to end. But that disruption cannot exist without the metrical norm, so how does it work with free verse, nonmetrical poetry? One answer is to be found in the work of Ezra Pound. As Marjorie Perloff notes, Pound's "great contribution to modern prosody was his focus on the line, rather than the larger stanza block." She also points out that "Pound's line repeatedly violates the iambic norm," and his lineation is characterized by "its heavy stressing, its spondaic, amphibrachic, and cretic feet, its long sonorous vowels in assonant patterns." These characteristics were "taken over by a score of poets," according to Perloff, including Eigner (she scans the first four lines of "flake diamond of" [*CP* 2:398]).[60]

Eigner considered his poetry to have lines and stanzas, though he rarely used a regular metrical pattern or stanzaic organization. He did not think of the line in terms of syllables or stresses, so, in one sense, identifying iamb, trochees, spondees, and the like doesn't really give us a sense of how Eigner approached lineation and line breaks. For Eigner, lines are an effect of spacing. In a letter to his sister-in-law Janet, he explains:

> Indentations whatever else they may be are partial turns, not going all the way back, and though even i have sometimes gone back farther left than my 1st line, I've thought it might be true enough that my rightward bent, besides being slapdash and ad lib, is due to a feeling that there was always a past, same as this other cause for the sotto voce especially at the opening (lower case and indent too, again), a wariness—of course some things begin with a cap. letter, unforced—of the implication that this is the Beginning (of Words, say) Speech going on before and after the poem, which is a slice of speech. So, this rightward bent of mine, out of a doubt that x is a Beginning, I mean a BEGINNING[61]

These comments are the first draft of the statement later titled "Method from Happenstance." There, Eigner writes, "Don't like to begin with a big B, as if I was at the Beginning of all speech, or anything; which may also have something to do with why usually I've had an aversion more or less to going back to the left margin after beginning a poem."[62]

Along with gaps and lacunae between letters, words, lines, and stanzas, the texts of Eigner's poems often have a distinct visual shape on the page, his "rightward bent," which spacing produces. In the letter, Eigner describes how the variable margins and indentations are composed:

> when i delete 1st word (suppress, art. . conj. . . .) from a line I feel pretty strongly against pushing 2nd word leftward, (3rd wrd etc) accordingly, even if the line has bn indented already, which is often as not ‡at least‡ A fixation of lay-out so to speak, maybe as a letting stand of the place where the suppressed word was as well. Then too, its happened often enough that something will appear in print and I won't care for it, then ill see it in typescript again and it will come back—while sometimes it come back without reference to ts, and of course at other times nothing seems like much anyway, after all[63]

In "fix[ing]" the "lay-out" of a poem's text by not returning the line to the left margin, Eigner lets the gap stand as an indicator of absence. The blank is a witness to the absent presence, or, as Derrida says, "all graphemes are of a testamentary essence." Derrida also theorizes that spacing is where language is not fully under control of the subject: "spacing as writing is the becoming-absent and the becoming-unconscious of the subject. By the movement of its drift/derivation [*dérive*] the emancipation of the sign constitutes in return the desire of presence."[64]

To *drift* is to be carried along by currents of air or water, to proceed or move unhurriedly and smoothly, to wander from a set course or point of attention (to stray), to be piled up in banks or heaps by the force of a current.[65] The Indo-European root means "to drive, push; snow." Drifting can be the act of driving a herd, or it can the passive drifting of snow or sand. Morton also points out that drifting is one way that art is ecological: "Psychogeography, the practice invented by Guy Debord and the Situationists of Paris 1968 fame, reclaims the environment through the *dérive*, or 'drifting,' aimless wandering. Debord explicitly states that psychogeography is ecological. The *dérive* is 'a technique of rapid passage through varied ambiences.' "[66] Eigner's drifting is both an active and a passive movement through space in the environment and on the page. Spacing is the hinge that articulates the individual units, joining them together and separating them at the same time, pushing the drift along as it meanders down the page-space. In this way, Eigner's form exposes what Morton calls "the ecological-ness of all art."[67] However, is this "ecological-ness" part of the poem's meaning, or is it just a supplemental effect that contributes to the poem's ecological "feel"? Morton says nothing regarding where *meaning* might come from in the ecological-ness of art.

Indeed, he sounds something like an Olsonian projectivist in that he turns *writing* into a form of *action*: "Ecological art *is* something, or maybe it *does* something." As he says elsewhere, "form just is the substance of a literary text," and, as Derrida reminds us, Saussure asserted that language is a form, not a substance. Meaning comes from the form, not the content.[68] Therefore, for Morton, "something about language shows you something about how meaning is also spectral."[69] Morton uses the term *subscendence* to counter the logocentric notion that truth *transcends* the particulars that constitute it. Rather than transcending parts and particulars, uniting them in a coherent, meaningful whole that is somehow more than the sum of its parts, Morton argues, ecological truth and meaning *subscend* their parts: "Being authentic doesn't really mean being totally and utterly something that transcends its parts. Being an author and being authentic in that sense aren't things we need to abolish or feel bad about or reduce to something else, because authorship already contains all kinds of other beings, a spectral, haunting otherness."[70] Consider how many "kinds of other beings" are part of Eigner's authorship: a variety of manual typewriters; his parents, who helped with his correspondence and submissions; his brothers, who shared their books and interests; his contemporaries such as Corman, Levertov, Creeley, and Duncan, who selected, typed, and published his work; the Language writers of the next generation who did the same. All authorship subscends its parts, it is just that Eigner's embodiment made this "spectral" quality of writing more apparent.

Meaning to flicker in and out

What if poetry's contribution to ecology is to make poems into objects, words into things?[71] If meaning is spectral because language is spectral, then objects may have the same characteristic:

```
An object

 words

air

  motion

   elusive

       again
```

(*CP* 3:968)

Eigner wrote this poem, which is tagged number 428 in *The Collected Poetry*, after receiving his copy of the *Inside Outer Space* anthology discussed in the previous chapter. In the editor's introduction, Robert Vas Dias traces the history of the technological image in poetry from French surrealism and Anglo-American modernism to the current scene, and he writes, "the poem itself is regarded as an object."[72] Describing Vas Dias's introduction to his friends David and Maria Gitin on August 27, 1970, Eigner writes,

> I guess the observation on the preceding page that Williams et al let "the object define the pattern of the poem" brought to mind the (mis)quotation from Wms, "a poem is an object made of words" and led to this p.m.'s piece, #428. I do like to think, ". . .organism. . ." wher W C W said ". . .machine. . ."
>
> And, of course, theres Zukofsky. . . .
>
> . . .
>
> Words do glimmer
> Regards
> Larry[73]

If a poem is an object, what constitutes its ontological status? Words. What are spoken words made of? Air. Air that is moving, being exhaled from lungs, vibrating vocal chords, making waves of sound. Yet, what is more elusive than air; how can it make an object? There are two possibilities in this poem: either the object has eluded him again—he just can't tell for sure whether an object is there—or it needs to be repeated, put into motion again, to exist. Poems have an ecological impact on the world when they are written down: they require paper made from trees, ink made from chemicals, and processes of printing and distribution that use energy and require infrastructure such as roads, rail lines, and shipping ports. As we have seen, Eigner is well aware of this fact. But, is the printed poem an object? No. The poem is a virtual object—it has the *effect* of being an object.

"Zukofsky" is here a metonym for objectivist poetics, the antipoetry that followed from modernist poetics, in general, and Imagism, in particular. "There[']s Zukofsky" is Eigner's way of saying, yes, a poem can be an object. But Eigner also indicates that he is thinking the ecological thought when he adds "Words do glimmer." Though not etymologically connected, *glimmer* rhymes with *shimmer* both in sound and meaning. For Morton, "shimmering" is a deconstructive means for thinking past binaries that is distinctly ecological: "Lifeforms play (a cat's nip says 'This is a bite and this is not a bite') because play is structural to reality, because things shimmer."[74] Words as things, as they *glimmer*, "emit a dim or intermittent light" or "appear faintly or indistinctly"; as a synonym for *flash*, *glimmer* "refers to faint, fleeting light," and *shimmer* "means to shine with a soft, tremulous light."[75] Written words, in Wallace Stevens's formulation, are "ghostlier demarcations" that indicate "keener sounds."[76] An object made of this material is a strange object indeed. In order to think about this play in language, and to ground ecocriticism in deconstruction, Morton adapts Derrida's notion of arche-writing, the trace of writing that is logically prior to logocentrism, in his term "arche-lithic," the structure that is logically prior to what he calls "agrilogistics," which grounds the metaphysics of presence by distinguishing culture from nature. Morton writes, "Perhaps what we now recognize as writing, done explicitly with wax and stylus and stone and papyrus, develops in the agricultural era to *contain* the implicit shimmer of arche-writing, just as agrilogistics contains the arche-lithic. The containment of the shimmer must constantly risk revealing that shimmer happening not only in what we conventionally recognize as writing, but also in ecological, social, and psychic space."[77] The ecology of Eigner's ecrippoetics is seen in this ambiguous glimmering of meaning, which in turn is based in the objectivist notion that poems can be objects. "Meaning . . . flicker[s] in and out" in a poetics that determines the weight of things in weightless words.

J. Hillis Miller associates the "shimmer" with words that take the *para-* prefix: " 'Para' is an 'uncanny' double antithetical prefix, signifying at once proximity and distance, similarity and difference, interiority and exteriority."[78] *Para-* signifies the in-between, both/and state in which firm, rigid distinctions lose their meaning. If the metaphysics of presence attempts to contain the shimmer of arche-writing, if agrilogistics attempts to contain the shimmer of the arche-lithic, then closed forms and linear syntax attempt to contain the shimmer of the open-form, nonlinear poetry that is Language writing. As Steve McCaffery observes, " 'Language writing' . . . involved not only a consensual denial of the difference between poetry and theory, but also a deliberate erosion of the fixed partitions between prose and poetic genres."[79] The shimmer, or play, of antipoetry refuses these distinctions and questions the basis of any binary opposition. Derrida's formulation is "the advent of writing is the advent of play," and Eigner agrees: "Writing can have more play than speech or talk."[80] As Miller points out, although a *para-* word may appear to mean one thing and not its opposite, "the other meanings are always there as a shimmering or wavering in the word which makes it refuse to stay still in a sentence."[81] When "proximity and distance, similarity and difference, interiority and exteriority" cannot be firmly distinguished, when their meanings shimmer and play around us in language, words and world become the ecological wor(l)d; as Morton puts it, "ecological reality resembles the shimmering, squiggly space of marks and signs underwriting the very scripts that underwrite agrilogistic space, with its neatly plowed lines of words."[82]

Of course, *para-* words are associated with disability as well (paraplegia, Paralympics), and Eigner's ecrippoetics, as we have seen, has always refused binary distinctions such as near and far, inside and outside, identity and difference. As he continued to participate in the Language-writing community of the Bay Area through the 1980s and into the 1990s, this deconstructive aspect of Eigner's ecrippoetics deepened. Two poems from October 1993 demonstrate Eigner's ongoing engagement with the interrelation of Language writing and ecology. The first poem is dated October 12, and it begins:

```
   l i n e s ,   d i v i s i o n s

        same as connections

              not always   or else

                where might be a shift

                 from one thing to another

                  along some scale
                                    or band
```

(*CP* 4:1662)

The poem seems to ask: Does a line separate or connect? Rather than black-and-white distinctions, is there a gradient along which we could go "from one thing to another" without insisting on a clear break or demarcation? It continues,

```
complete or not

    if there is any

     like, say, a wire in the air

        jointed or straight

      running through a town

          or state or county

           which is all
```

```
                    one place

         with none too few parts

           or quite a few places

            set up together in

                a certain time
```

(*CP* 4:1662)

The familiar question about the relationship of part to whole comes to mind as he thinks about lines and divisions. One place—whether town, county, or state—has "none too few parts" that make it up. Is the "jointed or straight" wire some sort of boundary? Could it be a description of electric and phone lines that would connect/separate places? The poem concludes with a bullet point followed by two more lines: "nice fresh apple / sliced not skinned," an image of a whole divided into parts.

The poem is dedicated to Lyn Hejinian and Scott Bentley, and this note is added below the dedication: "‡even as this piece here may come / mostly from hearing of 'fuzzy / logic' on the radio‡." "Fuzzy logic" is the branch of logical philosophy that attempts to account for degrees of truth rather than a binary true and false. It is a form of logic that would be seen as nonlogical in Western metaphysics, but, as Morton argues, this is the type of logic needed for the ecological thought: "Unless you allow for modal, paraconsistent and even dialetheic logics (that can say things are more or less true, or both true and false under some circumstances), you can't allow ecological beings to exist," because ecological beings are always in between, both inside and outside, both part and whole.[83]

The second poem, dated about two weeks later, bears the title, "one or two / things can be / speculated," and it has an unusual format even for Eigner. Two columns appear on the page: the left column is composed of single-word lines (with two exceptions) justified to the left margin; the right column uses a bit more spacing between lines and has a more irregular margin, though it doesn't have the rightward drift of Eigner's typical page-length poems. The poem that follows it in *The Collected Poems* is in a similar format, and Eigner indicates that with it he is imitating his friend Kit Robinson's "Ice Cubes," which appeared in Bentley's magazine *Letterbox* (*CP* 4:1664). It seems like he is doing the same in "one or two / things can be / speculated." The left column reads:

in
(to)
an
empty
sky
surrounding
so
many
****

comes
the
 (penetrant,   certain)
light

of
dawn
and

a
cloud

from the horizon

and
or

cd
we
say

space
what's
between

things
filled

no
solid

```
occupied

vacant

pervasive


divides
and
connects
```

(*CP* 4:1663)

The lines up to "and / or" restate Eigner's great poem "Again dawn" (discussed in the introduction). As dawn occurs, the "empty / sky" framing the stars ("****") is penetrated by light, and a cloud becomes visible. Twilight is a gradient: where can one draw the line between morning and night precisely? Eigner is still thinking about lines and divisions, and the "fuzzy logic" he heard about on the radio would accommodate the gloaming he witnesses here. The lines after "and / or" might be paraphrased: could we say that space, whether occupied or vacant, both divides and connects? Here, again, is Derrida's hinge, which both divides and connects, and which opens the experience of space-time.

And, to the extent that we can see the stars themselves before the light penetrates the sky, Eigner is giving us an ecological view through his typed asterisks. Morton uses the "twinkling" of stars as another example of the ambiguity of the shimmer: "Starlight is refracted through the atmosphere and comes onto my retina just so. It twinkles, twinkles. When I see that, I am seeing evidence of a thing I can't quite see called *atmosphere*, thus *biosphere*, thus Earth's magnetic shield. Where does one draw the line, ecologically speaking?"[84] It is unclear whether the right column is a continuation of the left, or whether it is a set of comments on the left side's statements. Are these the things that can be "speculated"? The first block of text appears to comment on the lines about the dawn light:

```
always

it seems

there's

some
```

```
    of the time

      of the whole
```

Perhaps if the light is "certain"—inevitable, dependable—then some part of it is always there, some of the daytime is present in the nighttime, and vice versa. A quadruple space is between this block of text and the rest of the right column:

```
that's
latin

to
deduce
first you

induce



   experience

        sense

     common   among

        whoever



     nothing
     too
     absolute


     nor infinite   ly

     mysterious

          - maybe
```

If, as the title suggests, "one or two things can be speculated," then Eigner seems to be suggesting here that his speculation can be either deductive or inductive. Or, rather, it's both. To be able to reason from the general to the particular (deduction), we have to start with our experience, reasoning from the particulars to the general (induction). This might be just a "common" thing to do with our "sense[s]," or it may be the basis of anyone's common sense. In any case, nothing can be determined to be "too / absolute," or too infinite, or too infinitely "mysterious." He concludes with the adverb that exists in between *yes* and *no*, which turns *maybe* itself into a hinge. For Morton, "to remain in indecision" is the philosophical position that ecology requires.[85] As we will see in the next chapter, this indeterminacy, which is the central characteristic of postmodernism, is how Eigner's ecrippoetics attunes to climate change.

CHAPTER FIVE

CO2 and All

Eigner's Ecrippoetics and Climate Change

To what are we tuning when we attune to the hyperobject?

TIMOTHY MORTON, *Hyperobjects*

JUST AS ENVIRONMENTAL pollution and toxicity seeped into the public consciousness with the *New Yorker*'s preview of Rachel Carson's *Silent Spring* in 1962, awareness of global warming was focused by an excerpt of Bill McKibben's *The End of Nature* in that magazine's September 11, 1989, issue.[1] In August 1988, about a year before McKibben's *New Yorker* article appeared, Eigner wrote this global warming poem:

```
c o 2   a n d   a l l

   penguins  ?  gulls ?   ducks ?

       "  . . .   to sit still  "

           we are so many
         we should live off the sun
```

(*CP* 4:1613)

As we will see in this chapter, Eigner's awareness of global warming and its consequences developed over decades through his extensive consumption of both popular and scientific media. Through the compression and ellipsis of his ecrippoetics, Eigner packs a number of issues into his poem: the primary driver of global warming (excessive carbon dioxide emitted by human activity), the impact that climate change will have on other species (in this case, waterbirds), the need to slow things down and think about them (sitting still), the growing human population that will require more and more energy, and a possible solution to that problem (solar energy). Timothy Morton makes the case for literature's contribution to dealing with climate change in a similar way: "While tackling global warming with all deliberate speed and trusting near total scientific consensus, we should be using culture . . . to create a framework in which global warming science becomes recognizable and legible. And in general, we should be slowing down, reflecting, and using this moment as an opportunity to change and develop."[2] Eigner's poem certainly trusts the scientific consensus (as we will see in this chapter he was deeply informed about the science), and the quotation from T. S. Eliot's "Ash-Wednesday" ("to sit still") confirms Morton's sense that we must use stillness as a space for reflection even as we take immediate action to address the crisis. Eigner's defamiliar body made him distinctly aware of the difficulty of sitting still. As he recalled in an autobiographical essay, "my left arm and leg pretty wild till I had cryosurgery about 6 weeks into my 36th year, I had to keep my attention away from myself to sit still, yet not too far away either."[3] Repurposing Eliot's prayer for God "to teach us to care and not to care, to sit still" from his disability perspective, Eigner indicates how embodiment is a central issue for understanding global warming and climate change. As Robert Grenier insists, "Larry's work does not *derive* from his palsy," but his worldview does, in large part because, Grenier also notes, "*he lived in his body* as few do."[4]

a matter // of // tune in // everything

It has taken some time for ecocriticism itself to adapt to climate change and global warming, just as with disability and defamiliar bodies.[5] Morton observes that "global warming is a 'super wicked problem': a wicked problem for which time is running out, for which there is no central authority; those seeking the solution are also creating it, and policies discount the future irrationally."[6] Ursula Heise concludes that the very literary forms ecocritics examine are not at the right scale for thinking climate change: "Like other processes of global systemic transformation, ecological or not, climate change poses a challenge for narrative and lyrical forms that have conventionally focused above all on individuals, families, or nations, since it requires the articulation of connections between events at vastly different scales."[7] The scale at which we need to think, according to Morton, is "Earth magnitude," but, he notes, "humanistic tools for thought at Earth magnitude are lacking, and often because we have deliberately resisted fashioning them."[8] To think at Earth magnitude risks erasing the cultural difference that the humanities define as their object of study, but to fail to think at Earth magnitude means we cannot "see" or "think," let alone begin to address, climate change. Furthermore, as Timothy Clark points out, "we understand distance, height and breadth in terms of the given dimensionality of our embodied existence. A particular human scale is inherent to the intelligibility of the Earth around us. . . . The Anthropocene entails the realization of how deeply this scale may be misleading."[9]

Clark refers to this as the scale of terrestriality, and it is a scale that Eigner's ecrippoetics defamiliarizes. As Alan Ramón Clinton observes, "the most peculiar—and to me most promising—aspect of Eigner's poetry . . . is its ability, or property, of sometimes instantly and vastly changing its scale of reference."[10] Clinton proposes the notion of "parability" as a way of understanding a poetics of embodiment refracted through disability. He "provisionally" defines parability "as the ability to tell improper stories, write improper poems, whose leaps from one image to another cannot be 'justified' in traditional ways," and he associates this impropriety with Eigner's specific disability: "the study of cerebral palsy has taught us about the uncanny workings of not only 'damaged' pyramidal tracts but 'normally' functioning pyramidal tracts as well. . . . [This] can help us see how Eigner's work, which seldom addresses cerebral palsy, represents a series of parabilities that allow us to imagine writing and thought processes that exceed traditional forms of poetry and observation. Eigner's poems are a panoply of paralogical tracts/traces/tracks (all related etymologically) without organs which, unlike traditional tracts, evade continuity, theme, and predictability."[11] The cryosurgery that Eigner had in 1962 was a direct intervention into his pyramidal tract to alleviate the spasticity on his left side. Combining Clark's and Clinton's approaches, we can see that Eigner's ecrippoetics defamiliarizes terrestriality because it is based in an "improper" body.

As discussed in the introduction, Morton and others have pointed out that environmentalism and ecocriticism largely assume a normate body that interacts with its environment in predicable and controllable ways. As ecocriticism has absorbed more gender, disability, and social justice theory, it has begun to allow for defamiliar bodies. In *From Apocalypse to Way of Life*, Frederick Buell writes, "thoroughgoing and persistent awareness of 'embodiment' and 'embeddedness' in ecosystems . . . has been clearly elaborated and advocated in ecofeminism for some time. It is, to translate it into my terms, a way of dwelling actively within rather than accommodating oneself to environmental crisis."[12] The ecofeminist sense of bodily enmeshment is elaborated by Stacy Alaimo as "transcorporeality."[13] For both Buell and Alaimo, embodiment thus conceived becomes a way of dwelling in the environmental crisis, or, in Alaimo's formulation, "dwelling in the dissolve." In *Exposed*, Alaimo extends transcorporeality into the Anthropocene and proposes the acidification of the Earth's oceans as a counterpoint to the carbonization of its atmosphere. She observes that "the acidifying seas, the liquid index of the Anthropocene, are disregarded, even as billions of tiny shelled creatures will meet their end in a catastrophic dissolve, reverberating through the food webs of the ocean."[14]

"Dwelling in the dissolve" means abandoning our notion of an interior subjectivity protected by an impermeable skin, a subject that transcends its embodiment and is unconnected to its environs ("transcorporeality originates with a recognition of the self as solidly located and denies the splitting of subject and object").[15] Transcorporeality means that we are all "exposed" to the risks—and pleasures—of being embodied in an environment. While Alaimo considers among her examples of exposure forms of protest that use the naked human body to draw attention to environmental crises, exposure is not simply nakedness. "Exposures may be differential, uneven, or incommensurate," Alaimo writes, "yet to practice exposure entails the intuitive sense or the philosophical conviction that the impermeable Western human subject is no longer tenable." Eigner's particular disability means that he was always "exposed" as a transcorporeal subject, manifesting a type of embodiment that most would want to "cure" or cover up. As we saw in chapter 3, such embodiment entails its own ethics, and Alaimo agrees that this embodiment also recalibrates our sense of justice: "The exposed subject is always already penetrated by substances and forces that can never be properly accounted for—ethics and politics must proceed from there."[16]

In order to conceptualize how life-forms are exposed to global warming, Morton coined the term *hyperobject* to describe entities "that are massively distributed in time and space relative to humans." Hyperobjects have a set of characteristics—viscosity, nonlocality, temporal undulation, phasing, and interobjectivity, each of which gets a chapter in Morton's *Hyperobjects*—and they have "already ushered in a new human phase of *hypocrisy*, *weakness*, and *lameness*."[17] It is not coincidental that Morton's terms encompass disability, and "weakness" and "lameness" are especially apt for Eigner's ecrippoetics. Morton explains, "The coexistence of beings, without an agenda, is predicated on what I call *lameness*. *Lameness* is the third human attunement to the time of hyperobjects, the first two being *hypocrisy* and *weakness*." He observes that "weakness determines the capacity for tuning"—that is, something has to be susceptible to tightening or loosening—and that "every aspect of hyperobjects reinforces our particular lameness with regard to them."[18] For example, their viscosity means that any attempt to unstick ourselves from them will be "lame," ineffectual; their undulating temporality "cripples" us by exposure to vastly different timescales on which we don't know how to act. We have considered the deconstructive aspects of Eigner's spacing elsewhere in this study, and spacing is also a form of tuning: "Gaps between stanzas, and other kinds of broken lineation, create tone out of sheer blankness."[19] We can *see* the tone or timbre of an Eigner poem as it tunes us to its objects through spacing. For Morton, this brings us back to the embodiment: "tone is useful because it ambiguously refers both to the body and to the environment."[20]

There is a dialectic, rather than a binary, between the passivity that allows for tuning and the activity of being a subject, and this dialectic means we have to revalue passivity and "sitting still."

In *Humankind*, Morton writes, "we have a disastrous fear of passivity. What if passivity were not the opposite of activity, like black versus white, but a way of thinking a spectral version of activity?"[21] We can now see Morton's tuning as a form of this spectral activity. Another musical example he cites is guitarist Keith Rowe's *un-intention*, which is his term for silence, "since 'silence' is only when humans stop making sounds. The improvisations of Rowe allow nonhumans to jut through the art into human space."[22] Un-intention would be a spectrally active way to make meaning, to allow the other beings involved to determine what their meaning is rather than having it imposed on them by a subject. And the bias against passivity needs to be addressed as a matter of politics: "One of the principal rules of polite speech is never to mention the unconscious in public, because it suggests that part of the way we talk and act is unintended, passive in some sense. But ecological awareness is about acknowledging what one avant-garde musician calls *un-intention*."[23] As the previous chapter demonstrated, Eigner's visual texts manifest this ambiguity between active and passive intention, and this ambiguity is directly related to his embodiment.

Thus, Eigner's ecrippoetics produces (un)intentional compositions that, by attuning to their surroundings through proprioceptive acts as well as by absorbing data and information through the media, make their readers aware of the scale effects of the Anthropocene. For Morton, awareness is not the same as "passive" contemplation: "Awareness oscillates or undulates or vibrates all by itself, neither doing or feeling exclusively, neither active or passive."[24] Whereas Alaimo invites us to contemplate our shells on acid, Morton proposes that we attune to hyperobjects to bring about ecological awareness, which is just the awareness of our transcorporeality. Morton's attunement allows for a spectral subject rather than a dissolved one: "at a basic level, to be alive is to adapt, without disappearing completely—to be protected by one's attunement, but not to the point of dissolving altogether."[25] The sections of this chapter will follow Eigner's ecrippoetics as it tunes to the hyperobject of global warming from the 1960s to the 1990s.

earth temperature rises

As we saw in chapter 2, Eigner's mesh excludes nothing, and images, ideas, and information enter into his poems from all directions, from any source, when he senses a connection to something else in the poem's unfolding.[26] With his growing awareness of environmental and ecological problems, his ecrippoetics continued to integrate more and more specific references to the sources that fed his increasing concern, and he began identifying poems to his correspondents as "ecological pieces." As an avid consumer of all sorts of media—popular television programs, but also "educational" television, as early public broadcasting was called, as well as newspapers, popular magazines, and scientific journals—Eigner is a model of contemporary ecological awareness, pre-internet but proto-hyperlinked. In December 1961, he told Denise Levertov: "what with the world at my fingertips pouring in—obverse to my remoteness—Congo, disc jockey, and all, day by day."[27] With so much information coming in from so many sources, how can one make any sense of it or decide what to do based on it?

In 1969, Eigner heard Nobel laureate George Wald's lecture "A Generation in Search of a Future" on the radio. The lecture is one of the first instances of a scientist publicly using his authority to address political matters of the day. In the *New York Times*, Richard Todd noted other scientists' critiques of Wald's outspokenness, and described the speech's effect as "an abrupt change in scale, as if one were suddenly orbited and forced to see the world not as a matter of street corners and marriages, an endless succession of privacies, but as the astronaut's delicate, vulnerable blue ball."[28] Enclosing a poem in a letter to his brother Joseph and sister-in-law Janet, Eigner informs them, "#295 Ecological piece in part frm Geo. Wald's 3/4/69 spch at MIT! Et al."[29] He called the poem "you know where you're going," perhaps an ironic comment on Wald's title. It begins:

```
Life the placid
       time-bomb

             how long the
          other end of the fuse

                     earth
                     coiled up in

                  how backward running

                     brake to re-enter

                         you eat yourself out
                           all ways by the tail
```

(*CP* 3:899)

Of course, the major concern for the younger generation was the threat of nuclear destruction, but Wald added another issue: "And it isn't only nuclear war. Another overwhelming threat is in the population explosion. That has not yet even begun to come under control." Eigner's "placid / time-bomb" combines the nuclear threat with the title of Paul Erhlich's *The Population Bomb*, published in 1968. Eigner may in fact be thinking of a whole-earth image here, albeit a more urgent image than the ones described in chapter 3: pamphlets and advertisements at this time often featured a rendering of the earth, its continents covered by tightly packed, small human figures, with a lit fuse extending from the North Pole and a giant pair of "population control" scissors about to slice through the fuse (figure 7). And Wald adds another of Eigner's ecological concerns to his list: "There is every indication that the world population will double before the year 2000; and there is a widespread expectation of famine on an unprecedented scale in many parts of the world. The experts tend to differ only in their estimates of when those famines will begin."[30]

However, what is most significant about "you know where you're going" is that it is the first time Eigner tunes to global warming, known at the time as the "greenhouse effect," in a poem. In the middle section of the poem, Eigner writes,

```
earth temperature rises
     towards
    the boiling point of water

       with power plants

    cool lighting and fires

      or fluorescents could dim
```

(*CP* 3:899)

Eigner is not speculating; he is drawing his information from the March 1969 issue of *Scientific American*, which presented an interesting array of articles. One of Eigner's ecological essays, "Integration Interchange," began as a letter to the magazine, commenting on a brief article, "Pollution by Fertilizer," in a section called Science and the Citizen.[31] The article cites Barry Commoner's report on "the rise in nitrogen production in the U.S. during the past 25 years." The "painful dilemma" that Commoner presents is the trade-off between higher food production and pollution reduction: "To impose limitations on the use of fertilizers would be to reduce food supplies at a time of

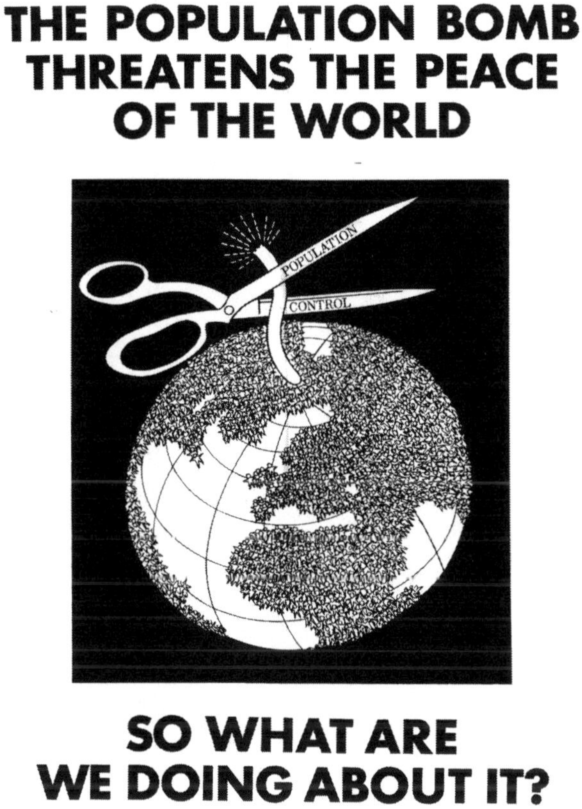

Figure 7. "Population Bomb" illustration, from a 1969 advertisement by the Campaign to Check the Population Explosion.

mounting worldwide needs. . . . To fail to do so exposes the environment to steady degradation." Eigner would have been interested in Commoner's last comment, too: "Science can reveal the depths of this crisis . . . but only social action can resolve it."[32] It seems that "humptydumpty" and the "grass roots" do indeed, as we saw in chapter 3, always go together.

In that March issue of *Scientific American*, Eigner would have also come across two articles that appear to inform this poem: "Thermal Pollution and Aquatic Life" and "The Atmospheres of Venus and Mars."[33] The former would contribute to his discussion of power plants and efforts at reducing the temperature of water used in industrial cooling, and the latter introduces the idea of the greenhouse effect. The article on Venus and Mars states, "If Earth were as hot as Venus, the oceans would evaporate," and it continues: "*Mariner V* found that the temperature of Venus' atmosphere increased nearly 10 degrees C. for each kilometer of decrease in altitude, reaching 100 degrees C.—the boiling point of water at sea level on earth—at an altitude of about 45 kilometers."[34] The article later describes the greenhouse effect and links it to the presence of CO_2 in the atmosphere, so population, consumption, pollution, and global warming are all elements of Eigner's "ecological piece" sparked by Wald's lecture.[35]

The poem concludes with some aspects of humptydumpty that the grass roots should be concerned with:

```
    travel's a descent or
          pulls   or a tendency
                among the stars

      it gets heavy
           it grows light

     feathers are good for clouds

          and rain streaks

 the artificial cavern under Denver

    the poisoned lake
              the shivering land
```

(*CP* 3:899)

Perhaps the "travel" here is the Mariner V probe mentioned in *Scientific American*, or perhaps he is thinking of travel in general (and, something that Eigner first experienced in the 1960s, air travel in particular, as discussed earlier). Traveling gets heavy when one considers its externalities, what we now call its "carbon footprint," and it may "grow[] light" if the grass roots does something about it. (Eigner once noted, "'Travel light' was Thoreau's thesis.")[36] But the poem ends on images of environmental degradation as a reminder that social action is still required. Eigner picked up this information from Wald's lecture:

> The Defense Department is always broke; but some of the things it does with that eighty billion dollars a year would make Buck Rogers envious. For example, the Rocky Mountain Arsenal, on the outskirts of Denver, was manufacturing a deadly nerve poison on such a scale that there was a problem of waste disposal. Nothing daunted, the people there dug a tunnel two miles deep under Denver, into which they have injected so much poisoned water

> that, beginning a couple of years ago, Denver has experienced a series of earth tremors of increasing severity. Now there is grave fear of a major earthquake. An interesting debate is in progress as to whether Denver will be safer if that lake of poisoned water is removed or is left in place.[37]

This clarifies the "artificial cavern" and "the shivering land," and perhaps the poisoned water mentioned by Wald is the "poisoned lake," but that phrase could also combine the information from Wald with "Pollution by Fertilizer": "a recent Federal Water Pollution Commission study of Lake Erie . . . estimates that municipal sewage annually contributes 90 million pounds of nitrogen to the lake yearly."[38]

About a year later, Eigner heard another lecture by Wald on the radio, which produced another "ecological piece" that tunes to hyperobjects. Writing to fellow poet and friend David Gitin in September 1970, Eigner observes,

> Continues to look more and more like we're overdoing things - while living great. Read that nxt to coal-mines or maybe it was mines in general, paper-mills are the unhealthiest places for workers. Well, priorities become pure guesswork in an outsized tribe, or kind of indeterminate, and at the same time the only real safe and intact beings continue to be mummies and armchair citizens like firebuffs transported cooly via huntley/brinkley and bob Hope and lawrentian whelk etc. nightly to a few of the hot and bright life/riley spots around the world. Maybe Fuller wd know better than I if radio/tv steps lighter in earth existence than the gutenberg (goodmountain) invention after the various alphabet channels. (This is the first I've heard of "World Game" Thinking abt the stars and synergy integrated whole or anyway coalesced whole greater than sundered parts and shards yet humpty-dumpty entropy, business, politics, death, taxes, and whatever wont be blinked, Refuse to pass out.)
>
> 2 nights ago heard George Wald as he spoke to entering class of Babson Institute. In the midst of telling things like there are signs of oil slick frm the states to europe. he says he's not pessimistic but optimist, bcz he's a scientist. Stoical, he seemed to me, as he also spoke of eons and the universe, ie, the long-range view. Maybe optimist *is* a better word for it, at that. As words go. Who can tell? Thats another indeterminate.[39]

Eigner continues to follow current events, which, as he says, continue to get worse. As we saw in chapter 3, Eigner worried that his own production was "overdoing things," and he wonders here whether a futurist such as Buckminster Fuller has calculated the energy consumption of print versus broadcast media. His own parents become figures of isolated media consumers, "firebuffs" entertained in the safety of their home through the "cool" medium of television. When priorities and language become indeterminate, it *is* difficult to figure out what to do.

And, as always, Eigner also feels overwhelmed by the amount of information arriving at Twenty-Three Bates Road. In a note in the bottom left margin in the letter to Gitin, he writes,

> This mrning came frm The Center For The Stu- Of Cultural Morphology & Mutation (RFD Tunbridge, Vermont 05077), #1 of ROOT, BRANCH & Mammal, A Monthly Bulletin Of Animal Discourse. Toward an "Environment that works so well we can run wild in it." Olson's NEW MAN AND WOMAN, March 70, Gloucester Edited and Interpolated by the Millenia Foundation So many Study Centers—hm. 1-, 2-, 3- . . . 80-yr-olds perennially. And cultural heritage piling up huge mountains.

The following day, he begins a poem:

```
  and cultural heritage piling up
 huge mountains

       1, 2, 3-,  ... 80-year-olds
     perennially

                   plant

                      bombs

                  how slow a seed can be

                      dynamite

                            of some

                          interest

                         explosive
                              disentropy
```

(*CP* 3:973)

The "goodmountain" produced by movable type is the "cultural heritage" that is piling up around him. The population bomb has been planted, and it grows "perennially," year after year. Eigner creates a time-lapse image through his pun on "plant": a seed slowly germinates and grows, but in a time-lapse video it would appear to explode, like dynamite. Life is a form of "explosive / disentropy" because it increases in complexity and capacity as the population explodes. In the next two lines, Eigner includes his insight from hearing that Wald is optimistic about the future: "and stoicism might better be / optimism." The "long-range view" can be optimistic as well as stoic.

As the decade progressed, Eigner continued to take in the abundant reports of environmental degradation, food and energy shortages, nuclear proliferation, and global conflict, and he absorbed and processed this information in his letters and poems. In a letter to Paul Auster dated January 1974, Eigner writes,

> I've recurrently wond what people shd be concerned with or should develop, or how much any particular thing, a garden, neck of the woods or biosphere ("man . . . less . . . nature more"?? Well, nothing too much from a lot of thinking, though to think excessively about what may be an optimum amount of thought doesn't make life whole in the daily humpty-dumpty world either. (Man now over-heating Earth of course, so many raw materials processed into productions already. Fatigue. Work ethic, Quixotic, easily disposable in time/areas areas of abundance, anyway, as generally, at least (in future) the chances of too much being done are as great as of too little being taken care of. Well, work for its own sake is play, sport, if not insisted on - a needed thing, "dance/ sitting down," as Olson wrote, or otherwise, idleness no good if you've energy, every day a new day. . . . .)[40]

Eigner sees reflection and contemplation as a supplement, or even replacement, for action; doing less, reflecting more, might turn down the heat a bit. We should learn to "dance / sitting down."[41] His thinking on this subject produced two types of global warming poems: longer ones that essentially collage together bits of information and perceptions to examine the complexity of the issue, such as "you know where you're going," and brief epigrammatic bursts that encapsulate the problem, such as "CO2 and All." Another fine example of the latter, written on March 18, 1974, might relate to the details of the letter to Auster:

```
Fiddle

   world

      inside

       burn
```

(*CP* 3:1197)[42]

One thing that kept Eigner up to date and aware of environmental matters was the fact that his brother Joseph was a biochemist with an interest in political and social causes. Eigner regularly visited both of his siblings in the 1960s and 1970s—Joseph in Saint Louis and Richard in San Francisco. When he commented on the lines "casualness in / so many causes" from his poem "High piled / clouds" (written after one of these Saint Louis visits) to one of the librarians at Kansas, he explained, "I got [them] in re St. Louis folks, Eigners and others. Quite a miscellany of concerns. Inevitable. How can there be priorities? Grass-roots, humptydumpty, all needing words and give-and-take - as I thght when we went to a benefit for Rev. Charles Koen and the blacks of Cairo, Ill."[43]

In the mid-1970s, Joseph became the head of the Hazardous Wastes Project of the Missouri Department of Natural Resources. He would send Eigner copies of *Missouri's Environment*, and Eigner would relay what he had been hearing about environmental issues. In January 1975, Eigner writes to Joseph and his family:

> And - after I hrd ma telling Aunt Edith when she rang Sunday abt yr commute etc., your new job, I inquired and so heard what she got from you Saturday nght - Jan 13 Newsweek (p. 54) is an article* [*seen 10 days ago, Howard Odum] on an "environmental engineer" at U of Florida, Gainesville, who's figured (with computer aid of course) "net energy" in calories (6.5 gained for one spent in production, strip-mined coal 3 for 1, current nuclr pwr 2/1, fusion development wd take as much elal capacity as the RS has now, besides a doubling of it, solar or likewise wdnt net much, nor would oil from shale pay), fantastically enough he sights the only real solution to be a stdy-state economy like that envisioned by J S Kill dependent on nature's energy systems, with an agriculture as organic (minimizing use of chemical fertilizers) and demechanized as possible the main economic activity.[44]

And in a note in the left margin, he adds, "A letter on seeing the article written Newsweek, abt the weather, limits to food (fertilizer), weekly fast/sharing, greenhouse effect, dormant imagination, 'triage' some last resort. Today a reply therefrom, none of it will see print, ah well - ouph!"[45] Joseph himself studied the effects of climate change related to ozone depletion and increased ultraviolet radiation, publishing an article titled "Unshielding the Sun" in *Environment* magazine in 1975. The article's emphasis is that the *biological* impacts—skin cancer, crop failure, fishery collapse, and so forth—of increased ultraviolet radiation require much more research and analysis; until that happens, it concludes, "we will continue to live in ignorance of technology's influence on the biosphere."[46]

As we have seen, it is not only his scientist brother with whom Eigner shares information about climate change and related matters. Writing to George Butterick in early 1975 as well, Eigner includes his discovery of "Odum's Law" among his comments about Charles Olson and the *Black Mountain Review*:

> No ideas but in acts (individual ones . . . ?) - wow! OLSON #2 has sure given me a substantial (head/eye-opening/-filling) view of BMR as a re..vv/involving center, for one thing as straining (trying) to be down-to-earth and integrate trees into forest.or put the humptydumpty wrld together (again?) Clarification on pp 11 et al what Olson was onto in strssing the active - the context I have now decreases puzzlement over his not seeming to or not con- hyperactivity along with underactivity and doing enough (as to what there is). The emphasis of process, e.g., though I knew of Whitehead through Olson in 56 or 57 or 58 (and Goethe's idea in *Faust* that the great thing isn't the destination but the journey, not succeeding but trying - I recall that too). Oh well, oi! In January 13th (or 23rd?) *Newsweek* (pp. 53-54) is a story abt an "environmental engineer" at the U of Florida, Howard Odum, who after figuring 6.5 calories are got from one put into oil production, 3 for 1 of energy into strip-mining, 2/1 fission poer plants, and there'd hardly be any net energy from shale oil or fusion or solar power, sees as the only real solution a no-growth, steady-state economy with an agriculture as organic and demechanized as possible the "main economic activity." Well, an impossibly way-out prospect, it seems, but also an idea less gloomy than "triage". Anyway I wrote N..week a letter with that stuff abt the fast and fund drive . . . I sent you . . . et al.[47]

Finding an example of the attempt to "integrate trees into forest" in postmodern poetry seems the same, for Eigner, as trying to calculate the net energy yield of various technologies. In this context, another brief poem from 1973 captures the dilemma of determining what is enough, not too much or too little, when taking action:

```
the forest

          trees

     together

          how
```

(*CP* 3:1138)

The particulars discovered and analyzed by science have to be put together to form a whole so that we may take action to avoid disaster. As Commoner noted, it is social action that will do this, not science.

Eigner's poems and letters from the 1970s offer evidence for Nathaniel Rich's claim that "everything we understand about global warming was understood in 1979." He observes, "by 1979 the main points were already settled beyond debate. . . . The 'greenhouse effect'—a metaphor dating back to the early twentieth century—was ancient history, described in any intro-to-biology textbook."[48] Rich's *Losing Earth* is the history of a single decade (1979–89), the ten years it took for the fossil fuel industry and its lobbyists to convince politicians that global warming was not caused by humans putting excessive amounts of carbon dioxide into the atmosphere. According to Rich, by the end of the 1970s, "it was widely accepted that action would have to come immediately."[49] As *Losing Earth* demonstrates, that action did not come, despite the determined efforts of a few lobbyists, scientists, and politicians. Eigner's ecrippoetics tracks the emerging scientific consensus about the greenhouse effect in the 1970s, and Eigner himself serves as a figure for what we tune to when we attune to the hyperobject of global warming.

because of man [. . .] Earth might heat

Because he was so concerned about global warming, it is perhaps one of the ironies of climate change that Eigner's move from Swampscott, Massachusetts, to Berkeley, California, happened just after the "Great Blizzard" of 1977–78.[50] When he edited Eigner's *Windows / Walls / Yard / Ways*, Robert Grenier chose to mark this transition by arranging the collection in three sections: "Swampscott," "Winter," and "Berkeley." The second section is a series of poems written during the blizzard (in the Northeast it was most severe during the first week of February), a version of which had been published in the 1979 "Objectivist Tradition" issue of the *Chicago Review* as "Snow Sequence." In "A Note on the Text," Grenier, in his idiosyncratic style, explains, "It is difficult to suppress the *inclination* to remark that there is something improvisatorially 'Eastern' about these verses, which *may* have to do with that coast of Massachusetts' long-standing 'interest' in the Far East (e.g., Hawthorne's post at the Custom-House, the Peabody Museum in Salem, 'Bowditch,' etc.)—see the eight poems, for instance, forming the *interlude* of section two; but, *it's throughout*—EXPLAINS the move west!"[51] "Snow Sequence" is indeed influenced by Eigner's study of haiku, and he uses the condensed format to comment on the storm itself ("snow / blinding / cold"), as well as its impact ("politics / suspended in snow") (*CP* 3:1331, 3:1333).

The nonliterary explanation for "the move west" was that Eigner's father died in March and his mother was too old to care for Eigner herself. Eigner first resided in a home for adults with disabilities, and though he complained of the disruptions and distractions of communal living (within a year, a household with Grenier and Kathleen Frumkin was established), he still had ample time to follow the environmental news. Thinking about the coming presidential election, Eigner writes to Cid Corman in July 1979,

> Seems US and world is enough to drive any Prs or anyone crazy. But synfuel? Oil from shale? Well, B Commoner as prs or sec'y mght be ½-way adequate. For a while. Decentralizing power source I've thought wd add to the falling apart. Like overkill?? (I hrd Commoner a few yrs ago at Ford Hall Forum via radio in what seemed a smashing spch on the whole, long enough in fact to leave little or no time for q.. period. Guess I figured there might not be material for too many solar cells, anyhow from a PBS-TV hour it somehow looked best to generate energy from the temperature gradient, 1 depth to another. Hm. I bet enough production wd destroy the gradient. Besides of crs the limits on copper wire, insulation etc there ultimately are. Ah - just now on Natl Pblc Radio news mag word of 2-hr power failure frm the usual thing, air-conditioning.) Sharing rather than production, getting and spending ... is the thing, but millions lack the imagination to, for one thing enough material goods ~~over~~ sink it. A hungry man in the White Hse might make popular a weekly, say, fast day with a March of Dimes to get cash from food-budgets pushing existint (food) supplies towards ppl below par and offering recompense or a subsidy to food retailers and restaurant men. F.. Day Thrdsday perhaps to include Thanksgiving in USA. A reminder of limits an increase fear and isolation, the dieing by itself, without the sharing, wd diminish community.[52]

Eigner understands the need for alternative energy sources, but he also knows that there is a significant difference between solar and other renewables, on the one hand, and synthetic fuel and what would come to be known as "fracking," on the other. As Morton proposes, the first human attunement to hyperobjects is hypocrisy:

> hyperobjects make hypocrites of us all. . . . Doing nothing evidently won't do at all. Drive a Prius? Why not (I do)? But it won't solve the problem in the long run. Sit around criticizing Prius drivers? Won't help at all. Form a people's army and seize control of the state? Will the new society have the time and resources to tackle global warming? Solar panels? They take a lot of energy to make. Nuclear power? Fukushima and Chernobyl, anyone? Stop burning fossil fuels now? Are we ready for such a colossal transition? Every position is "wrong": every position, including and especially the know-it-all cynicism that thinks it knows better than anything else.[53]

President Carter took leadership on climate change seriously enough to install solar panels on the White House, but, as Rich points out, "Carter's plan to stimulate production of synthetic fuels was a dangerous lurch in the direction of auto-annihilation."[54] In other words, "every position is 'wrong.'"

By 1986, Eigner observes in one poem that it is "down to the wire," we should not "expect everything // or too much," and the main thing we should do is "think, think, think" (*CP* 4:1572). *The Collected Poems of Larry Eigner* includes a note from Eigner's typescript of this poem:

> Everything, as seems inevitable, gets to be a specialty, like, say, the long view as much as the short run. For instance came over National Public Radio a couple of weeks ago half an hour of an interview on the Greenhouse effect, which a Walter Roberts (*if* that was his name) had it we can with advantage and had better start getting ready, planning, now, for the 6 degree warmer weather the world'll have in general by 2050, around 98% of the studious in the field agree, whereby the Midwestern U.S. corn belt will have to move 600 miles northwards, and Minnesota will be good to grow rice in, though there won't be enough groundwater for wheat. Various things could be done, he said: ample time enough at this point. Calling for a 25- or 43- or 60-year plan? Well, it's true, Barry Commoner, an ecologist and advocate of a big nationwide boost to solar energy (as Israel has done) industry, did run for President in 1980. And further research, better than none, seems a good sport. I like the idea of it pretty much. The flatulence of cattle produces methane, he said. 3 degrees of the rise in temperature (during the next 60-odd years) will be from carbon dioxide, or so it's expected, and 3 degrees from various other things. (*CP* 4:xxii–xxiii)

So, by the mid-1980s, Eigner was more or less fully informed about global warming, its causes, and its impacts, as well as what might be done about them. An August 1987 poem attunes to multiple hyperobjects, including black holes, supernovas, overpopulation, radiation, and agriculture. It begins its tuning by means of spacing:

```
                    s t a r r y   f i g u r e s

  n o d e s

o p e n w o r k   e a r t h w o r k s

      f a m i l i e s
                        i n   t h e   s e a ' s   t i d e s
```

Constellations are "starry figures," individual stars being the "nodes" that are connected to produce the figures, and the night sky looks like "openwork" (a term from embroidery or metalsmithing). Perhaps the term "openwork" reminds Eigner of the sculptures produced by earthwork artists, or perhaps the contrast is just between airy openness and solid earth. The families could be the constellations themselves, or perhaps they are neither celestial nor terrestrial but rather oceanic: families of fish in the sea. In any case, the spacing here creates the effect of openwork in the words, the letters clustering or spreading out in a wavering spatial field. The following lines, without spacing between the letters, extend the overlay of sky, earth, and ocean: "then ships crowding the channel // and planets a narrow space // in the galaxies" (*CP* 4:1598). The sense of "crowding" and "narrow[ing] space" introduces overpopulation, which is one of Eigner's motivations for writing the poem:

a yugoslav newborn designated
(July '87)
our 5 billionth contemporary
(promotion
for the World University Games)

then out of 12 1/2 quintillion less 2 1/2 billion
2-way daily exchanges

how few (many) to
slip by the rocks, avoid black holes[55]

The next lines are the poem's pivot; they come almost to the dead center of the page and are also spaced out in the text, and they explain the focus on the stars: "(year / of the supernova)." A supernova—the final explosion of a dying star—was discovered in February 1987. The hyperobjects of black holes (supernovas that have burned out) and human population are superimposed, presenting the Scylla and Charybdis that are hard to avoid.

After this pivot, the second half of the poem reads:

faint hope again a film right now seen

h o w farmers reducing chemicals
e.g.
in 3 or 4 states
for about these past ten years
not only to save costs

```
      a sense of the world still

  1,000 saved 2 million bucks

     (Pan-American Games starting
                 in Indianapolis
                  where the speedway is
      the day after my birthday
                       Hiroshima Day

"the most productive agricultural county in the East"
                 (Nat'l Geographic, April '84)
  where the Amish and Mennonites be

      near Three Mile Island

             in the piling-up continents
```

(*CP* 4:1598)

Eigner is heartened to find out that some farmers are trying to reduce fertilizer usage, one of his concerns since he read about nitrogen pollution in 1969. He remarks on the fact that it wasn't just to save money (though "1,000 saved 2 million bucks"); such concern shows that these farmers have "a sense of the world still." What Eigner detects here is one of the effects of the hyperobject: "*World* is a function of a very long-lasting and complex set of social forms that we could roughly call the logistics of agriculture." According to Morton, "*World* as the background of events is an objectification of a hyperobject: the biosphere, climate, evolution, capitalism (yes, perhaps economic relations compose hyperobjects)."[56] Eigner's ecrippoetics destabilizes the foreground-background distinction, and the graphic form of his poems accounts for this effect; white space is just supposed to be the background for a poem. Eigner's ecrippoetics is a form of attunement to the hyperobject.

Eigner also tunes to the timescale of hyperobjects in this poem. Morton coined the term "agrilogistics" in *Dark Ecology* to encompass the 12,500-year history of agriculture.[57] That is one hyperobject, distributed over a fairly comprehensible timescale. In this poem, population and radiation are also hyperobjects. To quote Morton, "Even the massive density of the exponentially increasing human population itself could be seen as a hyperobject created by leaps in agricultural technology and logistics since the eighteenth-century Agricultural Revolution, and even more so since 1945. What should we do about substances that will be around many centuries after our culture has radically changed or disappeared entirely?"[58] Juxtaposing "the most productive agricultural county in the East" with the partial meltdown of the nuclear reactor at Three Mile Island in Pennsylvania gives us a sense of the contradictions of the Anthropocene, as well as a feel for the overlapping of past and future that belies the present moment.[59] Amish and Mennonite farmers mostly eschew post-eighteenth-century technology, but that is only a slight resistance to agrilogistics: "the gigantic machinery of agriculture" is "not just specific machines, but *the machine that is agriculture as such*, a machine that predates Industrial Age machinery."[60] And autobiography intersects with hyperobjects here, too, in that the date of Eigner's birth (which was actually the day before the dropping of the atomic bomb on Hiroshima) coincides with the definitive advent of a human-made hyperobject (nuclear fallout). With "ships crowding the channel," billions of "2-way daily exchanges," and "the piling-up continents," perhaps "faint hope" is the best ratio of optimism to stoicism we can achieve.

As Thoreau might say

"CO2 and All," discussed at the beginning of this chapter, is dated August 21, 1988. Eigner was evidently responding to James Hansen's statement to Congress on the greenhouse effect in June 1988.[61] As Bill McKibben reports, after Hansen's testimony before the Senate, the *New York Times* ran a headline declaring "Global Warming Has Begun, Expert Tells Senate."[62] The hearing was motivated in part by the severe drought that gripped the Midwest in 1987–88. Hansen informed Congress that "1988 will be the warmest year on record," and that he "believe[d] that this change in frequency of hot summers is large enough to be noticeable to the average person."[63] As McKibben points out, the climate scientists who authored the report for Congress wrote that the inability to imagine the consequences of global warming limited their ability to predict what may come; the intricate interconnections between society, environment, and climate prevented them from analyzing "the reductions in barge shipments due to lower river levels, the increases in forest fires due to dry conditions, or the impacts on ducks due to disappearing prairie potholes."[64] As I have argued throughout this chapter, Eigner's tuning to the hyperobject of global warming is a significant component of his ecrippoetics, and his concern about environmental issues was deeply informed by his reading of newspapers and journal articles, his listening to public radio, and his watching of the news on television. Yet, Eigner also feels hampered by the disorienting number of interconnections that must be accounted for.

This is the reason why he (much like the ecocritics I have been citing) points out the need "to sit still" in "CO2 and All."

In his 1978 essay that opens the inaugural *L=A=N=G=U=A=G=E* newsletter, Eigner provides a little more of the quote from Eliot's "Ash-Wednesday": "'. . . to care and not to care . . . to sit still' Careful of earth air and water mainly perhaps, and other lives, but some (how many?) other things too. Walden, ah! The dancer and the dance."[65] As noted in the first chapter, Eigner lived about thirty miles from Concord and Walden Pond, and as a New Englander he was well aware of the transcendentalist legacy. "Walden" serves for him as a shorthand term for the deliberate life that would attend to these matters of care. Eigner agrees with Eliot that we need to be *taught* "to care and not to care," that we need to be *taught* "to sit still" so that we might figure out the relationship of part to whole, actor to action, that William Butler Yeats's "Among School Children" posits as central questions (Yeats's poem ends with the line "How can we know the dancer from the dance?").[66] Starting in the mid-1960s, Eigner began to use "Thoreau" or "Walden" or "Walden Pond" as metonyms for an ecological ideal. One of the earliest examples of this comes in a poem from 1966:

```
 Thoreau's 2 or 3
affairs   but the air-pressure
   from birds, wow,   or snow,or they

  rest on the branches
    and weigh them down

       while cloud motion
          may light time
```

(*CP* 2:711)

Eigner cited a longer passage from *Walden* in one of his letters to the editor; the quotation comes from the "Where I Lived, and What I Lived For" chapter: "Simplicity, simplicity, simplicity! I say let your affairs be as two or three, and not a hundred or a thousand; instead of a million count half a dozen, and keep your accounts on your thumbnail."[67] As we saw earlier in this chapter, Eigner felt that "to care" involved one in so many different causes and concerns that getting anything accomplished diminished with each additional commitment. Morton points out the pun in "careless" in *Being Ecological*, that to care *less* is to also be *carefree*, a pretty good condition for thinking and reflecting, and that is why Morton exhorts us not to "hit delete on your indifference."[68]

"Walden" is the best option for finding the golden mean between caring and not caring, balancing one's cares by reducing how many one should be concerned with at any given time. Writing to Levertov on September 1, 1968, Eigner complained, "Abt everyone around here is so idle in talk, indifferent, and *dumb* - and so much worn on the sleeve, *fantastic* doing! A Thoreau must be one in a million. And it wd take a certain respectable % of Th.'s for mankind not over-eat and the opposite, to husband resource and wear materials lightly."[69] In March of the following year, Eigner began the letter that would become the essay "Integration Interchange." He starts with his proposal for a weekly fast day as a response to rising populations and decreasing food yields; yet, "by itself a reminder of limits magnifies fear and rifts," Eigner observes. He continues, "But there's little enough chance of a world more or less fit for life. . . . And it's been foreseen that if enough energy is produced the earth will become overheated, or it will if enough ozone (is it?),* blocking the escape of heat from the planet gets into the atmosphere."[70] The note that he appends to his uncertainty about what causes the "greenhouse effect" clarifies: "CO_2 it is, firstly, and then methane (CH_4), then CFCs." It was only in the mid-1950s that scientists—specifically Roger Revelle and Hans E. Suess—began investigating the connection between CO_2 in the atmosphere and global temperatures. By June 1988, as McKibben observes, the "message was finally getting across, nearly a century after Arrhenius and three decades past Revelle and Suess."[71] Yet, as Nathaniel Rich's *Losing Earth* demonstrates, that message might not have been as clearly received as necessary.

Eigner himself had trouble keeping track of it all. After Hansen's testimony before Congress and the related news coverage, Eigner writes to his friend and publisher James Weil in late October 1988, "I heard of th grhouse effect yrs back, yet, eventually forgot it, virtually inevitably. Well, no business and/or sport (while prticular cmflict fase) can have moratorium without, say, us all going into dpfreeze or hibernating evry yr, taking trns at it. More'n 5 bllion ppl on eart now."[72] Eigner enclosed a copy of a letter he wrote to his family in August, which includes this note at the bottom of the first page:

```
More and more extras ! So many! Walden Pond
runneth  over
                 CO2 ,
                      CO2,   CO2
                   I've forgotten you
                     enough times too
```

Because hyperobjects make hypocrites of us all, Eigner points out that some of these "extras" overflowing "Walden Pond" are the very things required to avoid, or adapt to, climate change. On the back of the envelope containing the letter to Weil, Eigner types out "CO2 and All" and adds this note directly below the line "we should live off the sun":

```
            ‡?‡
Yet soon enough, needs with luxuries spiraling,
 there'd    be too many solar panels covering ye

earth; so cnrvatin and moderate activity, so much
 as they're possible, is the thing
```

By August 1989, he boils it down to:

```
A s  T h o r e a u   m i g h t   s a y


       cool it

          whoever can
```

(*CP* 4:1623)

Eigner sent this poem and another to Charles Bernstein in September, telling him, "these two latest (August 15) seem really all I can say (by) now." The other poem was a retrospective look back at "A long life (/history)" and what it produced: "a few things (poems) // how many" (*CP* 4:1623). He tells Bernstein, "well, how much shop to talk, whether poet writing is a big problem, in comparison with the rest of life, or a little one, or whatever, something to dwell on a good bit, at that."[73] Whether solar panels or poems, Eigner is worried about the "extras," the things that "Thoreau's 2 or 3 / affairs" were supposed to help reduce.

It should come as no surprise that Eigner found more to say about these things. Writing to a cousin in August 1990, he comments, "And I've Walden Pond on the brain, it gets increasingly clear how we're at the end of our history, and mankind, so hyperagile and numerous, is burning up himself and the life system (so, now, here is G.. Bush defending our ‡gassy‡ way of life) Well, really formidable dilemma is: continue the destruction, excess and waste or, stop much or 9/10ths ‡?‡ of the busynes, ie the buying/selling/advertising, and thus make destitute, throw out of work, and home, a lot more people. Or lower the speedlimit on the highways again, etc??"[74] In one of his last global warming poems, written in 1992, Eigner switches his literary reference point from Thoreau to the broader English literary tradition with allusions to John Donne, Thomas Hardy, and William Shakespeare:

```
" a n y  m a n ' s  d e a t h . . . "
```

```
how near and far away
   to/from Frisco, Watts, L.A.,   - W o w !
                                             the madding
                                               crowd

   and 2030 or so
   when cities, towns, islands,
   under salt water will go,
   under the oceans' flow -

      ding-dong  ho well  heigh-ho
```

(*CP* 4:1645)

Eigner's use of allusion, compression, and spacing engage some of the concepts required for comprehending climate change. Three main allusions—to Donne's Meditation 17 ("any man's death"), Hardy's novel *Far from the Madding Crowd* (and by extension Thomas Gray's "Elegy in a Country Churchyard," from which Hardy's title derives), and Ariel's second song from *The Tempest* ("ding-dong," in a song about "a sea-change")—combine to produce a commentary on rising sea levels. If we take each author's name, as Eigner did with "Thoreau" or "Walden," as a metonym for an idea associated with climate change, we might get: Donne, interconnectedness; Hardy, population; Shakespeare, metamorphosis (sea change). Allusion allows Eigner to compress these core ideas into a statement about climate change without discursive explanation. Also, typical concerns such as scale, time, and space are involved. Eigner informed Clayton Eshleman that the idea of San Francisco under water came to him from hearing Lawrence Ferlinghetti read a poem about it on the radio. He also tells Eshleman: "And only a cple of months ago it occured to me (nvr before then did I think it) that nobody knows really how far to look into the future, and maybe no one ever knew or cd decide, except that engh millions have looked and still do look forward to the rest of time or eternity, an endless future, a bright one for at least theirselves and thr biological descendents. Like the horizon, earth and heaven, Or beyond."[75] How near or far are we from the population centers, "the madding crowd[s]," how near in time are we to the "sea change" brought on by global warming? Ariel's bell that signals the sea change is at the same time Donne's bell that tolls for us all.

These two bells are perhaps the English literary tradition's prime figures for "feeling" or "sensing" climate rhetorically. As he comes to the end of

Losing Earth, Nathaniel Rich observes, "an underexamined worst-case scenario is the violence done to our belief in a shared humanity. The failure to act erodes our trust in human fellowship as it does our glaciers." He concludes: "There can be no civil society without a stable climate. There can be no stable climate without a civil society. The fight to preserve one is the same as the fight to preserve the other. If a clod be washed away by the sea, all are diminished."[76] Eigner's ecrippoetics may be primarily derived from the objectivist-projectivist tradition, but even Olson himself says, in "Projective Verse," that "each of us must save himself after his own fashion and how much, for that matter, each of us owes to the non-projective, and will continue to owe, as both go alongside each other."[77] To "save himself," and everything else, Eigner would use any literary tradition that fit the bill. Eigner's experience in his defamiliar body produces an ecrippoetics that can tune to the hyperobject of global warming. The hard-to-control muscles of his left side prior to cryosurgery showed Eigner the importance of sitting still, how "hyperactivity" has unintended consequences not just for the person but the planet. Morton sees the ability to sit still as a form of being ecological because it lets us just be what we are: "stillness is the quantum of action, of species-being: species-being, nothing else."[78] As Eigner puts it in his dedication to *Windows / Walls / Yard / Ways*: "health and stillness to us all, as much as can be."[79]

Coda: Readiness / Enough / Depends / On

Shortly before his death in February 1996, Eigner contracted with Green Integer to publish a collection of poems. It was posthumously released in 2000, and it was titled after its preface, which Eigner called "Readiness / Enough / Depends / On." As we have seen, Eigner's ecrippoetics was a continual search for what is enough, for balance, for a golden mean between contemplation and action. In this phrase, he frames the key concept of his ecrippoetics with William Shakespeare and William Carlos Williams. We have seen Eigner punning on the title of Williams's modernist masterpiece *Spring and All*; here he alludes to that book's most famous poem, "The Red Wheelbarrow," recasting Williams's modernist "so much" as an ecrippoetic "enough." He appropriates "readiness" from *Hamlet*. In the letter to Clayton Eshleman cited above, as Eigner is discussing "every man's death," he quotes the relevant passage from act 5, scene 2 of *Hamlet*: "So, at that, there's the end of Hamlet, and near it H.'s stoicism: 'We defy augury. If it be not now . . . yet it will come . . . a special providence . . .' And oft engh we overestimate what's humanly possible, human respons/ibility. While if we see milk spilled by a cat, or baby, say, it's an act of nature, and there's no crying."[80] The last three sentences of the passage that Eigner omits read: "The readiness is all. Since no man has aught of what he leaves, what is't to leave betimes? Let be." To be ready for death, to meet one's fate, to accept providence, requires stoicism, which, as we saw in this chapter, for Eigner is also a form of optimism about the future. Yet, Hamlet is also the ultimate figure of thought preempting action, so a state of "readiness" is a type of spectral activity that allows for awareness, which meaningful action requires.

It has been over twenty years since Eigner's death, and stoicism may be at risk of becoming pessimism, instead of optimism, as he feared. As we approach "2030 or so," the time for Eigner's ecrippoetics has come. Let's hope it is not too late. I want to give Eigner the last word, and his statement from *Readiness / Enough / Depends / On* deserves renewed attention. Its main paragraph reads:

> Mankind is so numerous now, and enough of us are more active than ever, hopeless or just hyperactive, people are getting farther and farther from being able to get together enough to stop global warming and its consequences, doomsday or just about, for instance, yet the long run is made of many short terms, never could there be next week without tomorrow, and the momentary is maybe about as meaningful as what lasts for some generations. The more you do the less you see, too, the narrower is your tunnel of vision (vision is itself the more blurred the more you're in motion), as well as vice versa, and while doing anything you're more or less specializing, even when you try to see a whole it may be like the biosphere it's so big and/or complicated you can't get enough detail to be realistic about it. So, all in all, enough is enough. It's great enough to keep your head in the air while your feet are on the ground.[81]

Notes

Introduction

Epigraph: Larry Eigner, "Qs & As (?) Large and Small / Parts of a Collaborate," in *Areas Lights Heights: Selected Writings 1954–1989*, by Larry Eigner, ed. Benjamin Friedlander (New York: Roof Books, 1989), 150.

1. Early ecocritical studies of twentieth-century American poetry include John Elder, *Imagining the Earth: Poetry and the Vision of Nature* (Urbana: University of Illinois Press, 1985); Leonard M. Scigaj, *Sustainable Poetry: Four American Ecopoets* (Lexington: University of Kentucky Press, 1999); and J. Scott Bryson, ed., *Ecopoetry: A Critical Introduction* (Salt Lake City: University of Utah Press, 2002). Recent studies of experimental ecopoetry that accommodate a disability poetics like Eigner's include Sarah Nolan, *Unnatural Ecopoetics: Unlikely Spaces in Contemporary Poetry* (Reno: University of Nevada Press, 2017); Lynn Keller, *Recomposing Ecopoetics: North American Poetry of the Self-Conscious Anthropocene* (Charlottesville: University of Virginia Press, 2017); Angela Hume and Gillian Osborne, eds., *Ecopoetics: Essays in the Field* (Iowa City: University of Iowa Press, 2018); and David Farrier, *Anthropocene Poetics: Deep Time, Sacrifice Zones, and Extinction* (Minneapolis: University of Minnesota Press, 2019). Language-oriented approaches to ecopoetics that are appropriate for thinking about Eigner's ecrippoetics include Brenda Iijima, ed., *The Eco Language Reader* (New York: Portable Press, 2010); and *ecopoetics*, a journal edited by Jonathan Skinner from 2001 to 2007. Eigner's work is also included in two recent anthologies of ecopoetry: Ann Fisher-Wirth and Laura-Gray Street, eds., *The Ecopoetry Anthology* (San Antonio, TX: Trinity University Press, 2013); and David Hinton, ed., *The Wilds of Poetry: Adventures in Mind and Landscape* (Boulder, CO: Shambhala, 2017).

2. Forrest Gander and John Kinsella, *Redstart: An Ecological Poetics* (Iowa City: University of Iowa Press, 2012), 37.

3. Timothy Morton, *Ecology without Nature: Rethinking Environmental Aesthetics* (Cambridge, MA: Harvard University Press, 2007), 34.

4. Morton, 33.

5. For another account of the development of Eigner's ecopoetic form, see George Hart, "Walking the Walk: Ammons, Eigner, and Ecopoetic Form in the 1960s," *ISLE: Interdisciplinary Studies in Literature and Environment* 21, no. 1 (2018): 680–706.

6. The section heading, "I can only play one note at a time," is from Larry Eigner, *The Collected Poems of Larry Eigner*, 4 vols., ed. Curtis Faville and Robert Grenier

(Stanford, CA: Stanford University Press, 2010), 1:47. Subsequent citations to *The Collected Poems* are parenthetical and use the abbreviation *CP* with corresponding volume and page numbers.

7. Michael Davidson, *Concerto for the Left Hand: Disability and the Defamiliar Body* (Ann Arbor: University of Michigan Press, 2008), 226.

8. Michael Davidson, "Disability Poetics," in *The Oxford Handbook of Modern and Contemporary American Poetry*, ed. Cary Nelson (Oxford: Oxford University Press, 2012), 597; Davidson provides another account of Eigner's use of the manual typewriter in *Concerto for the Left Hand*, 124–25. Once asked in an interview what the primary effect of his cerebral palsy was, Eigner replied, "I don't know. Being jerky in my movements." Eigner, "Larry Eigner, 1927–1996," in *Contemporary Authors Autobiography Series*, vol. 23, ed. Joyce Nakamura (Detroit, MI: Gale Research, 1996), 56.

9. Barrett Watten argues that Eigner should be considered a "distributed author" in that his authorial intentions are distributed among the other poets, friends, and editors who helped him make typescripts, select poems for collections, and arrange typesetting and printing. See "Scenes of Decision: Larry Eigner as a Distributed Author," in *Momentous Inconclusions: The Life and Work of Larry Eigner*, edited by Jennifer Bartlett and George Hart (Albuquerque: University of New Mexico Press, 2020), 87–120.

10. Davidson, *Concerto for the Left Hand*, 118.

11. Grenier's poem for Eigner is quoted in Stephen Ratcliffe, *Listening to Reading* (Albany: State University of New York Press, 2000), 121 (emphasis in original).

12. Larry Eigner, "Twenty-One Poems and an Interview," *Kaleidoscope*, Spring 1982, 13.

13. Jacques Derrida, *Of Grammatology*, trans. Gayatri Chakravorty Spivak, 40th anniversary ed. (Baltimore, MD: Johns Hopkins University Press, 2016), 64.

14. Derrida, 99–100.

15. Jerome McGann, *The Textual Condition* (Princeton, NJ: Princeton University Press, 1991), 60.

16. "Established texts" is the phrase that Faville and Robert Grenier use in *The Collected Poems of Larry Eigner* to refer to texts based on typescripts prepared by Eigner with the help of Grenier (*CP* 1:xiv).

17. Peter L. Shillingsburg, "Text as Matter, Concept, and Action." *Studies in Bibliography* 44 (1991): 54.

18. Lennard Davis, "From *Enforcing Normalcy: Disability, Deafness, and the Body*," in *The Norton Anthology of Theory and Criticism*, ed. Jeffrey J. Williams, John McGowan, Laurie A. Finke, T. Denean Sharpley-Whiting, Vincent B. Leitch, and William E. Cain, 3rd ed. (New York: Norton, 2018), 2175.

19. Ratcliffe, *Listening to Reading*, 155.

20. Raphael Allison, *Bodies on the Line: Performance and the Sixties Poetry Reading* (Iowa City: University of Iowa Press, 2014), 174. Eigner used the phrase "momentous layouts" in a letter to Charles Bernstein; Charles Bernstein Papers (MSS 0519), box 18, folder 5, Special Collections and Archives, University of California, San Diego.

21. Ratcliffe, *Listening to Reading*, 155 (emphasis in original).

22. Allison, *Bodies on the Line*, 185.

23. Eigner's family encouraged him to speak and write clearly so that he could be understood. In "Course Matter," recounting a recovery from an injury he suffered from a wheelchair accident, Eigner says he was still getting "speech therapy" that "brother and s..-in-law got me to take [. . .] as I was talking strenuously enough as yet, often enough, hence poorly, words coming out skewed" (*Areas Lights Heights*, 141).

24. Allison, *Bodies on the Line*, 188.

25. Ratcliffe, *Listening to Reading*, 155.

26. Eigner, *Areas Lights Heights*, 121.

27. Charles Olson, "Projective Verse." In *The Collected Prose of Charles Olson*, ed. Donald Allen and Benjamin Friedlander (Berkeley: University of California Press, 1997), 245.

28. G. Thomas Tanselle, "The Textual Criticism of Visual and Aural Works." *Studies in Bibliography* 57 (2005–6): 5–6.

29. Eigner, *Areas Lights Heights*, 47.

30. Eigner, 55.

31. Eigner, 150.

32. The phrase "voice of the body" is David Hinton's. In *The Wilds of Poetry*, he traces the ecopoetic tradition back to Walt Whitman, who, he claims, "reinvented language as the voice of the body" (16).

33. Larry Eigner, *Country Harbor Quiet Act Around: Selected Prose*, ed. Barrett Watten (Berkeley, CA: This Press, 1978).

34. Barrett Watten, *Total Syntax* (Carbondale: Southern Illinois University Press, 1985), 178 (emphasis in original).

35. Timothy Morton, *The Ecological Thought* (Cambridge, MA: Harvard University Press, 2010), 15, 36.

36. Davidson, *Concerto for the Left Hand*, 122.

37. Watten, *Total Syntax*, 180.

38. Davidson, *Concerto for the Left Hand*, 121.

39. Watten, *Total Syntax*, 190 (emphasis in original).

40. Olson, "Projective Verse," in *The Collected Prose of Charles Olson*, 247.

41. Morton, *The Ecological Thought*, 11 (emphasis in original).

42. Morton, *Ecology without Nature*, 171.

43. Robert Grenier, "Three Possibilities—for Larry Eigner," collected in Matthew Hofer and Michael Golston, eds., *The L=A=N=G=U=A=G=E Letters: Selected 1970s Correspondence of Bruce Andrews, Charles Bernstein, and Ron Silliman* (Albuquerque: University of New Mexico Press, 2019), 359.

44. Robert Grenier to Bruce Andrews, October 9, 1977, collected in Hofer and Golston, 350 (emphasis in original).

45. Albert Hofstadter, "Enownment," *Boundary 2*, vol. 4, no. 2 (1976): 372 (emphasis in original). Hofstadter provides a more extensive explanation of Heidegger's playful etymology for the term in his introduction to Martin Heidegger, *Poetry, Language, Thought*, trans. Albert Hofstadter (New York: Harper and Row, 1971), xviii–xxii.

46. Hofstadter emphasizes that this is not the same as ownership or property: "It is clear that Heidegger here is making use of the 'own' meaning of '*eigen*' to read the

sense of the verb *ereignen* as *to make one's own, to appropriate*. But instead of 'appropriate' in the sense of one's own appropriating of something for oneself. . . . Heidegger wants to speak of an activity or process by which nothing 'selfish' occurs, but rather by which the different members of the world are brought into belonging to and with one another and are helped to realize themselves and each other in realizing this belonging" (introduction to Heidegger, *Poetry, Language, Thought*, xix–xx). I take "realizing this belonging" to be another way of saying "coexistence."

47. Morton, *Ecology without Nature*, 172 (emphasis in original). Morton's deconstructive ecocriticism derives in part from Heidegger, directly and through object-oriented ontology. For a Heideggerian ecopoetics presented as "a post-phenomenological inflection of High Romantic poetics" (262), see Jonathan Bate, *Song of the Earth* (Cambridge, MA: Harvard University Press, 2000), 243–83.

48. Hofstadter, "Enownment," 371.

49. Robert Grenier to Bruce Andrews, October 9, 1977, collected in Hofer and Golston, *The L=A=N=G=U=A=G=E Letters*, 350–51 (emphasis in original).

50. Morton, *Ecology without Nature*, 174, 175 (emphasis in original).

51. For a discussion of Eigner and walking, see George Hart, " 'Enough Defined': Disability, Ecopoetics, and Larry Eigner," *Contemporary Literature* 51, no. 1 (2010): 152–79.

52. Eigner, *Areas Lights Heights*, 125.

53. Heidegger, *Poetry, Language, Thought*, 3.

54. Eigner, *Areas Lights Heights*, 3.

55. For an example of such a reading, see George Hart, "Postmodernist Nature/Poetry: The Example of Larry Eigner," in *Reading under the Sign of Nature: New Essays in Ecocriticism*, ed. John Tallmadge and Henry Harrington (Salt Lake City: University of Utah Press, 2000), 324–26.

56. The parascript is included in the notes, so even without the facsimile *The Collected Poems* includes this information. Eigner himself was ambivalent about when to include such information and when to leave it out, noting in 1977: "If anything isn't intrinsic, better to do without it, or sum up with something else. Immediacy and force take priority over notes clarifying allusions. A dedication 'To So-and-So,' for instance, doesn't seem to interfere with a piece as much as I felt it did 15 or 20 years ago. Then, I felt less sure of my poems at the time of writing them and was aiming to write big and perfect poems," *Areas Lights Heights*, 149–50.

57. Larry Eigner to George Butterick, November 6, 1974, George Butterick Papers (PCMS-0118), Poetry Collection of the University Libraries, University at Buffalo, State University of New York.

58. This line is Charles Bernstein's transcription of a comment by Eigner after a reading of "Again dawn"; see PennSound: Center for Programs in Contemporary Writing, "Larry Eigner," accessed February 10, 2021, https://writing.upenn.edu/pennsound/x/Eigner.php. Eigner uses the phrase "immediacy and force" in a number of essays; see Eigner, *Areas Lights Heights*, 15, 109, 135.

59. An image of the envelope appeared on the cover of *Sagetrieb* 18, no. 1 (1999), and Friedlander's transcription is included in that issue. For Friedlander's reflections

on transcribing this text, see "Typos and Abbrevs," *National Poetry Foundation* (blog), April 8, 2010, https://nationalpoetryfoundation.wordpress.com/2010/04/08/typos-and-abbrevs/.

60. I have followed Friedlander's transcription as closely as possible.

61. Morton, *Ecology without Nature*, 37, 38.

62. Eigner, *Areas Lights Heights*, 149.

63. Morton, *Ecology without Nature*, 40.

64. Jacques Derrida, *Margins of Philosophy*, trans. Alan Bass (Chicago: University of Chicago Press, 1982), xv.

65. Derrida, xix.

66. The phrase "constant ephemerals" is from an early poem (*CP* 1:76). *From the Sustaining Air* was published by Robert Creeley's Divers Press in 1953. Jonathan Skinner discusses the wide variety of sounds that Eigner responded to in his "soundscape" and produced in his poems in "What Sounds: Larry Eigner's Environments," in Bartlett and Hart, *Momentous Inconclusions*, 171–91.

67. It is for this reason that I will not be using the social model of disability to frame Eigner's poetics very much. As Susan Schweik has pointed out, poets with disabilities who do not associate themselves with disability activism that acknowledges the *social* construction of disability pose a problem for interpretations using this model. Whereas Josephine Miles herself refused to engage in disability activism or investigate disability as a constructed identity, Schweik asserts that "one can attend to how someone like Miles was 'disabled' not by rheumatoid arthritis per se but by a society that sometimes denied her access to schooling, saw her as desexualized, tokenized her, infantilized her, and medicalized her." Schweik points out that poets with disabilities who wrote in the middle decades of the twentieth century often avoided the social model of disability by "travelling off the body." She writes, "Take, for example, the views through window frames that occur so frequently in the poems of another Bay Area writer, Larry Eigner—texts that also uneasily invoke poetic tradition's usual mode of 'travelling off,' lyric transcendence. Like Eigner's work, Miles's poetry both complicates and accentuates a social model of disability by making it clear what poetry travels into, and what it travels in, is (accessible and inaccessible) language." Schweik, "The Voice of 'Reason,'" *Public Culture* 13, no. 3 (2001); 488n4, 499. In other words, as I see it, the social model and the structural model are both doing activist work, and Davidson's account of disability poetics as a counterbalance to disability politics accommodates poets who do not explicitly write from a disability identity.

68. Davidson, "Disability Poetics," 584. Both Leonard M. Scigaj and Scott Knickerbocker put foregrounding, which is another term for defamiliarization, at the center of ecopoetics. Knickerbocker asserts that "ecopoetics [is] the foregrounding of poetic artifice as a manifestation of our interrelation with the rest of nature"; Knickerbocker, *Ecopoetics: The Language of Nature, the Nature of Language* (Amherst: University of Massachusetts Press, 2012), 159. For his part, Scigaj argues that "within ecopoetry and environmental poetry, language is often foregrounded only to reveal its limitations, and this is accomplished in such a way that the reader's gaze is thrust beyond language back into the less limited natural world that language refers to, the inhabited place

where humans must live in harmony with ecological cycles"; Scigaj, *Sustainable Poetry*, 37. Neither critic, however, uses foregrounding in its technical sense. Rather than "thrust[ing]" the "reader's gaze" toward the world outside of the text, as Scigaj would have it, foregrounded language, as Russian formalism and Language poetry deploy it, brings us deeper into the text. Or, more precisely, deeper into language: its grammar, syntax, and structure. For a technical definition of defamiliarization and foregrounding, see Jan Mukarovsky, "Standard Language and Poetic Language," in *Chapters from the History of Czech Functional Linguistics*, ed. Jan Chovanec (Brno: Masarykova univerzita, 2014), 41–53.

69. Ellen Samuels, "Six Ways of Looking at Crip Time," *Disability Studies Quarterly* 37, no. 3 (2017), https://dsq-sds.org/article/view/5824/4684 (emphasis in original); Hillary Gravendyk, "Chronic Poetics," *Journal of Modern Literature* 38, no. 1 (2014): 7, 8.

70. Jesse Matz, *Modernist Time Ecology* (Baltimore, MD: Johns Hopkins University Press, 2019), 5 (emphasis in original).

71. Henri Lefebvre, *The Production of Space*, trans. Donald Nicholson-Smith (New York: Blackwell, 1991), 95–96.

72. Susan Schweik, *The Ugly Laws: Disability in Public* (New York: New York University Press, 2009), 3.

73. Timothy Morton, *Being Ecological* (Cambridge: MIT Press, 2018), 116.

74. The last lines were used as the title for *Another Time in Fragments* (London: Fulcrum Press, 1967), which Grenier calls Eigner's "definitive 'book'" of the 1960s (*CP* 2:286), and the poem appeared on the facade of the Berkeley University Art Museum as a tribute to Eigner, June through October 1993.

75. William James, *The Principles of Psychology*, vol. 1 (Boston: Henry Holt, 1910), 609–10. James cites E. R. Clay as the coiner of the phrase "specious present."

76. James, 613.

77. Derrida, *Of Grammatology*, 71 (bracketed enclosure in original).

78. Matz, *Modernist Time Ecology*, 3, 41.

79. Morton, *Being Ecological*, 82 (emphasis in original); Morton introduced "nowness" in *Humankind: Solidarity with Nonhuman People* (London: Verso, 2017), 81.

80. Morton, *Being Ecological*, 117.

Chapter One

Epigraph: Larry Eigner to Jonathan Williams, December 1957, collected in *Letters to Jargon: The Correspondence between Larry Eigner and Jonathan Williams*, ed. Andrew Rippeon (Tuscaloosa: University of Alabama Press, 2019), 49.

1. Robert Grenier, "A Note on the Text," in *Windows / Walls / Yard / Ways*, by Larry Eigner, ed. Robert Grenier (Santa Rosa, CA: Black Sparrow Press, 1994), 17.

2. Larry Eigner, *Areas Lights Heights: Selected Writings 1954–1989*, ed. Benjamin Friedlander (New York: Roof Books, 1989), 130.

3. Stephen Fredman, *The Grounding of American Poetry: Charles Olson and the Emersonian Tradition* (Cambridge: Cambridge University Press, 1993), 143, 144 (emphasis in the original). Albert Gelpi describes this Emersonian–New England tradition in relation to Fredman's picture-writing, which also establishes its relation to David Hin-

ton's innovative/ecopoetic tradition in *The Wilds of Poetry*. In his account of Language poetry, Gelpi notes Eigner's influence on Robert Grenier as part of this lineage: "The progression from Williams to Creeley to Eigner to Grenier traces a clear trajectory in American poetry. . . . Grenier's drawing poems are a kind of American haiku, and behind them stands Pound's notion of the ideogram as a more accurate analogy. Pound thought the Chinese language superior to English in having words written as pictographs of the things they represent, thus fusing word and thing;" Gelpi, *American Poetry after Modernism: The Power of the Word* (Cambridge: Cambridge University Press, 2015), 243; see also David Hinton, ed., *The Wilds of Poetry: Adventures in Mind and Landscape* (Boulder, CO: Shambhala, 2017).

4. Fredman, *The Grounding of American Poetry*, 145.

5. In a letter dated January 7, 1953, Eigner tells Corman that he has a copy of *The Maximus Poems*; in a letter dated May 9, 1953, Eigner reports to Corman that he obtained Williams's *Paterson* on trip to New York City. Cid Corman Papers, Harry Ransom Center, University of Texas at Austin.

6. Fredman, *The Grounding of American Poetry*, 146.

7. See George Hart, "'Enough Defined': Disability, Ecopoetics, and Larry Eigner," *Contemporary Literature* 51, no. 1 (2010): 152–79.

8. Edward Halsey Foster's characterization of Robert Creeley as a New England poet is apt for Eigner as well. Foster writes that Creeley's sense of limitation—his family's poverty after his father's death, his impaired eyesight—"has a parallel in the Puritan's assumption, rooted in Calvinist theology, that life offers individual opportunities but only within a profoundly determined and limited universe. . . . Edward Taylor's pastoral study, Thoreau's hut at Walden, Dickinson's upstairs room in Amherst, and Charles Ives's Spartan studio were not prisons but private worlds that helped to define the artist's objective. The pattern in each instance was to accept imposed (or self-imposed) limits and then to look to the imagination. . . . The New England artist begins with a recognition of limits." Foster, *Understanding the Black Mountain Poets* (Columbia: University of South Carolina Press, 1995), 89–90.

9. J. B. Jackson, "The Order of a Landscape," in *The Interpretation of Ordinary Landscapes: Geographical Essays*, ed. D. W. Meinig (Oxford: Oxford University Press, 1979), 157.

10. H. Daniel Peck, *Thoreau's Morning Work: Memory and Perception in "A Week on the Concord and Merrimack Rivers," the Journal, and "Walden"* (New Haven, CT: Yale University Press, 1994), ix, 73–74.

11. Peck, 118; Henry David Thoreau, *A Week on the Concord and Merrimack Rivers, Walden; or Life in the Woods, The Maine Woods, Cape Cod* (New York: Library of America, 1985), 395.

12. Peck, *Thoreau's Morning Work*, 129.

13. Eigner, *Areas Lights Heights*, 125.

14. Larry Eigner, "What A Time Distance," in *Selected Poems*, by Larry Eigner, ed. Samuel Charters and Andrea Wyatt (Berkeley, CA: Oyez, 1972), 111–25. The actual genre of "What A Time Distance" is ambiguous. I call it a "story" because Eigner uses pseudonyms when referring to himself and his brothers in the narrative.

15. Eigner, *Areas Lights Heights*, 128.

16. Eigner, *Selected Poems*, 111, 112.

17. Eigner, *Selected Poems*, 116. Eigner's brother Richard summarizes the history of Twenty-Three Bates Road in the afterword to *The Collected Poems*: "During the years of Larry's boyhood—which were the years of the Depression—the neighborhood was settled by a colony of immigrants from Basilicata, one of the most impoverished and least known Italian provinces. . . . They built their own houses, most on double lots that left space for vegetable and flower gardens. After the War the incursion of suburbia filled what remained of the tract's vacant spaces. This process diminished but never supplanted—at least on his eyes and in his ears—the particularities of Larry's world" (*CP* 4:xxxv).

18. See *CP* 1:xxii; Eigner, *Areas Lights Heights*, 131.

19. Eigner, *Country Harbor Quiet Act Around: Selected Prose*, ed. Barrett Watten (Berkeley, CA: This Press, 1978), 158.

20. Eigner, 23, 24, 25.

21. Eigner, 35.

22. The section heading, "we must be animate, and walk // turn abruptly // the lines are irregular," is from *CP* 1:179.

23. Nicholas Royle, *Veering: A Theory of Literature* (Edinburgh: Edinburgh University Press, 2011), 2–3.

24. Jeffrey Jerome Cohen and Lowell Duckert, "Introduction: Welcome to the Whirled," in *Veer Ecology: A Companion for Environmental Thinking*, ed. Jeffrey Jerome Cohen and Lowell Duckert (Minneapolis: University of Minnesota Press, 2017), 2.

25. For a previous reading of this poem, see Hart, "Enough Defined," 168–70.

26. Jim Ferris, "The Enjambed Body: A Step toward a Crippled Poetics," *Georgia Review* 58, no. 2 (2004): 219 (emphasis in original).

27. Eigner, *Selected Poems*, 123.

28. Anne F. Harris, "Tend," in Cohen and Duckert, *Veer Ecology*, 393.

29. Timothy Morton, "Attune," Cohen and Duckert, *Veer Ecology*, 164; Morton's chapter from this collection has been incorporated into his *Being Ecological* (Cambridge: MIT Press, 2018).

30. Nicholas Royle, "Afterword: On the Veer," in Cohen and Duckert, *Veer Ecology*, 472.

31. Eigner, *Selected Poems*, 125.

32. Eigner, *Areas Lights Heights*, 68.

33. Karen Barad, *Meeting the Universe Halfway: Quantum Physics and the Entanglement of Matter and Meaning* (Durham, NC: Duke University Press, 2007), 170.

34. Eigner, *Areas Lights Heights*, 69.

35. The section heading, "and commonly parts of the world / are more than the absolute whole," is from *CP* 1:139.

36. Morton, *Humankind: Solidarity with Nonhuman People* (London: Verso, 2017), 70.

37. William James observes, "we see that in the time-world and the space-world alike the first known things are not elements, but combinations, not separate units,

but wholes already formed. The condition of *being* of the wholes may be the elements; but the condition of our *knowing* the elements is our having already felt the wholes as wholes." See James, *The Principles of Psychology*, vol. 1 (Boston: Henry Holt, 1910), 622.

38. Henri Lefebvre, *The Production of Space*, trans. Donald Nicholson-Smith (New York: Blackwell, 1991), 95–96. Eigner can be seen as practicing what Siobhan Phillips calls "the poetics of the everyday" or "ordinary poetics." She writes, "Anyone can pattern his or her life and work by diurnal time. . . . Ordinary poetics describes a pastoralism of habits rather than habitats. If environmental criticism has, rightly and usefully, often focused its theoretical efforts on a definition of place and space, environmental readings continue to demand new ways of describing the interrelations of nature and culture. Time, and daily time in particular, might prove a significant category in this effort"; see Phillips, *The Poetics of Everyday: Creative Repetition in Modern American Verse* (New York: Columbia University Press, 2010), 210.

39. Larry Eigner, "A light illness. . . . ," unpublished poem, Paul Blackburn Papers (MSS 4), box 37, folder 34, Special Collections and Archives, University of California, San Diego.

40. Morton, *Hyperobjects: Philosophy and Ecology after the End of the World* (Minneapolis: University of Minnesota Press, 2013), 81, 82, 83.

41. See Heidi Cullen, *The Weather of the Future: Heat Waves, Extreme Storms, and Other Scenes from a Climate-Changed Planet* (New York: HarperCollins, 2010), 8–10. Morton observes, "When the environment becomes intimate . . . it is decisively no longer an environment, since it no longer just happens around us: that's the difference between weather and climate." Timothy Morton, "Queer Ecology," *PMLA* 125, no. 2 (2010): 274.

42. Larry Eigner to Robert Creeley, August 1953, Robert Creeley Papers (M662), series 1, box 44, folder 18, Department of Special Collections, Stanford University Libraries.

43. Larry Eigner to Robert Creeley, June 18, 1952, Robert Creeley Papers (M662), series 1, box 44, folder 18, Department of Special Collections, Stanford University Libraries.

44. Larry Eigner to Robert Creeley, February 7, 1953, Robert Creeley Papers (M662), series 1, box 44, folder 19. The text of the poem looks like it is a carbon copy—with name and address included but not the date—and the text of the letter is in lighter type, so probably it was later typed directly onto the carbon of the poem with the salutation ("Dear Bob") and date ("Sunday Feb 7, '53") typed at top; a note on spacing begins immediately below the last line, canceled with pencil, and then the commentary appears. If Eigner had already sent the poem to Souster by February 7, 1953, then the composition date of the poem is likely prior to February and could possibly be August 1952. Along with the canceled last line, this version differs from that in *The Collected Poems* by its use of the article in the phrase "a shore."

45. I have found no evidence that Eigner had read *Prometheus Unbound* at this point in his life (or ever, for that matter), but it is possible that his title is an allusion to Shelley's verse drama. Toward the end of the first act, the Earth Mother calls forth "those subtle and fair spirits / Whose homes are the dim caves of human thought /

And who inhabit, as birds wing the wind, / Its world-surrounding ether" in order to "cheer [Prometheus's] state," Percy B. Shelley, *Prometheus Unbound*, in *Shelley's Poetry and Prose*, ed. Donald H. Reiman and Sharon B. Powers (New York: Norton, 1977), I.ll.657–58. After the spirits speak, Ione describes them as "twin nurslings of the all-sustaining air / on swift still wings glid[ing] down the atmosphere" (I.ll. 754–55). If Eigner's title is an allusion to Shelley's play, it would be a further instance of Eigner's early ecrippoetics. Karl Kroeber reads *Prometheus Unbound* as a central ecopoetic text: "Prometheus embodies self-consciousness as a natural phenomenon manifesting the emergence of culture from material nature," and he proposes that "if we can but properly imagine materialistically both 'mind' and 'nature,' we may hope to attain nontranscendent deconstructive reconstructions of cultural life for which the most beautiful of previous paradisal fantasies will seem faint and inadequate representations"; Kroeber, *Ecological Literary Criticism: Romantic Imagining and the Biology of Mind* (New York: Columbia University Press, 1994), 125, 133.

46. *CP* 2:286. Benjamin Friedlander has observed that as Eigner's life experience expanded in the 1960s (he took his first airplane trips, to the Midwest and West Coast, to visit his brothers), a corresponding expansion of his sense of the poetic space on the page occurred: "Eigner began more and more to explore the *syntactic* possibilities afforded by the new relation of the poem to space." See Friedlander, "Larry Eigner," in *American Poets Since World War II*, 6th ser., ed. Joseph Conte, vol. 193 of *Dictionary of Literary Biography* (Detroit, MI: Gale Research, 1998), 121.

47. See the diagram "Four Basic Shapes of the Projective Poem," included among the photographs in Paul Christensen, *Charles Olson: Call Him Ishmael* (Austin: University of Texas Press, 1979), n.p.

48. Eigner, *Areas Lights Heights*, 25–26.

49. Yi-Fu Tuan, *Space and Place: The Perspective of Experience* (Minneapolis: University of Minnesota Press, 1977), 170–71.

Chapter Two

Epigraph: Ralph Waldo Emerson, *Essays and Lectures* (New York: Library of America, 1983), 961.

1. Eliza Griswold, "How *Silent Spring* Ignited the Environmental Movement," *New York Times Magazine*, September 21, 2012.

2. Joshua Schuster, *The Ecology of Modernism: American Environments and Avant-Garde Poetics* (Tuscaloosa: University of Alabama Press, 2015), 134.

3. Schuster, *The Ecology of Modernism*, 134.

4. In fact, Eigner might be indicating a stylistic affinity with Carson. In *The Ecology of Modernism*, Schuster describes Carson's style: "Carson finds she must narrate using a twisty, jumpy, multi-layered prose just to keep up with how pesticides spread both slowly and quickly, with short and long term chemicals coursing through all levels of life from tiny cells to major organs," and he continues, "The narrator must track down multiple agents that can act at differing times, make sense of the ambiguity of numerous causal events, question some forms of scientific and political practice while validating others, and bring coherence to disparate materials, languages, and human

and nonhuman actors. It bears mentioning that these are indeed the same referential difficulties that modernist poetics thrive on" (136).

5. Larry Eigner to Cid Corman, September 14, 1962, Cid Corman Papers, Harry Ransom Center, University of Texas at Austin.

6. Larry Eigner to Denise Levertov, October 15, 1963, Denise Levertov Papers (M601), box 33, folder 9, Department of Special Collections, Stanford University Libraries.

7. Denise Levertov to Robert Duncan, December 11, 1957, collected in Robert J. Bertholf and Albert Gelpi, eds., *The Letters of Robert Duncan and Denise Levertov* (Stanford, CA: Stanford University Press, 2004), 87–88.

8. It is an intriguing fact that three of Eigner's early admirers, each of whom praised the clarity of his vision, were themselves visually impaired. Levertov mentions her nearsightedness here; Robert Duncan and Robert Creeley both suffered injuries early in life that resulted in impairment: a split visual field for Duncan and the loss of one eye for Creeley.

9. Larry Eigner to Denise Levertov, October 15, 1963, Denise Levertov Papers (M601), box 33, folder 9, Department of Special Collections, Stanford University Libraries.

10. Larry Eigner to Donald Allen, November 20, 1963, Donald Allen Papers (MSS 3), box 63, folder 18, Special Collections and Archives, University of California, San Diego.

11. Timothy Morton, *The Ecological Thought* (Cambridge, MA: Harvard University Press, 2010), 28.

12. Schuster, *The Ecology of Modernism*, 141.

13. This section heading, "my old machine / new like strange," is from *CP* 4:1387.

14. Quoted in Friedrich A. Kittler, *Gramophone, Film, Typewriter*, trans. Geoffrey Winthrop-Young and Michael Wutz (Stanford, CA: Stanford University Press, 1999), 199.

15. William Carlos Williams, *The Autobiography of William Carlos Williams* (New York: Random House, 1951), xiii–xiv.

16. William Carlos Williams, *The Collected Poems of William Carlos Williams*, vol. 2, *1939–1962*, ed. A. Walton Litz and Christopher MacGowan (New York: New Directions, 1988), 54.

17. Kittler, *Gramaphone, Film, Typewriter*, 210–11. Interestingly, Kittler also documents the historical association of typewriters and disability: "Hans Rasmus Johann Malling Hansen (1835–90), pastor and head of the royal Døvstummeinstitut in Copenhagen, developed his *skrivekugle* / writing ball / *sphere ècrivante* out of the observation that his deaf-mute patients' sign language was faster than handwriting. The machine 'did not take into account the needs of business' but rather was meant to compensate for physiological deficiencies and to increase writing speed. . . . According to Burghagen, this hemispheric arrangement of the keys had the advantage of allowing 'the blind, for whom this writing ball was primarily designed, to learn writing on it in a surprising short time' " (202).

18. J. Scott Bryson, ed., *Ecopoetry: A Critical Introduction* (Salt Lake City: University

of Utah Press, 2002), 6. In a twist on Heidegger, Wendell Berry rejects the computer as a means of composition because it makes his writing dependent on electricity produced by burning coal. In "Why I Am Not Going to Buy a Computer," he asks, "How could I write conscientiously against the rape of nature if I were, in the act of writing, implicated in the rape? For the same reason, it matters to me that my writing is done in the daytime, without electric light"; Berry, *What Are People For?* (Berkeley, CA: North Point Press, 1990), 170. Although he sees no "irruption" of the machine in the word when his wife then types his manuscripts, such a stance does seem based in an impossible purity. Timothy Morton explains such environmental choices as being based in hypocrisy; see Morton, *Hyperobjects: Philosophy and Ecology after the End of the World* (Minneapolis: University of Minnesota Press, 2013), 136.

19. Timothy Morton, "Ecology as Text, Text as Ecology," *Oxford Literary Review* 32, no. 1 (2010): 7.

20. X. J. Kennedy, rev. of *The New American Poetry*, ed. Donald Allen, *Poetry* 98, no. 4 (July 1961): 244. Charles Olson also referred to typewriters as machines in "Projective Verse": "It is time we picked the fruits of the experiments of Cummings, Pound, Williams, each of whom has, after his way, already used the machine as a scoring to his composing, as a script to its vocalization"; Olson, *The Collected Prose of Charles Olson*, ed. Donald Allen and Benjamin Friedlander (Berkeley: University of California Press, 1997), 245.

21. Galway Kinnell, rev. of *On My Eyes*, by Larry Eigner, *Poetry* 100, no. 6 (September 1962): 402. Raphael Allison echoes this critique in his discussion of Eigner's recorded readings: "The editors [of *The Collected Poems of Larry Eigner*] make a virtual fetish out of the typewriter's centrality to Eigner's work, including numerous references to his 1940 Royal typewriter in the preface. . . . They also draw on a term Eigner himself devised, referring to Eigner's 'typewriter calligraphy'"; Allison, *Bodies on the Line: Performance and the Sixties Poetry Reading* (Iowa City: University of Iowa Press, 2014), 176. Allison's *phonocentric* approach to Eigner is discussed in the introduction.

22. Larry Eigner to Paul Blackburn, July 9, 1961, Paul Blackburn Papers (MSS 4), box 37, folder 34, Special Collections and Archives, University of California, San Diego.

23. Allen Ginsberg's "To an Old Poet in Peru" appeared in the first issue (1960), and three of Eigner's poems, in English with German translations, were published in *Rhinozeros* 5 (1961). The entire run of *Rhinozeros* is available at Jed Birmingham, "*Rhinozeros* Archive," RealityStudio, July 9, 2012, http://realitystudio.org/bibliographic-bunker/rhinozeros/.

24. Larry Eigner to Paul Blackburn, July 9, 1961, Paul Blackburn Papers (MSS 4), box 37, folder 34, Special Collections and Archives, University of California, San Diego. Eigner also refers to beginnings as "stentorian" in a 1961 letter published in *Poet and Critic* and reprinted in Eigner, *Areas Lights Heights: Selected Writings 1954–1989*, ed. Benjamin Friedlander (New York: Roof Books, 1989), 16. The "comment" Eigner mentions is likely from the paper "A Feeling of Eternity: Larry Eigner: The Man and His Poetry," by Joan Avioli, held in Larry Eigner Papers (M0902), box 24, folder 7, Department of Special Collections, Stanford University Libraries.

25. Morton, *Hyperobjects*, 130.

26. Morton, *The Ecological Thought*, 33.

27. In a twist on Kinnell's anti-mechanistic organicism, Eigner writes to his friends Todd and Maria Gitin in August 1970, "I do like to think, '. . .organism. . .' wher W C W said '. . .machine. . .'" Larry Eigner Papers (MSS 1974-0001), Archives and Special Collections at the Thomas J. Dodd Research Center, University of Connecticut Library.

28. David Schneider, *Crowded by Beauty: The Life and Zen of Poet Philip Whalen* (Berkeley: University of California Press, 2015), 94.

29. *American Heritage Dictionary*, 3rd ed., s.v. "hat" and "bureau."

30. For a related examination of Eigner's "mediascape" in the 1960s and early 1970s, see Lytle Shaw, *Narrowcast: Poetry and Audio Research* (Stanford, CA: Stanford University Press, 2018).

31. Jonathan Skinner, "What Sounds: Larry Eigner's Environments," in *Momentous Inconclusions: The Life and Work of Larry Eigner*, ed. Jennifer Bartlett and George Hart (Albuquerque: University of New Mexico Press, 2020), 190. The section heading, "it takes imagination / to supplement / the water," is from *CP* 2:611.

32. Skinner, "What Sounds," 180.

33. For a comparison of Ammons and Eigner, see George Hart, "Walking the Walk: Ammons, Eigner, and Ecopoetic Form in the 1960s," *ISLE: Interdisciplinary Studies in Literature and Environment* 24, no. 4 (2018): 680–706.

34. Skinner, "What Sounds," 179.

35. Andrew Rippeon, ed., *Letters to Jargon: The Correspondence between Larry Eigner and Jonathan Williams* (Tuscaloosa: University of Alabama Press, 2019), 128.

36. Michael Davidson, *Concerto for the Left Hand: Disability and the Defamiliar Body* (Ann Arbor: University of Michigan Press, 2008), 128.

37. Rachel Carson, *The Sea around Us* (Oxford: Oxford University Press, 1951), 95–96.

38. Carson, 93, 96.

39. Carson, 96.

40. Ursula Heise, *Imagining Extinction: The Cultural Meanings of Endangered Species* (Chicago: University of Chicago Press, 2016), 48.

41. Carson, *The Sea around Us*, 151.

42. Carson, 40.

43. Carson, 45, 49–50. This interpretation does not exhaust the references to Carson's book in this poem. Others that I can detect, but don't have room for in this reading, include the mention of spiders settling the islands, as described by Carson earlier, in "The Birth of an Island" (90). Eigner's lines "rock crumbles to earth / under rain / the seas" also might refer to a quote from Algernon Charles Swinburne that Carson uses as the epigraph for the next chapter: "Till the slow Sea rise and the sheer cliff crumble, / Till terrace and meadow the deep gulfs drink" (97). This quote might also inform the poem's paratextual note that Eigner's slow poem corresponds to the slow sea.

44. Henry David Thoreau, *A Week on the Concord and Merrimack Rivers, Walden; or Life in the Woods, The Maine Woods, Cape Cod* (New York: Library of America, 1985), 34.

45. Andrew Rippeon's transcription of Eigner's letter to Williams includes additional lines that appear to conclude this poem: "beat against the night // quiet nevertheless / as the sea-wall // 'these simple sounds relate us to the stars' // no other / fit medium // the remoteness a reflecting // music / is half a drum // the poem is a pool." Rippeon identifies the quotation as coming from the "Monday" chapter of Thoreau's *A Week on the Concord and Merrimack Rivers*; see Rippeon, *Letters to Jargon*, 129, 277.

46. Rippeon, 128.

47. Thoreau, *A Week on the Concord and Merrimack Rivers*, 34.

48. Thoreau, 35 (emphasis in original).

49. As with the poem drawn from *The Sea around Us*, there are more citations of *A Week on the Concord and Merrimack Rivers* in this poem than I can fit into this reading. For example, the lines "no torrent slight / tilt of this river" refer to Thoreau's description of the Concord River: "Concord River is remarkable for the gentleness of its current. . . . I have read that a descent of an eighth of an inch is sufficient to produce a flow. Our river has, probably, very near the smallest allowance." Thoreau, 143.

50. Larry Eigner to Cid Corman, April 19, 1965, Cid Corman Papers, Harry Ransom Center, University of Texas at Austin.

51. Font size reduced to reproduce Eigner's typing exactly.

52. Rachel Carson, *Under the Sea Wind: A Naturalist's Picture of Ocean Life* (Oxford: Oxford University Press, 1952), 111. In June 1965, Eigner was still thinking about his reading of Carson and the bird book: "the birds expand / the neighborhood / however many / they once broke trees" (*CP* 2:644).

53. Gilbert T Pearson, ed., *Birds of America*, vol. 2 (New York: University Society, 1923), 45.

54. Ursula Heise observes that the passenger pigeon is "the species most often mentioned in discussions about extinction in the United States"; see Heise, *Imagining Extinction*, 43.

55. The section heading, "But if you don't fly, you can't come to a value of the earth," is Eigner's note on a copy of "i sneeze" (*CP* 2:528), sent to LeRoi Jones, Amiri Baraka Papers (Collection 491), Library Special Collections, Charles E. Young Research Library, University of California, Los Angeles.

56. Olson, *The Collected Prose of Charles Olson*, 306–7 (emphasis in original).

57. For example, writing to his sister-in-law Janet in July 1963, Eigner remarked, "This brings to mind Lectures given at Black Mtn College by Olson (I have specially unmanageable photostats on left/right curly paper)." Olson's *The Special View of History*, ed. Ann Charters (Berkeley, CA: Oyez, 1970), is the "photostat" he was likely trying to read. Larry Eigner to Janet Eigner, July 2, 1963, Larry Eigner Papers (M0902), Department of Special Collections, Stanford University Libraries.

58. For a more detailed account of Eigner's Civil War poems, see George Hart, "'My Nose on the Ground': Larry Eigner's Civil War," in Bartlett and Hart, *Momentous Inconclusions*, 49–68. Portions of that contribution have been incorporated into this chapter.

59. Larry Eigner to Cid Corman, February 11, 1960, Cid Corman Papers, Harry Ransom Center, University of Texas at Austin.

60. Larry Eigner to Cid Corman, January 4, 1965, Cid Corman Papers, Harry Ransom Center, University of Texas at Austin.

61. Larry Eigner to Hettie Cohen, April 29, 1966, Amiri Baraka Papers (Collection 491), Library Special Collections, Charles E. Young Research Library, University of California, Los Angeles.

62. Eigner was concerned about the safety of air travel for a while. In a letter to Corman written just before his surgery, he says, "In fact I've bn thinking this brn-operation is less risky thn flying, and may be like having a tooth pulled, sort of—but come to think of it i still have all my teeth (some of em patched up to be sure), while i lost some brains in '41"; Larry Eigner to Cid Corman, September 14, 1962, Cid Corman Papers, Harry Ransom Center, University of Texas at Austin.

63. "Freedom in the Air" was the first song featured on Radio New York's *Folk Music Worldwide* program on civil rights movement songs, broadcast on August 10, 17, and 20, 1963. As a voracious consumer of educational programs on television and radio, Eigner may have heard the song through this shortwave radio program. See "Civil Rights Movement Songs with Tom Murray of SNCC," *Folk Music Worldwide*, August 10, 17, and 20, 1963, http://folkmusicworldwide.com/sncc-civil-rights-songs-1.html.

64. Larry Eigner, "Letters to the Editor, 1963–69," *PMLA* 131, no. 3 (2016): 782.

65. Walt Whitman, *Complete Poetry and Collected Prose* (New York: Library of America, 1982), 764.

66. Eigner, "Letters to the Editor," 782.

67. Eigner, 784.

Chapter Three

Epigraph: Ralph Waldo Emerson, *Essays and Lectures* (New York: Library of America, 1983), 481–82.

1. Aldo Leopold, *A Sand County Almanac* (Oxford: Oxford University Press, 1949), 224.

2. Raphael Allison, *Bodies on the Line: Performance and the Sixties Poetry Reading* (Iowa City: University of Iowa Press, 2014), xv. Allison includes a chapter on the recorded readings of Eigner and William Carlos Williams. See the introduction for a discussion of his work on Eigner.

3. Larry Eigner, *Areas Lights Heights: Selected Writings 1954–1989*, ed. Benjamin Friedlander (New York: Roof Books, 1989), 162, 163.

4. Eigner, 114.

5. Benjamin Friedlander, note to Larry Eigner, "Unpublished Letter to Ina Forster," *Passages* 5 (April 1998), http://writing.upenn.edu/epc/ezines/passages/passages5/forster.html.

6. Bill McKibben, *Enough: Staying Human in an Engineered Age* (New York: Times Books / Henry Holt, 2003), 210.

7. McKibben, 222.

8. Timothy Morton, *The Ecological Thought* (Cambridge, MA: Harvard University Press, 2010), 120.

9. The section heading, "Copies will flood me frm Kansas maybe in no time," is from a letter that Larry Eigner sent to Joe and Janet Eigner, December 10, 1970, Larry Eigner Papers (M0902), box 21, folder 3, Department of Special Collections, Stanford University Libraries.

10. Edwin M. Eigner was the author of *Robert Louis Stevenson and the Romantic Tradition* (Princeton, NJ: Princeton University Press, 1966). The repository was established in August 1965; see *CP* 1:xiv.

11. Larry Eigner to Robert Duncan, December 29, 1969, Robert Duncan Papers (PCMS-0110), Poetry Collection of the University Libraries, University at Buffalo, State University of New York.

12. Larry Eigner to Alexandra Mason, July 20, 1971, Larry Eigner Papers (MS 39), box 17, folder 18, Kenneth Spencer Research Library, University of Kansas.

13. Larry Eigner to Ian Tyson, November 19, 1970, Ian Tyson Collection (MSS 0413), box 1, folder 3, Special Collections and Archives, University of California, San Diego.

14. Joseph H. Hertz, ed., *The Pentateuch and Haftorahs: Hebrew Text, English Translation, and Commentary*, vol. 1 (Oxford: Soncino Press, 1928), 6–7.

15. Hertz, 1:2. Eigner's interest in the names of God connects him to Jewish mysticism: "Jewish magic has frequently employed phrases from the Bible to invoke God's protection or help. Names in particular could conjure up power, and by the Middle Ages all words, all incantations, were understood as names capable of calling forth and unleashing forces on earth"; Ruth Gruber Fredman, *The Passover Seder: Afrikoman in Exile* (Philadelphia: University of Pennsylvania Press, 1981), 99.

16. Larry Eigner to George Butterick, June 4, 1974, George Butterick Papers (PCMS-0118), Poetry Collection of the University Libraries, University at Buffalo, State University of New York. In the parenthetical aside where I have placed the second set of ellipses, Eigner gives a more complete account of how he acquired the Hertz Chumash:

> (copies in the hands of all the congregation, no such book hereabts in the 30s when I was a kid and went to hbrew school in the vestry of temple and at times upstairs into pews with bookracks, while f Beth El in Lynn mother knew a word for hebrew/vernacular annotated text all along, chumesh, the word she spoke when I talked of it after she brought it to me sitting in the lobby of the Marblehead Temple as I didnt feel up to attending the service, never absorbing in the mouths of businessmen, I get unease anyway)

Eigner adds a note in the margin with further information:

> A cousin-in-law, at some time Pres of this temple, sent my mother to me with the bk open to whr Noah boards the Ark, the kid's passage, portion, sedrah. I took it home, allowed to borrow it - and a week later, just as Dad was nosing his chevvy out of our driveway to return it, a mail-truck brought me a new copy, a surprise gift from my proselytizing relation, who advised me to take it all in little by little over about 2 yrs

Eigner also mentions his encounter with the Chumash, and its link to "The closed system," in *Areas Lights Heights*, 13.

17. Hertz, *The Pentateuch and Haftorahs*, 1:215 (emphasis in original).

18. Likely quoting from memory, Eigner actually corrects a typo that Olson kept in the final version of this poem. The published lines (complete with unclosed parenthesis) read, "the thing you're after / may lie around the bend / of the nest (second, time slain, the bird! the bird!" Charles Olson, *The Maximus Poems*, ed. George Butterick (Berkeley: University of California Press, 1983), 5. See Tom Clark's biography of Olson for the composition history of this poem; Clark, *Charles Olson: The Allegory of a Poet's Life* (New York: W. W. Norton, 1991), 166.

19. Larry Eigner to George Butterick, June 4, 1974, George Butterick Papers (PCMS-0118), Poetry Collection of the University Libraries, University at Buffalo, State University of New York.

20. Alvin Toffler, *Future Shock* (New York: Random House, 1970), 28.

21. Toffler, 30–31 (emphasis in original).

22. Larry Eigner to Alexandra Mason, July 20, 1971, Larry Eigner Papers (MS 39), box 17, folder 18, Kenneth Spencer Research Library, University of Kansas.

23. Hertz, *The Pentateuch and Haftorahs*, 1:29 (emphasis in original). For the discussion of Eigner's cousin's bar mitzvah, see note 16 in this chapter.

24. Hertz, 1:7.

25. Larry Eigner to Douglas Calhoun, September 11, 1970, *Athanor* Collection (PCMS-0003), box 26, folder 14, Poetry Collection of the University Libraries, University at Buffalo, State University of New York.

26. Larry Eigner to Allen De Loach, August 25, 1970, *Intrepid* Collection (PCMS-0005), box 21, folder 1, Poetry Collection of the University Libraries, University at Buffalo, State University of New York.

27. Larry Eigner to Douglas Calhoun, September 23, 1970, *Athanor* Collection (PCMS-0003), box 26, folder 15, Poetry Collection of the University Libraries, University at Buffalo, State University of New York.

28. Eigner describes such devices in a letter to Denise Levertov, October 15, 1963, Denise Levertov Papers (M601), series 4, box 33, folder 9, Department of Special Collections, Stanford University Libraries.

29. The section heading here is taken from a letter that Larry Eigner sent to Robert Duncan, December 29, 1969, Robert Duncan Papers (PCMS-0110), Poetry Collection of the University Libraries, University at Buffalo, State University of New York.

30. Larry Eigner to George Butterick, June 4, 1974, George Butterick Papers (PCMS-0118), Poetry Collection of the University Libraries, University at Buffalo, State University of New York; *CP* 3:1161.

31. Larry Eigner to Robert Duncan, December 29, 1969, Robert Duncan Papers (PCMS-0110), Poetry Collection of the University Libraries, University at Buffalo, State University of New York.

32. Hertz, *The Pentateuch and Haftorahs*, 1:595–96; Num. 24–26.

33. Robert Duncan, *The Years as Catches, First Poems (1939–1946)* (Berkeley, CA: Oyez, 1966), ii.

34. Larry Eigner to Robert Duncan, December 29, 1969, Robert Duncan Papers (PCMS-0110), Poetry Collection of the University Libraries, University at Buffalo, State University of New York.

35. Larry Eigner to Joseph and Janet Eigner, October 11, 1969, Larry Eigner Papers (MS 39), box 16, folder 25, Kenneth Spencer Research Library, University of Kansas.

36. Olson, *The Maximus Poems*, 168.

37. Robert Vas Dias, ed., *Inside Outer Space: New Poems of the Space Age* (New York: Doubleday, 1970), xxxiii–xxxiv.

38. Vas Dias, ix, 300.

39. Vas Dias, xxxviii.

40. Vas Dias, xxxiv.

41. Vas Dias, xxxvi.

42. Vas Dias, xxxvi–xxxvii; and see p. 75.

43. Ursula Heise, *Sense of Place and Sense of Planet: The Environmental Imagination of the Global* (Oxford: Oxford University Press, 2008), 22.

44. Timothy Clark, *Ecocriticism on the Edge: The Anthropocene as a Threshold Concept* (London: Bloomsbury, 2015), 31.

45. Clark, 33, 34 (emphasis in original).

46. Clark, 33.

47. Clark, 40.

48. Timothy Morton, *Dark Ecology: For a Logic of Future Coexistence* (New York: Columbia University Press, 2015), 25.

49. Morton, 25.

50. The section heading here is from a letter that Larry Eigner wrote to the editors of *WIN*, 1972. Jackson Mac Low Papers (MSS 180), box 14, folder 16, Special Collections and Archives, University of California, San Diego.

51. Adam Rome, "'Give Earth a Chance': The Environmental Movement and the Sixties," *Journal of American History* 90, no. 2 (2003): 546, 547.

52. Stephanie LeMenager, *Living Oil: Petroleum Culture in the American Century* (Oxford: Oxford University Press, 2014), 24.

53. LeMenager, 23. Adam Rome also associates grassroots activism, especially by women, with the Santa Barbara oil spill: "After the Santa Barbara, California, oil spill in 1969, women were the driving force behind Get Oil Out (GOO), a grass-roots group that sought to end offshore drilling. . . . No matter what the issue, environmentalism at the grass roots depended on a volunteer corps of women"; Rome, "'Give Earth a Chance,'" 537.

54. LeMenager, *Living Oil*, 25. "Slow violence" is a term coined by Rob Nixon. He writes, "By slow violence I mean a violence that occurs gradually and out of sight, a violence of delayed destruction that is dispersed across time and space, an attritional violence that is typically not viewed as violence at all"; Nixon, *Slow Violence and the Environmentalism of the Poor* (Cambridge, MA: Harvard University Press, 2011), 2.

55. Rome, "'Give Earth a Chance,'" 543.

56. Prominent examples of such action include Allen Ginsberg's participation in "levitating" the Pentagon in 1967 and Gary Snyder's and Michael McClure's attendance

at the United Nations' 1972 conference on the environment in Stockholm, Sweden.

57. Snyder's list includes "Michael McClure, Richard Brautigan, Steve Beckwitt, Keith Lampe, Cliff Humphreys, Alan Watts, Allen Hoffman, Stewart Brand, and Diane de [*sic*] Prima"; Gary Snyder, "Four Changes," in *Turtle Island* (New York: New Directions, 1974), 91.

58. Larry Eigner to Jackson Mac Low, March 31, 1970, Jackson Mac Low Papers (MSS 180), box 14, folder 16, Special Collections and Archives, University of California, San Diego; a full transcription of this letter can be found in Jennifer Bartlett and George Hart, eds., *Momentous Inconclusions: The Life and Work of Larry Eigner* (Albuquerque: University of New Mexico Press, 2020), 251–53. Eigner's comment regarding "Earth Read Out" indicates his awareness of the emerging radical ecology movement on the West Coast. In an examination of the underground papers the *Berkeley Barb* and the *Berkeley Tribe*, which featured the journalism of Keith Lampe, environmental historian Keith M. Woodhouse has shown that the People's Park protest in Berkeley, California, is one of the emergence points for this activism. Woodhouse writes, "Lampe, a one-time instructor at Queens College who moved to California to write for the underground press, had already been reporting about the ecology movement before People's Park. After the Berkeley showdown, he started a column called 'Earth Read-Out.' . . . Earth Read-Out ran in many of the most widely read alternative newspapers, and Lampe became an authority on environmental activism for the radical left." Woodhouse, "The Politics of Ecology: Environmentalism and Liberalism in the 1960s," *Journal for the Study of Radicalism* 2, no. 2 (2008): 72.

59. Eigner, "Integration Interchange," in Eigner, *Areas Lights Heights*, 43–44. The article Eigner mentions is "Pollution by Fertilizer" in *Scientific American* 220, no. 3 (March 1969): 47.

60. Larry Eigner to George Butterick, November 6, 1974, George Butterick Papers (PCMS-0118), Poetry Collection of the University Libraries, University at Buffalo, State University of New York.

61. The fourth issue that Snyder names in his "Four Changes" is "Transformation."

62. Larry Eigner, "Letters to the Editor, 1963–69," *PMLA* 131, no. 3 (2016): 785.

63. Eigner, 785; Eigner, *Areas Lights Heights*, 44.

64. Fredman, *The Passover Seder*, 152.

65. Fredman, 137.

66. Larry Eigner to Joseph and Janet Eigner, October 11, 1969, Larry Eigner Papers (MS 39), box 16, folder 25, Kenneth Spencer Research Library, University of Kansas.

67. Snyder, "Four Changes," 100, 93.

68. Rome, "'Give Earth a Chance,'" 543, 548.

69. Draft letter, Larry Eigner Papers (MS 39), box 17, folder 21, Kenneth Spencer Research Library, University of Kansas.

70. The typographically playful "disease" is hard to interpret. As noted above, Eigner had been reading Duncan's introduction to *The Years as Catches* in late 1969, and he may have in mind Duncan's statement, "I saw the State and the War as diseases" (vii).

71. Eigner, *Areas Lights Heights*, 163; Larry Eigner, *Windows / Walls / Yard / Ways*, ed. Robert Grenier (Santa Rosa, CA: Black Sparrow Press, 1994), n.p. The section title

here is from a letter that Larry Eigner sent to George Butterick, June 4, 1974, George Butterick Papers (PCMS-0118), Poetry Collection of the University Libraries, University at Buffalo, State University of New York; a full transcription of this letter can be found in Bartlett and Hart, *Momentous Inconclusions*, 257–64 (this citation includes corrections).

72. This issue also contained two of Eigner's poems about Charles Olson and a letter about Olson written to George Butterick, all of which have been reprinted in Eigner, *Areas Lights Heights*, 106–13.

73. Larry Eigner to Douglas Calhoun, May 5, 1971, *Athanor* Collection (PCMS-003), box 26, folder 2, Poetry Collection of the University Libraries, University at Buffalo, State University of New York.

74. T. S. Eliot, *The Waste Land*, in *American Poetry: The Twentieth Century*, vol. 1, *Henry Adams to Dorothy Parker*, ed. Carolyn Kizer et al. (New York: Library of America, 2000), 755.

75. Fredman, *The Passover Seder*, 23.

76. Morton, *Dark Ecology*, 87–88.

77. Fredman, *The Passover Seder*, 83–84.

78. Morton, *The Ecological Thought*, 82.

79. Fredman, *The Passover Seder*, 19. "'Dayenu' means approximately 'it would have been enough for us,' 'it would have been sufficient,' or 'it would have sufficed' (*day* in Hebrew is 'enough,' and *-enu* the first person plural suffix, 'to us')"; Wikipedia, "Dayenu," last edited January 27, 2021, https://en.wikipedia.org/wiki/Dayenu.

80. Eigner, *Areas Lights Heights*, 125, 126.

Chapter Four

Epigraph: Charles Olson, *The Collected Prose of Charles Olson*, ed. Donald Allen and Benjamin Friedlander (Berkeley: University of California Press, 1997), 248.

1. Eigner, postcard, January 2, 1986, Larry Eigner Papers (MS 39), box 17, folder 30, Kenneth Spencer Research Library, University of Kansas.

2. Robert Creeley, rev. of *In the American Tree*, ed. Ron Silliman, *San Francisco Chronicle*, September 28, 1986.

3. Larry Eigner, *Areas Lights Heights: Selected Writings 1954–1989*, ed. Benjamin Friedlander (New York: Roof Books, 1989), 120–21.

4. Dorceta E. Taylor, *The Rise of the American Conservation Movement: Power, Privilege, and Environmental Protection* (Durham, NC: Duke University Press, 2016), 30.

5. Tom Beckett and Earel Neikirk, eds., *Difficulties* 1, no. 1 (1980): n.p.

6. Eigner, *Areas Lights Heights*, 10.

7. Matthew Hofer and Michael Golston, eds., *The L=A=N=G=U=A=G=E Letters: Selected 1970s Correspondence of Bruce Andrews, Charles Bernstein, and Ron Silliman* (Albuquerque: University of New Mexico Press, 2019), 7.

8. Robert Grenier, "On Speech," *This*, no. 1 (1971): 86–87, reprinted in *In the American Tree*, ed. Ron Silliman (Orono, ME: National Poetry Foundation, 2002), 477–78. *This* was edited by Grenier and Barrett Watten.

9. Hofer and Golston, *The L=A=N=G=U=A=G=E Letters*, 4.

10. Grenier, "On Speech," in Silliman, *In the American Tree*, 477.

11. Albert Gelpi, *American Poetry after Modernism: The Power of the Word* (Cambridge: Cambridge University Press, 2015), 243.

12. The section heading is from *CP* 3:1145.

13. Ron Silliman, "Surprised by Sign (Notes on Nine)," *Alcheringa*, n.s., 1, no. 2 (1975): 119.

14. Robert Creeley, *A Quick Graph: Collected Notes and Essays* (San Francisco: Four Seasons, 1970), 54.

15. Silliman derives his title from Roland Barthes's account of "the Word" in *Writing Degree Zero*. In a letter to Bruce Andrews, dated December 6, 1971, Silliman copies a long quote from Barthes, which includes the following: "in modern poetry, connections are only an extension of the word, it is the Word which is 'the dwelling place' "; Hofer and Golston, *The L=A=N=G=U=A=G=E Letters*, 35.

16. Charles Olson, *Causal Mythology* (San Francisco: Four Seasons Foundation, 1969), 1, 2.

17. Creeley, *A Quick Graph*, 53–54.

18. Creeley, 54.

19. Stephen Fredman, *The Grounding of American Poetry: Charles Olson and the Emersonian Tradition* (Cambridge: Cambridge University Press, 1993), 63, 64.

20. In a letter to George Butterick, Eigner identifies the *Earth Ship* "preface" as the second of such statements: "I used to more or less question what's the good of theory, e.g. prosody. A few in/hindsights I've had along the way, like maybe you've seen the statement I wrote in 64 for Rbt Kelly and Paris Leary's 1965 anthology *A Controversy Of Poets*, which may be the first time I wrote down anything like a treatise except for remarks in letters [. . .] second time I guess in Dec or Nov 71, intro I did for a solo issue EARTH SHIP." Larry Eigner to Butterick, November 6, 1974, George Butterick Papers (PCMS-0118), Poetry Collection of the University Libraries, University at Buffalo, State University of New York.

21. Eigner, *Areas Lights Heights*, 47 (emphasis in Eigner).

22. Creeley, *A Quick Graph*, 152.

23. Eigner, *Areas Lights Heights*, 47.

24. On "thinking big," see Timothy Morton, *The Ecological Thought* (Cambridge, MA: Harvard University Press, 2010), 20–58; for the idea of "Earth magnitude," see Timothy Morton, *Dark Ecology: For a Logic of Future Coexistence* (New York: Columbia University Press, 2015), 24–27.

25. Eigner, *Areas Lights Heights*, 47 (italics in original).

26. Richard Poirier, *Poetry and Pragmatism* (Cambridge, MA: Harvard University Press, 1992), 86.

27. Eigner, *Areas Lights Heights*, 47–48.

28. As the Language writers were brainstorming names for their approach to poetry, one possibility was "new thing." Bruce Andrews writes, "OK: In 'New Thing Poetry' or whatever ~~you~~ i call it, there's no real Establishment, made up of older accepted poets"; Hofer and Golston, *The L=A=N=G=U=A=G=E Letters*, 102.

29. Eigner, *Areas Lights Heights*, 48 (ellipsis in original).

30. Comparing poetic production to industrial production is something Eigner had thought about for a long time. In a letter to Cid Corman, he writes, "The greed for community, beyond need of it, and if the oceans of poetry get big enough how should it be different from oceans of cars?" Larry Eigner to Corman, January 26, 1959, Henry W. and Albert A. Berg Collection, New York Public Library.

31. Larry Eigner, letter addressed to "Dear Folks," May 15, 1972, Larry Eigner Papers (M0902), box 21, folder 3, Department of Special Collections, Stanford University Libraries.

32. Eigner, "Dear Folks."

33. Larry Eigner to Robert Grenier, December 19, 1971, Larry Eigner Papers (MS 39), box 16, folder 13, Kenneth Spencer Research Library, University of Kansas.

34. *American Heritage Dictionary*, 3rd ed., s.v. "continuous."

35. Irving P. Leif, *Larry Eigner: A Bibliography of His Works* (Metuchen, NJ: Scarecrow Press, 1989), 30.

36. Larry Eigner to Cid Corman, February 21, 1962, Cid Corman Papers, Harry Ransom Center, University of Texas at Austin.

37. Paris Leary and Robert Kelly, eds., *A Controversy of Poets* (New York: Doubleday, 1965), 528–29, reprinted as "Method from Happenstance" in Eigner, *Areas Lights Heights*, 6.

38. The section heading is from *CP* 3:1191.

39. Jacques Derrida, *Of Grammatology*, trans. Gayatri Chakravorty Spivak, 40th anniversary ed. (Baltimore, MD: Johns Hopkins University Press, 2016), 76.

40. Ron Silliman to Bruce Andrews, December 26, 1971, collected in Hofer and Golston, *The L=A=N=G=U=A=G=E Letters*, 52.

41. Robert Grenier, "Three Possibilities—for Larry Eigner," in Hofer and Golston, 359.

42. Olson, *The Collected Prose of Charles Olson*, 239.

43. Olson, 246.

44. *American Heritage Dictionary*, 3rd ed., s.v. "composition" and "register."

45. Tom Clark, *Charles Olson: The Allegory of a Poet's Life* (New York: W. W. Norton, 1991), 161.

46. Charles Olson to Robert Giroux, June 16, 1950, collected in Charles Olson, *Selected Letters*, ed. Ralph Maud (Berkeley: University of California Press, 2000), 117.

47. Quoted in George F. Butterick, *A Guide to the Maximus Poems of Charles Olson* (Berkeley: University of California Press, 1981), xxxix (emphasis in original).

48. Quoted in Derrida, *Of Grammatology*, 71.

49. Derrida, 75.

50. Silliman, "Surprised by Sign (Notes on Nine)," 119.

51. Larry Eigner to Janet Eigner, July 2, 1963, Larry Eigner Papers (M0902), box 21, folder 3, Department of Special Collections, Stanford University Libraries; this letter is published in Jennifer Bartlett and George Hart, eds., *Momentous Inconclusions: The Life and Work of Larry Eigner* (Albuquerque: University of New Mexico Press, 2020), 227–35.

52. Eigner plays on the word *passive* in a letter to the editors of *El corno emplu-*

mado, dated December 29, 1966: "But I've been rather a passivist, as well as a pacifist, the past few years"; *El Cornado Emplumado* Papers, Harry Ransom Center, University of Texas at Austin.

53. Derrida, *Of Grammatology*, 75; I have omitted the French terms enclosed in brackets in this quotation.

54. Raphael Allison, *Bodies on the Line: Performance and the Sixties Poetry Reading* (Iowa City: University of Iowa Press, 2014), 177, 178, 176. The section heading here is from a letter that Larry Eigner wrote to Charles Bernstein, September 15, 1989, Charles Bernstein Papers (MSS 0519), Special Collections and Archives, University of California, San Diego.

55. Larry Eigner to Charles Bernstein, September 15, 1989, Charles Bernstein Papers (MSS 0519), Special Collections and Archives, University of California, San Diego.

56. Larry Eigner, letter to the editors of *El corno emplumado*, December 29, 1966; *El coronado emplumado* Papers, Harry Ransom Center, University of Texas at Austin.

57. The ambiguous nature of intention in Eigner is compounded by the fact that he sometimes let printers' errors stand. Writing to Joe and Janet Eigner about his poem "the music, the rooms," he tells them that "in the page proofs to [my *Selected Poems*] it looked at least as well with every line a stanza, ie. A double line-break after each line, so I left it that way." Letter dated February 2, 1974, Larry Eigner Papers (M0902), box 21, folder 3, Department of Special Collections, Stanford University Libraries.

58. Eigner, *Areas Lights Heights*, 47 (emphasis in Eigner). The section heading, "what kind of poetry is / a horizontal line," is from *CP* 3:1172.

59. See, for example, Paul Fussell, *Poetic Meter and Poetic Form*, rev. ed. (New York: McGraw-Hill, 1979), 12.

60. Marjorie Perloff, *Poetic License: Essays on Modernist and Postmodernist Lyric* (Evanston, IL: Northwestern University Press, 1990), 126, 127.

61. Letter to Janet Eigner, July 2, 1963, Larry Eigner Papers (M0902), box 21, folder 3, Department of Special Collections, Stanford University Libraries.

62. Eigner, *Areas Lights Heights*, 6.

63. Letter to Janet Eigner, July 2, 1963, Larry Eigner Papers (M0902), box 21, folder 3, Department of Special Collections, Stanford University Libraries.

64. Derrida, *Of Grammatology*, 74.

65. *American Heritage Dictionary*, 3rd ed., s.v. "drift."

66. Morton, *The Ecological Thought*, 106.

67. Morton, 11; the "ecological-ness" of form is also discussed in the introduction.

68. Morton, 11 (emphasis in original); Timothy Morton, "An Object-Oriented Defense of Poetry," *New Literary History* 43, no. 2 (2012): 219.

69. Timothy Morton, *Humankind: Solidarity with Nonhuman People* (London: Verso, 2017), 116.

70. Morton, 116.

71. The section heading is from Eigner, *Areas Lights Heights*, 22.

72. Robert Vas Dias, *Inside Outer Space: New Poems of the Space Age* (New York: Doubleday, 1970), xxxiv.

73. Larry Eigner to David and Maria Gitin, August 27, 1970, Larry Eigner Papers (MSS 1974-0001), Archives and Special Collections, Thomas J. Dodd Research Center, University of Connecticut Library.

74. Morton, *Dark Ecology*, 115.

75. *American Heritage Dictionary*, 3rd ed., s.v. "glimmer" and "shimmer."

76. Wallace Stevens, "The Idea of Order at Key West," in *American Poetry: The Twentieth Century*, vol. 1, *Henry Adams to Dorothy Parker*, ed. Carolyn Kizer et al. (New York: Library of America, 2000), 310–11.

77. Morton, *Dark Ecology*, 82 (emphasis in original).

78. J. Hillis Miller, "The Critic as Host," *Critical Inquiry* 3, no. 3 (1977): 441.

79. Steve McCaffery, "Language Writing," in *The Cambridge Companion to American Poetry since 1945*, ed. Jennifer Ashton (Cambridge: Cambridge University Press, 2013), 143.

80. Derrida, *Of Grammatology*, 7; Larry Eigner, "Twenty-One Poems and an Interview," *Kaleidoscope*, Spring 1982, 13.

81. Miller, "The Critic as Host," 441.

82. Morton, *Dark Ecology*, 50.

83. Morton, *Humankind*, 123.

84. Morton, *Dark Ecology*, 108 (emphasis in original).

85. Morton, 109.

Chapter Five

Epigraph: Timothy Morton, *Hyperobjects: Philosophy and Ecology after the End of the World* (Minneapolis: University of Minnesota Press, 2013), 50.

1. Bill McKibben, *The End of Nature* (New York: Doubleday, 1989), excerpted in the *New Yorker*, September 11, 1989.

2. Timothy Morton, "Ecologocentrism: Unworking Animals," *SubStance* 37, no. 3 (2008): 92.

3. Larry Eigner, *Areas Lights Heights: Selected Writings 1954–1989*, ed. Benjamin Friedlander (New York: Roof Books, 1989), 128.

4. Robert Grenier, afterword to *Readiness / Enough / Depends / On*, by Larry Eigner, ed. Robert Grenier (Los Angeles: Green Integer, 2000), n.p. (emphasis in original); T. S. Eliot, "Ash-Wednesday," in *American Poetry: The Twentieth Century*, vol. 1, *Henry Adams to Dorothy Parker*, ed. Carolyn Kizer et al. (New York: Library of America, 2000), 766.

5. The section heading is from *CP* 3:1067.

6. Timothy Morton, *Dark Ecology: For a Logic of Future Coexistence* (New York: Columbia University Press, 2015), 37.

7. Ursula Heise, *Sense of Place and Sense of Planet: The Environmental Imagination of the Global* (Oxford: Oxford University Press, 2008), 205.

8. Morton, *Dark Ecology*, 26.

9. Timothy Clark, *Ecocriticism on the Edge: The Anthropocene as a Threshold Concept* (London: Bloomsbury, 2015), 30.

10. Alan Ramón Clinton, *Intuitions in Literature, Technology, and Politics: Parabilities* (New York: Palgrave Macmillan, 2012), 161.

11. Clinton, 1, 153.

12. Frederick Buell, *From Apocalypse to Way of Life: Environmental Crisis in the American Century* (New York: Routledge, 2003), 190.

13. The term was first introduced in Stacy Alaimo, *Bodily Natures: Science, Environment, and the Material Self* (Bloomington: Indiana University Press, 2010), 2:

> Imagining human corporeality as trans-corporeality, in which the human is always intermeshed with the more-than-human world, underlines the extent to which the substance of the human is ultimately inseparable from "the environment." It makes it difficult to pose nature as mere background. . . . Indeed, thinking across bodies may catalyze the recognition that the environment, which is too often imagined as inert, empty space or as a resource for human use, is, in fact, a world of fleshy beings with their own needs, claims, and actions. By emphasizing the movement across bodies, trans-corporeality reveals the interchanges and interconnections between various bodily natures. But by underscoring that *trans* indicates movement across different sites, trans-corporeality also opens up a mobile space that acknowledges the often unpredictable and unwanted actions of human bodies, nonhuman creatures, ecological systems, chemical agents, and other actors

14. Stacy Alaimo, *Exposed: Environmental Politics and Pleasures in Posthuman Times* (Minneapolis: University of Minnesota Press, 2016), 143.

15. Alaimo, 7.

16. Alaimo, 5.

17. Morton, *Hyperobjects*, 1, 2 (emphasis in original).

18. Morton, 195, 176, 197 (emphasis in original).

19. Timothy Morton, *Ecology without Nature: Rethinking Environmental Aesthetics* (Cambridge, MA: Harvard University Press, 2007), 45.

20. Morton, 43.

21. Timothy Morton, *Humankind: Solidarity with Nonhuman People* (London: Verso, 2017), 139.

22. Morton, *Hyperobjects*, 165.

23. Morton, *Humankind*, 181 (emphasis in original).

24. Morton, 186.

25. Timothy Morton, *Being Ecological* (Cambridge: MIT Press, 2018), 91.

26. The section heading is from *CP* 3:899.

27. Larry Eigner to Denise Levertov, December 1, 1961, Denise Levertov Papers (M601), series 4, box 33, folder 9, Department of Special Collections, Stanford University Libraries.

28. Todd also reported that "The *Boston Globe* reprinted the speech from a tape recording. The *New Yorker* published about 3,000 words of it. Many other papers around the country have reprinted the speech. And so an extraordinary number of people have read 'A Generation in Search of a Future.'" Richard Todd, "George Wald: The Man, *the* Speech," *New York Times*, August 17, 1969.

29. Larry Eigner to Joseph and Janet Eigner, December 10, 1970, Larry Eigner Papers

(MS 39), box 16, folder 36, Kenneth Spencer Research Library, University of Kansas.

30. George Wald, "A Generation in Search of a Future," lecture delivered at MIT, March 4, 1969, available at the website of Elijah Wald, son of George Wald, accessed February 10, 2021, https://www.elijahwald.com/generation.html.

31. For the text of this letter, see Larry Eigner, "Letters to the Editor, 1963–69," *PMLA* 131, no. 3 (2016): 785–86; for the essay, see Eigner, *Areas Lights Heights*, 43–44.

32. "Pollution by Fertilizer," *Scientific American* 220, no. 3 (March 1969): 47.

33. John R. Clark, "Thermal Pollution and Aquatic Life," *Scientific American* 220, no. 3 (March 1969): 19–27; Von R. Eshleman, "The Atmospheres of Mars and Venus," *Scientific American* 220, no. 3 (March 1969): 79–88.

34. Eshleman, "The Atmospheres of Mars and Venus," 79.

35. In "The Atmospheres of Venus and Mars," Eshleman explains, "the hypothesis that is favored at present is that solar radiation is trapped by the 'greenhouse' effect. Carl Sagan of Cornell University and James Pollack of the Smithsonian Astrophysical Observatory have studied this problem in detail. Their view, in brief, is that the carbon dioxide and water vapor in the atmosphere of Venus act as a highly efficient glass in the greenhouse" (86). The article concludes, "it behooves us to take strong steps to eliminate the known harmful effects of man's activities and to minimize those effects that are not yet fully understood. Whatever else we may wish to know, we hardly wish to test whether a lifeless earth would become like Mars or like Venus" (88).

36. Note on an envelope postmarked March 3, 1967, Larry Eigner Papers (MS 39), Kenneth Spencer Research Library, University of Kansas.

37. Wald, "A Generation in Search of a Future."

38. "Pollution by Fertilizer," 47.

39. Larry Eigner to David Gitin, September 14, 1970, Larry Eigner Papers (MSS 1974-0001), Archives and Special Collections, Thomas J. Dodd Research Center, University of Connecticut Library. I have been unable to determine whether a text of Wald's address at the Babson Institute exists. Wald also delivered the 1970 Massey Lectures broadcast by the Canadian Broadcasting Corporation, later published as *Therefore Choose Life* (Toronto: Anansi, 2017), and he mentions the "oil slick" there: "Now we are being told by experts . . . that the oil residues present in th[e] upper layers of the oceans are equal in bulk to all the algae" (68).

40. Larry Eigner to Paul Auster, January 1974, Henry W. and Albert A. Berg Collection, New York Public Library.

41. Morton refers to such activity as "rocking"; see Morton, *Humankind*, 179.

42. Eigner associates himself with the Nero figure in a 1978 essay: "And I feel my way in fiddling a little, or then sometimes more, on the roof of the burning or rusting world"; Eigner, *Areas Lights Heights*, 125.

43. See *CP* 3:1035; Larry Eigner, letter dated August 15, 1971, Larry Eigner Papers (MS 39), box 17, folder 18, Kenneth Spencer Research Library, University of Kansas.

44. Larry Eigner to Joseph Eigner and family, January 29, 1975, Larry Eigner Papers (M0902), box 21, folder 3, Department of Special Collections, Stanford University Libraries. Notably, the issue of *Newsweek* that Eigner cites here features, in the column space to the right of "Odum's Law," an ad for the United Cerebral Palsy Association (53). The copy reads: "Born Free! You can help your baby be born free and healthy.

You are bringing a brand new life into the world. Whether your child is born healthy or not, may well depend on what you do, or don't do, in the next 9 months. We'd like to help your baby be born free by giving you a little booklet explaining the 'Do's and Don'ts for the Most Important Nine Months in Life.' For your free copy contact your United Cerebral Palsy Association." A full-length picture of a smiling infant on its back accompanies the ad. The fact that Eigner makes no note of this ad might mean nothing. But from a disability perspective this ad's rhetoric is offensive (just the use of marketing language alone—"brand new"). Perhaps Eigner's reluctance to posit an origin is in part a response to this kind of stereotype, that a child born with a disability is not "born free." The important point here may be about Eigner's attention and interest. He does not respond to the ad as an opportunity for political statement. His interest is ecology.

45. The article Eigner refers to is likely "Running Out of Food?" One can see why the notion of "triage" would be especially problematic from Eigner's disability perspective: "a few Draconian solutions have been considered. Dr. Jay Forrester of the Massachusetts Institute of Technology created a storm recently by suggesting that one potential approach was triage—letting the least fit die in order to save the more robust victims of hunger." "Running Out of Food?," *Newsweek*, November 11, 1974, 60.

46. Joseph Eigner, "Unshielding the Sun: Environmental Effects." *Environment* 17, no. 3 (1975): 18.

47. Larry Eigner to George Butterick, February 9, 1975, George Butterick Papers (PCMS-0118), Poetry Collection of the University Libraries, University at Buffalo, State University of New York.

48. Nathaniel Rich, *Losing Earth: A Recent History* (New York: Farrar, Straus and Giroux, 2019), 3.

49. Rich, 7.

50. The section heading here comes from *CP* 4:1548.

51. Larry Eigner, *Windows / Walls / Yard / Ways*, ed. Robert Grenier (Santa Rosa, CA: Black Sparrow Press, 1994), 17 (emphasis in original).

52. Larry Eigner to Cid Corman, July 30, 1979, Henry W. and Albert A. Berg Collection, New York Public Library.

53. Morton, *Hyperobjects*, 136.

54. Rich, *Losing Earth*, 24.

55. These lines are genetically related to the prior poem in *The Collected Poetry*, which also comments on the "5 billionth contemporary" and asks how many of these "2-way daily exchanges" are needed "for community engh // among people // to survive to // avoid complete death" (*CP* 4:1597).

56. Morton, *Hyperobjects*, 1, 100 (emphasis in original).

57. Morton, *Dark Ecology*, 42.

58. Morton, *Hyperobjects*, 140.

59. It also evokes the idea of the "specious present," discussed in the introduction. Eigner's information about Amish and Mennonite farmers comes from an article on Lancaster County, Pennsylvania, in the April 1984 issue of *National Geographic*: "The Plain People of Pennsylvania," *National Geographic* 165, no. 4 (April 1984): 492–519. A previous poem (*CP* 4:1515) cites the same line about the "most productive agricultural

county" and collages together the lyrical names of the towns (e.g., Bird in Hand, Paradise, Safe Harbor) as they appeared on a map of Lancaster County that accompanied the article.

60. Morton, *Dark Ecology*, 42 (emphasis in original).

61. Bill McKibben, ed., *The Global Warming Reader: A Century of Writing about Climate Change* (New York: Penguin, 2012), 46.

62. McKibben, *End of Nature*, 24.

63. McKibben, *The Global Warming Reader*, 49, 51.

64. McKibben, *End of Nature*, 135.

65. Eigner, *Areas Lights Heights*, 126.

66. William Butler Yeats, "Among School Children" (1933), Poetry Foundation (website), accessed April 10, 2021, https://www.poetryfoundation.org/poems/43293/among-school-children.

67. Eigner, "Letters to the Editor," 782; Henry David Thoreau, *A Week on the Concord and Merrimack Rivers, Walden; or Life in the Woods, The Maine Woods, Cape Cod* (New York: Library of America, 1985), 395.

68. Morton, *Being Ecological*, xxxix.

69. Larry Eigner to Denise Levertov, September 1, 1968, Denise Levertov Papers (M601), n.s., box 33, folder 10, Department of Special Collections, Stanford University Libraries.

70. Eigner, *Areas Lights Heights*, 43, 44.

71. McKibben, *The Global Warming Reader*, 38; McKibben, *End of Nature*, 24.

72. Larry Eigner to James Weil, October 30, 1988, General Collection, box 585, folder 25B, Poetry Collection of the University Libraries, University at Buffalo, State University of New York.

73. Larry Eigner to Charles Bernstein, September 15, 1989, Charles Bernstein Papers (MSS 0519), box 18, folder 5, Special Collections and Archives, University of California, San Diego.

74. Larry Eigner to Ruth Polansky Bloom, August 18, 1990, Larry Eigner Papers (M0902), box 8, folder 1, Department of Special Collections, Stanford University Libraries.

75. Larry Eigner to Clayton Eshleman, December 13, 1991, Larry Eigner Papers (M0902), box 8, folder 1, Department of Special Collections, Stanford University Libraries.

76. Rich, *Losing Earth*, 199–200.

77. Charles Olson, *The Collected Prose of Charles Olson*, ed. Donald Allen and Benjamin Friedlander (Berkeley: University of California Press, 1997), 248.

78. Morton, *Humankind*, 171.

79. Eigner, *Windows / Walls / Yard / Ways*, n.p.

80. Larry Eigner to Clayton Eshleman, December 13, 1991, Larry Eigner Papers (M0902), box 8, folder 1, Department of Special Collections, Stanford University Libraries.

81. Eigner, *Readiness / Enough / Depends / On*, n.p.

Bibliography

Archival Collections

Allen, Donald. Papers (MSS 3). Special Collections and Archives, University of California, San Diego.

Athanor Collection (PCMS-0003). Poetry Collection of the University Libraries, University at Buffalo, State University of New York.

Baraka, Amiri. Papers (Collection 491). Library Special Collections, Charles E. Young Research Library, University of California, Los Angeles.

Berg, Henry W., and Albert A. Berg. Collection. New York Public Library.

Bernstein, Charles. Papers (MSS 0519). Special Collections and Archives, University of California, San Diego.

Blackburn, Paul. Papers (MSS 4). Special Collections and Archives, University of California, San Diego.

Butterick, George. Papers (PCMS-0118). Poetry Collection of the University Libraries, University at Buffalo, State University of New York.

Corman, Cid. Papers. Harry Ransom Center, University of Texas at Austin.

Creeley, Robert. Papers (M662). Department of Special Collections, Stanford University Libraries.

Duncan, Robert. Papers (PCMS-0110). Poetry Collection of the University Libraries, University at Buffalo, State University of New York.

Eigner, Larry. Papers (MSS 1974-0001). Archives and Special Collections at the Thomas J. Dodd Research Center, University of Connecticut Library.

———. Papers (MS 39). Kenneth Spencer Research Library, University of Kansas.

———. Papers (M0902). Department of Special Collections, Stanford University Libraries.

Eshleman, Clayton. Papers (MSS 21). Special Collections and Archives, University of California, San Diego.

General Collection. Poetry Collection of the University Libraries, University at Buffalo, State University of New York.

Intrepid Collection (PCMS-0005). Poetry Collection of the University Libraries, University at Buffalo, State University of New York.

Levertov, Denise. Papers (M601). Department of Special Collections, Stanford University Libraries.

Mac Low, Jackson. Papers (MSS 180). Special Collections and Archives, University of California, San Diego.

Olson, Charles. Research Collection (MSS 1969-0001). Archives and Special Collections at the Thomas J. Dodd Research Center, University of Connecticut Library.

Silliman, Ron. Papers (MSS 75). Special Collections and Archives, University of California, San Diego.

Tyson, Ian. Collection (MSS 0413). Special Collections and Archives, University of California, San Diego.

Published Sources

Alaimo, Stacy. *Bodily Natures: Science, Environment, and the Material Self*. Bloomington: Indiana University Press, 2010.

———. *Exposed: Environmental Politics and Pleasures in Posthuman Times*. Minneapolis: University of Minnesota Press, 2016.

Allen, Donald M., ed. *The New American Poetry*. New York: Grove Press, 1960.

Allison, Raphael. *Bodies on the Line: Performance and the Sixties Poetry Reading*. Iowa City: University of Iowa Press, 2014.

Barad, Karen. *Meeting the Universe Halfway: Quantum Physics and the Entanglement of Matter and Meaning*. Durham, NC: Duke University Press, 2007.

Bartlett, Jennifer, and George Hart, eds. *Momentous Inconclusions: The Life and Work of Larry Eigner*. Albuquerque: University of New Mexico Press, 2020.

Bate, Jonathan. *Song of the Earth*. Cambridge, MA: Harvard University Press, 2000.

Beckett, Tom, and Earel Neikirk, eds. *Difficulties* 1, no. 1 (1980).

Berry, Wendell. *What Are People For?* Berkeley, CA: North Point Press, 1990.

Bertholf, Robert J., and Albert Gelpi, eds. *The Letters of Robert Duncan and Denise Levertov*. Stanford, CA: Stanford University Press, 2004.

Birmingham, Jed. "*Rhinozeros* Archive." RealityStudio. July 9, 2012. https://realitystudio.org/bibliographic-bunker/rhinozeros/.

Bryson, J. Scott, ed. *Ecopoetry: A Critical Introduction*. Salt Lake City: University of Utah Press, 2002.

Buell, Frederick. *From Apocalypse to Way of Life: Environmental Crisis in the American Century*. New York: Routledge, 2003.

Butterick, George F. *A Guide to the Maximus Poems of Charles Olson*. Berkeley: University of California Press, 1981.

Carson, Rachel. *The Sea around Us*. Oxford: Oxford University Press, 1951.

———. *Silent Spring*. Boston: Houghton Mifflin, 1962.

———. *Under the Sea Wind: A Naturalist's Picture of Ocean Life*. Oxford: Oxford University Press, 1952.

Christensen, Paul. *Charles Olson: Call Him Ishmael*. Austin: University of Texas Press, 1979.

"Civil Rights Movement Songs with Tom Murray of SNCC." *Folk Music Worldwide*, August 10, 17, and 20, 1963. http://folkmusicworldwide.com/sncc-civil-rights-songs-1.html.

Clark, John R. "Thermal Pollution and Aquatic Life." *Scientific American* 220, no. 3 (March 1969): 19–27.

Clark, Timothy. *Ecocriticism on the Edge: The Anthropocene as a Threshold Concept*. London: Bloomsbury, 2015.

Clark, Tom. *Charles Olson: The Allegory of a Poet's Life*. New York: W. W. Norton, 1991.

Clinton, Alan Ramón. *Intuitions in Literature, Technology, and Politics: Parabilities*. New York: Palgrave Macmillan, 2012.

Cohen, Jeffrey Jerome, and Lowell Duckert. "Introduction: Welcome to the Whirled." In *Veer Ecology: A Companion for Environmental Thinking*, edited by Jeffrey Jerome Cohen and Lowell Duckert, 1–15. Minneapolis: University of Minnesota Press, 2017.

Creeley, Robert. *A Quick Graph: Collected Notes and Essays*. San Francisco: Four Seasons, 1970.

———. Rev. of *In the American Tree*, ed. Ron Silliman. *San Francisco Chronicle*, September 28, 1986.

Cullen, Heidi. *The Weather of the Future: Heat Waves, Extreme Storms, and Other Scenes from a Climate-Changed Planet*. New York: HarperCollins, 2010.

Davidson, Michael. *Concerto for the Left Hand: Disability and the Defamiliar Body*. Ann Arbor: University of Michigan Press, 2008.

———. "Disability Poetics." In *The Oxford Handbook of Modern and Contemporary American Poetry*, edited by Cary Nelson, 581–601. Oxford: Oxford University Press, 2012.

Davis, Lennard. "From *Enforcing Normalcy: Disability, Deafness, and the Body*." In *The Norton Anthology of Theory and Criticism*, edited by Jeffrey J. Williams, John McGowan, Laurie A. Finke, T. Denean Sharpley-Whiting, Vincent B. Leitch, and William E. Cain, 3rd ed., 2173–91. New York: W. W. Norton, 2018.

Derrida, Jacques. *Margins of Philosophy*. Translated by Alan Bass. Chicago: University of Chicago Press, 1982.

———. *Of Grammatology*. Translated by Gayatri Chakravorty Spivak. 40th anniversary ed. Baltimore, MD: Johns Hopkins University Press, 2016.

Duncan, Robert. *The Years as Catches, First Poems (1939–1946)*. Berkeley, CA: Oyez, 1966.

Eigner, Edwin M. *Robert Louis Stevenson and the Romantic Tradition*. Princeton, NJ: Princeton University Press, 1966.

Eigner, Joseph. "Unshielding the Sun: Environmental Effects." *Environment* 17, no. 3 (1975): 15–18.

Eigner, Larry. *Another Time in Fragments*. London: Fulcrum Press, 1967.

———. *Areas Lights Heights: Selected Writings 1954–1989*. Edited by Benjamin Friedlander. New York: Roof Books, 1989.

———. *The Collected Poems of Larry Eigner*. 4 vols. Edited by Curtis Faville and Robert Grenier. Stanford, CA: Stanford University Press, 2010.

———. *Country Harbor Quiet Act Around: Selected Prose*. Edited by Barrett Watten. Berkeley, CA: This Press, 1978.

———. *From the Sustaining Air*. Mallorca: Divers Press, 1953.

———. "Larry Eigner, 1927–1996." In *Contemporary Authors Autobiography Series*, vol. 23, edited by Joyce Nakamura, 19–62. Detroit, MI: Gale Research, 1996.

———. "Letters to the Editor, 1963–69." *PMLA* 131, no. 3 (2016): 774–86.

———. *Readiness / Enough / Depends / On*. Edited with an afterword by Robert Grenier. Los Angeles: Green Integer, 2000.

———. *Selected Poems*. Edited by Samuel Charters and Andrea Wyatt. Berkeley, CA: Oyez, 1972.

———. "Twenty-One Poems and an Interview." *Kaleidoscope*, Spring 1982, 10–20.

———. "Unpublished Letter to Ina Forster." *Passages* 5 (April 1998), http://writing.upenn.edu/epc/ezines/passages/passages5/forster.html.

———. *What You Hear*. London: Edible Magazine, 1972.

———. *Windows / Walls / Yard / Ways*, edited by Robert Grenier. Santa Rosa, CA: Black Sparrow Press, 1994.

Elder, John. *Imagining the Earth: Poetry and the Vision of Nature*. Urbana: University of Illinois Press, 1985.

Emerson, Ralph Waldo. *Essays and Lectures*. New York: Library of America, 1983.

Eshleman, Von R. "The Atmospheres of Mars and Venus." *Scientific American* 220, no. 3 (March 1969): 79–88.

Farrier, David. *Anthropocene Poetics: Deep Time, Sacrifice Zones, and Extinction*. Minneapolis: University of Minnesota Press, 2019.

Ferris, Jim. "The Enjambed Body: A Step toward a Crippled Poetics." *Georgia Review* 58, no. 2 (2004): 219–33.

Fisher-Wirth, Ann, and Laura-Gray Street, eds. *The Ecopoetry Anthology*. San Antonio, TX: Trinity University Press, 2013.

Foster, Edward Halsey. *Understanding the Black Mountain Poets*. Columbia: University of South Carolina Press, 1995.

Fredman, Ruth Gruber. *The Passover Seder: Afrikoman in Exile*. Philadelphia: University of Pennsylvania Press, 1981.

Fredman, Stephen. *The Grounding of American Poetry: Charles Olson and the Emersonian Tradition*. Cambridge: Cambridge University Press, 1993.

Friedlander, Benjamin. "Larry Eigner." In *American Poets since World War II*, 6th ser., edited by Joseph Conte, 114–26. Vol. 193 of *Dictionary of Literary Biography*. Detroit, MI: Gale Research Press, 1998.

———. Typescript of an unpublished poetics statement by Larry Eigner. *Sagetrieb* 18, no. 1 (1999): cover image.

———. "Typos and Abbrevs." *National Poetry Foundation* (blog), April 8, 2010. https://nationalpoetryfoundation.wordpress.com/2010/04/08/typos-and-abbrevs/.

Fussell, Paul. *Poetic Meter and Poetic Form*. Rev. ed. New York: McGraw-Hill, 1979.

Gander, Forrest, and John Kinsella. *Redstart: An Ecological Poetics*. Iowa City: University of Iowa Press, 2012.

Gelpi, Albert. *American Poetry after Modernism: The Power of the Word*. Cambridge: Cambridge University Press, 2015.

Gravendyk, Hillary. "Chronic Poetics." *Journal of Modern Literature* 38, no. 1 (2014): 1–19.

Grenier, Robert. "A Note on the Text." In *Windows / Walls / Yard / Ways*, by Larry Eigner, edited by Robert Grenier, 17. Santa Rosa, CA: Black Sparrow Press, 1994.

———. "On Speech." *This*, no. 1 (1971): 86–87, reprinted in *In the American Tree*, edited by Ron Silliman, 477–78. Orono, ME: National Poetry Foundation, 2002.

Griswold, Eliza. "How *Silent Spring* Ignited the Environmental Movement." *New York Times Magazine*, September 21, 2012.

Harris, Anne F. "Tend." In *Veer Ecology: A Companion for Environmental Thinking*, edited by Jeffrey Jerome Cohen and Lowell Duckert, 392–406. Minneapolis: University of Minnesota Press, 2017.

Hart, George. "'Enough Defined': Disability, Ecopoetics, and Larry Eigner." *Contemporary Literature* 51, no. 1 (2010): 152–79.

———. "'My Nose on the Ground': Larry Eigner's Civil War." In *Momentous Inconclusions: The Life and Work of Larry Eigner*, edited by Jennifer Bartlett and George Hart, 49–68. Albuquerque: University of New Mexico Press, 2020.

———."Postmodernist Nature/Poetry: The Example of Larry Eigner." In *Reading under the Sign of Nature: New Essays in Ecocriticism*, edited by John Tallmadge and Henry Harrington, 315–32. Salt Lake City: University of Utah Press, 2000.

———. "Walking the Walk: Ammons, Eigner, and Ecopoetic Form in the 1960s." *ISLE: Interdisciplinary Studies in Literature and Environment* 24, no. 4 (2018): 680–706.

Heidegger, Martin. *Poetry, Language, Thought*. Translated by Albert Hofstadter. New York: Harper and Row, 1971.

Heise, Ursula. *Imagining Extinction: The Cultural Meanings of Endangered Species*. Chicago: University of Chicago Press, 2016.

———. *Sense of Place and Sense of Planet: The Environmental Imagination of the Global*. Oxford: Oxford University Press, 2008.

Hertz, Joseph H., ed. *The Pentateuch and Haftorahs: Hebrew Text, English Translation, and Commentary*. Vol. 1. Oxford: Soncino Press, 1928.

Hinton, David, ed. *The Wilds of Poetry: Adventures in Mind and Landscape*. Boulder, CO: Shambhala, 2017.

Hofer, Matthew, and Michael Golston, eds. *The L=A=N=G=U=A=G=E Letters: Selected 1970s Correspondence of Bruce Andrews, Charles Bernstein, and Ron Silliman*. Albuquerque: University of New Mexico Press, 2019.

Hofstadter, Albert. "Enownment." *Boundary 2*, vol. 4, no. 2 (1976): 356–77.

Hume, Angela, and Gillian Osborne, eds. *Ecopoetics: Essays in the Field*. Iowa City: University of Iowa Press, 2018.

Iijima, Brenda, ed. *The Eco Language Reader*. New York: Portable Press, 2010.

Jackson, J. B., "The Order of a Landscape." In *The Interpretation of Ordinary Landscapes: Geographical Essays*, edited by D. W. Meinig, 153–63. Oxford: Oxford University Press, 1979.

James, William. *The Principles of Psychology*. Vol. 1. Boston: Henry Holt, 1910.

Keller, Lynn. *Recomposing Ecopoetics: North American Poetry of the Self-Conscious Anthropocene*. Charlottesville: University of Virginia Press, 2017.

Kennedy, X. J. Rev. of *The New American Poetry*, edited by Donald Allen. *Poetry* 98, no. 4 (July 1961): 242–44.

Kinnell, Galway. Rev. of *On My Eyes*, by Larry Eigner. *Poetry* 100, no. 6 (September 1962): 400–403.

Kittler, Friedrich A. *Gramophone, Film, Typewriter*. Translated by Geoffrey Winthrop-Young and Michael Wutz. Stanford, CA: Stanford University Press, 1999.

Kizer, Carolyn, Marjorie Perloff, Nathaniel Mackey, John Holander, and Robert Hass, eds. *American Poetry: The Twentieth Century*. Vol. 1, *Henry Adams to Dorothy Parker*. New York: Library of America, 2000.

Knickerbocker, Scott. *Ecopoetics: The Language of Nature, the Nature of Language*. Amherst: University of Massachusetts Press, 2012.

Kroeber, Karl. *Ecological Literary Criticism: Romantic Imagining and the Biology of Mind*. New York: Columbia University Press, 1994.

Leary, Paris, and Robert Kelly, eds. *A Controversy of Poets*. New York: Doubleday, 1965.

Lefebvre, Henri. *The Production of Space*. Translated by Donald Nicholson-Smith. New York: Blackwell, 1991.

Leif, Irving P., *Larry Eigner: A Bibliography of His Works*. Metuchen, NJ: Scarecrow Press, 1989.

LeMenager, Stephanie. *Living Oil: Petroleum Culture in the American Century*. Oxford: Oxford University Press, 2014.

Leopold, Aldo. *A Sand County Almanac*. Oxford: Oxford University Press, 1949.

Matz, Jesse. *Modernist Time Ecology*. Baltimore, MD: Johns Hopkins University Press, 2019.

McCaffery, Steve. "Language Writing." In *The Cambridge Companion to American Poetry since 1945*, edited by Jennifer Ashton, 143–57. Cambridge: Cambridge University Press, 2013.

McGann, Jerome. *The Textual Condition*. Princeton, NJ: Princeton University Press, 1991.

McKibben, Bill. *The End of Nature*. New York: Doubleday, 1989.

———. *Enough: Staying Human in an Engineered Age*. New York: Times Books / Henry Holt, 2003.

———, ed. *The Global Warming Reader: A Century of Writing about Climate Change*. New York: Penguin, 2012.

Miller, J. Hillis. "The Critic as Host." *Critical Inquiry* 3, no. 3 (1977): 439–47.

Morton, Timothy. "Attune." In *Veer Ecology: A Companion for Environmental Thinking*, edited by Jeffrey Jerome Cohen and Lowell Duckert, 151–67. Minneapolis: University of Minnesota Press, 2017.

———. *Being Ecological*. Cambridge: MIT Press, 2018.

———. *Dark Ecology: For a Logic of Future Coexistence*. New York: Columbia University Press, 2015.

———. *The Ecological Thought*. Cambridge, MA: Harvard University Press, 2010.

———. "Ecologocentrism: Unworking Animals." *SubStance* 37, no. 3 (2008): 73–96.

———. "Ecology as Text, Text as Ecology." *Oxford Literary Review* 32, no. 1 (2010): 1–17.

———. *Ecology without Nature: Rethinking Environmental Aesthetics*. Cambridge, MA: Harvard University Press, 2007.

———. *Humankind: Solidarity with Nonhuman People*. London: Verso, 2017.

———. *Hyperobjects: Philosophy and Ecology after the End of the World*. Minneapolis: University of Minnesota Press, 2013.

———. "An Object-Oriented Defense of Poetry." *New Literary History* 43, no. 2 (2012): 205–24.

———. "Queer Ecology." *PMLA* 125, no. 2 (2010): 273–82.

Mukarovsky, Jan. "Standard Language and Poetic Language." In *Chapters from the History of Czech Functional Linguistics*, edited by Jan Chovanec, 41–53. Brno: Masarykova univerzita, 2014.

National Geographic. "The Plain People of Pennsylvania." Vol. 165, no. 4 (April 1984): 492–519.

Newsweek. "Running Out of Food?" November 11, 1974, 56–68.

Nixon, Rob. *Slow Violence and the Environmentalism of the Poor*. Cambridge, MA: Harvard University Press, 2011.

Nolan, Sarah. *Unnatural Ecopoetics: Unlikely Spaces in Contemporary Poetry*. Reno: University of Nevada Press, 2017.

Olson, Charles. *Causal Mythology*. San Francisco: Four Seasons Foundation, 1969.

———. *The Collected Prose of Charles Olson*. Edited by Donald Allen and Benjamin Friedlander. Berkeley: University of California Press, 1997.

———. *The Maximus Poems*. Edited by George Butterick. Berkeley: University of California Press, 1983.

———. *Selected Letters*. Edited by Ralph Maud. Berkeley: University of California Press, 2000.

———. *The Special View of History*. Edited by Ann Charters. Berkeley, CA: Oyez, 1970.

Pearson, Gilbert T., ed. *Birds of America*. 2 vols. New York: University Society, 1923.

Peck, H. Daniel. *Thoreau's Morning Work: Memory and Perception in "A Week on the Concord and Merrimack Rivers," the Journal, and "Walden."* New Haven, CT: Yale University Press, 1994.

PennSound: Center for Programs in Contemporary Writing. "Larry Eigner." Accessed February 10, 2021. https://writing.upenn.edu/pennsound/x/Eigner.php.

Perloff, Marjorie. *Poetic License: Essays on Modernist and Postmodernist Lyric*. Evanston, IL: Northwestern University Press, 1990.

Phillips, Siobhan. *The Poetics of Everyday: Creative Repetition in Modern American Verse*. New York: Columbia University Press, 2010.

Poirier, Richard. *Poetry and Pragmatism*. Cambridge, MA: Harvard University Press, 1992.

Ratcliffe, Stephen. *Listening to Reading*. Albany: State University of New York Press, 2000.

Rich, Nathaniel. *Losing Earth: A Recent History*. New York: Farrar, Straus and Giroux, 2019.

Rippeon, Andrew, ed. *Letters to Jargon: The Correspondence between Larry Eigner and Jonathan Williams*. Tuscaloosa: University of Alabama Press, 2019.

Rome, Adam. "'Give Earth a Chance': The Environmental Movement and the Sixties." *Journal of American History* 90, no. 2 (2003): 525–54.

Roosevelt, Theodore. "Manhood and Statehood." In *The Strenuous Life*, 201–14. Vol. 12 of *The Works of Theodore Roosevelt*. New York: P. F. Collier, 1910.

Royle, Nicholas. "Afterword: On the Veer." In *Veer Ecology: A Companion for Environmental Thinking*, edited by Jeffrey Jerome Cohen and Lowell Duckert, 469–74. Minneapolis: University of Minnesota Press, 2017.

———. *Veering: A Theory of Literature*. Edinburgh: Edinburgh University Press, 2011.

Samuels, Ellen. "Six Ways of Looking at Crip Time." *Disability Studies Quarterly* 37, no. 3 (2017), https://dsq-sds.org/article/view/5824/4684.

Schneider, David. *Crowded by Beauty: The Life and Zen of Poet Philip Whalen*. Berkeley: University of California Press, 2015.

Schuster, Joshua. *The Ecology of Modernism: American Environments and Avant-Garde Poetics*. Tuscaloosa: University of Alabama Press, 2015.

Schweik, Susan. *The Ugly Laws: Disability in Public*. New York: New York University Press, 2009.

———. "The Voice of 'Reason.'" *Public Culture* 13, no. 3 (2001): 485–505.

Scientific American. "Pollution by Fertilizer." Vol. 220, no. 3 (March 1969): 47.

Scigaj, Leonard M. *Sustainable Poetry: Four American Ecopoets*. Lexington: University of Kentucky Press, 1999.

Shaw, Lytle. *Narrowcast: Poetry and Audio Research*. Stanford, CA: Stanford University Press, 2018.

Shelley, Percy B. *Shelley's Poetry and Prose*. Edited by Donald H. Reiman and Sharon B. Powers. New York: W. W. Norton, 1977.

Shillingsburg, Peter L. "Text as Matter, Concept, and Action." *Studies in Bibliography* 44 (1991): 31–82.

Silliman, Ron, ed. *In the American Tree*. Orono, ME: National Poetry Foundation, 2002.

———. "Surprised by Sign (Notes on Nine)." *Alcheringa*, n.s., 1, no. 2 (1975): 118–20.

Skinner, Jonathan, ed. *ecopoetics*, 2001–7.

———. "What Sounds: Larry Eigner's Environments." In *Momentous Inconclusions: The Life and Work of Larry Eigner*, edited by Jennifer Bartlett and George Hart, 171–91. Albuquerque: University of New Mexico Press, 2020.

Snyder, Gary. "Four Changes." In *Turtle Island*, by Gary Snyder, 91–102. New York: New Directions, 1974.

Tanselle, G. Thomas. "The Textual Criticism of Visual and Aural Works." *Studies in Bibliography* 57 (2005–6): 1–37.

Taylor, Dorceta E. *The Rise of the American Conservation Movement: Power, Privilege, and Environmental Protection*. Durham, NC: Duke University Press, 2016.

Thoreau, Henry David. *A Week on the Concord and Merrimack Rivers, Walden; or Life in the Woods, The Maine Woods, Cape Cod*. New York: Library of America, 1985.

Todd, Richard. "George Wald: The Man, *the* Speech." *New York Times*, August 17, 1969.

Toffler, Alvin. *Future Shock*. New York: Random House, 1970.

Tuan, Yi-Fu. *Space and Place: The Perspective of Experience*. Minneapolis: University of Minnesota Press, 1977.

Vas Dias, Robert, ed. *Inside Outer Space: New Poems of the Space Age*. New York: Doubleday, 1970.

Wald, George. "A Generation in Search of a Future." Lecture delivered at MIT, March 4, 1969. Available at the website of Elijah Wald, son of George Wald, accessed February 10, 2021, https://www.elijahwald.com/generation.html.

———. *Therefore Choose Life*. Toronto: Anansi, 2017.

Watten, Barrett. "Scenes of Decision: Larry Eigner as a Distributed Author." In *Momentous Inconclusions: The Life and Work of Larry Eigner*, edited by Jennifer Bartlett and George Hart, 87–120. Albuquerque: University of New Mexico Press, 2020.

———. *Total Syntax*. Carbondale: Southern Illinois University Press, 1985.

Whitman, Walt. *Complete Poetry and Collected Prose*. New York: Library of America, 1982.

Wikipedia, "Dayenu." Last edited January 27, 2021. https://en.wikipedia.org/wiki/Dayenu.

Williams, William Carlos. *The Autobiography of William Carlos Williams*. New York: Random House, 1951.

———. *The Collected Poems of William Carlos Williams*. Vol. 2, *1939–1962*, edited by A. Walton Litz and Christopher MacGowan. New York: New Directions, 1988.

———. *Paterson*. Edited by Christopher MacGowan. New York: New Directions, 1992.

Woodhouse, Keith M. "The Politics of Ecology: Environmentalism and Liberalism in the 1960s." *Journal for the Study of Radicalism* 2, no. 2 (2008): 53–88.

Worster, Donald. *Nature's Economy: A History of Ecological Ideas*. 2nd ed. Cambridge: Cambridge University Press, 1994.

Yeats, William Butler. "Among School Children." 1933. Poetry Foundation (website). Accessed April 10, 2021. https://www.poetryfoundation.org/poems/43293/among-school-children.

Index

Page numbers in italics refer to figures.